PENGUIN BOOKS

THE NATIONAL TRUST MANUAL OF HOUSEKEEPING

Hermione Sandwith has a degree in the history of art from London University. In the aftermath of the Florence floods of 1966 she had two years' valuable experience of the practical conservation of works of art at the Uffizi in Florence and at the Istituto del Restauro in Rome. She joined the National Trust in 1974 and has played a leading part in setting up the Trust's Conservation Service. She was formerly Deputy to the Surveyor of Conservation with special responsibility for paintings and is now carrying out a survey of the Trust's picture frames.

Sheila Stainton trained as an occupational therapist. She has a long-standing interest in the conservation of textiles and spent three years helping to establish the Textile Conservation Centre at Hampton Court. She has worked for the National Trust since 1961 on textile repairs and in 1977 was appointed the Trust's first Housekeeper. In this capacity she travelled extensively, giving advice on the maintenance of proper conservation standards in the houses in the care of the Trust. From 1985 until her retirement in 1990 she was Deputy Surveyor of Conservation.

11. PESTS, MOULDS AND INSECTS
189

12. PHOTOGRAPHS
197

13. PICTURES
205

14. STONE, INCLUDING MARBLE AND ALABASTER
239

15. TEXTILES
255

16. WALLS, CEILINGS AND WINDOWS
273

17. MISCELLANEOUS
291

APPENDICES
1. Methods of Protection against Light
301

2. Special Equipment and Protection
307

3. The Housemaids' Cupboard
317

4. Suppliers of Equipment and Materials
323

5. Suppliers' Addresses
331

PHOTOGRAPHIC ACKNOWLEDGEMENTS
338

INDEX
339

CONTENTS

FOREWORD
David Winfield
9

INTRODUCTION
John Cornforth
15

1. THE RIGHT ENVIRONMENT
19

2. BOOKS AND DOCUMENTS
35

3. CERAMICS
61

4. CLOCKS AND WATCHES
75

5. FLOORS
89

6. FURNITURE
103

7. GLASS
119

8. METALWORK
135

9. MUSICAL INSTRUMENTS
157

10. NATURAL HISTORY COLLECTIONS
177

PENGUIN BOOKS

Published by the Penguin Group
Penguin Books Ltd, 27 Wrights Lane, London W8 5TZ, England
Penguin Books USA Inc., 375 Hudson Street, New York, New York 10014, USA
Penguin Books Australia Ltd, Ringwood, Victoria, Australia
Penguin Books Canada Ltd, 10 Alcorn Avenue, Toronto, Ontario, Canada M4V 3B2
Penguin Books (NZ) Ltd, 182–190 Wairau Road, Auckland 10, New Zealand

Penguin Books Ltd, Registered Offices: Harmondsworth, Middlesex, England

First published by Allen Lane Ltd in association with The National Trust 1984
Published in Penguin Books 1985
Revised edition Viking 1991
Published in Penguin Books with minor revisions 1993
1 3 5 7 9 10 8 6 4 2

Copyright © The National Trust 1984
Revised edition copyright
© The National Trust 1991
All rights reserved

Made and printed in Great Britain by
Butler and Tanner Ltd, Frome and London
Filmset in Linotron Sabon by
Rowland Phototypesetting Ltd, Bury St Edmunds, Suffolk

THE
NATIONAL TRUST
MANUAL OF HOUSEKEEPING

A New Edition of the Practical Guide
to the Conservation of Old Houses and
Their Contents

Compiled by
HERMIONE SANDWITH
and
SHEILA STAINTON

PENGUIN BOOKS
in association with
THE NATIONAL TRUST

What we have delivered in this Treatise, we took not upon Trust or Hearsay, but by our own personal knowledge and experience do promise and aver, that if you punctually observe them, you must of necessity succeed well; and if any Gentlemen or Ladies, having met with disappointments in some of the Receipts, do question the truth and reality of them, they may for their satisfaction (if it stands with their convenience) see them tried by the Auther, according to the very rules set down . . .

Stalker and Parker,
A Treatise of Japanning and Varnishing, 1688

1. The servants at Erddig in 1912, carrying the implements of their occupations

FOREWORD

BY DAVID WINFIELD

Surveyor of Conservation to the National Trust

First edition, 1984

The housekeeper of a country house was concerned with the day-to-day upkeep of its contents, as well as the supervision of the female staff and the comfort of the owner and his family. The historic buildings representatives and house staff of the National Trust, for whom this Manual was first compiled, are concerned with the preservation of the Trust's possessions for ever.

These two words 'for ever' are simple enough to say, and even though the task they imply is impossible to achieve, they must never be forgotten, underlining as they do the difference between the housekeeper of old who was concerned only with maintenance and our far greater task today.

The purpose of maintenance is to preserve in good working order. Most of us spend some of our time in this way. We see that the car is serviced; we wash and mend clothes; we paint and decorate the house. In maintaining we are helping to preserve our possessions.

The National Trust's responsibility for preservation is different and ever-lasting, and that is why the Housekeeping Manual came into being. It is the first publication to bridge the gap between the old maintenance and modern conservation. We have called it a 'Housekeeping' rather than a 'Conservation' Manual, because good housekeeping is part of what we would call preventive conservation, and the Manual is for those who 'housekeep' or look after things rather than for the professional conservator. Our aim is to ensure that as few objects as possible decline to the point where they need repair. Neither accident nor *Anno Domini* can be avoided, and since all things begin to decay from the moment they are made, conservation treatment will be necessary over the years at more or less regular intervals. Nevertheless the skills of the conservator would be of no use without the continuing care taken by the 'housekeepers' – in a National Trust house, the staff.

One of the most important tasks is to maintain the right environment. We hope that, in the first place, the Manual will help you to recognize the conditions of light, heat and humidity in which the contents of a house can exist safely.

In the second place, the Manual tries to explain how to dust, handle, move and store the various categories of objects to be found in a historic house. More than common sense is needed, as will be clear to those who have ever benefited from the advice of skilled conservators.

Thirdly, the Manual contains a lot of important 'don'ts', the reasons for which we hope the reader will understand. We have tried to explain why 'do-it-yourself' treatment is no longer advisable for old and fragile objects. The phrase 'consult an expert' recurs constantly in these pages, and it cannot be stressed enough that repairs carried out by unsupervised amateurs will almost always cause more damage in the long run than the natural process of decay.

The conservator's job is increasingly separated from that of the traditional craftsman, partly because of the advance in scientific knowledge of what might be called the chemistry of decay and partly because of its long-term purpose. In his quest after the causes of decay the conservator is making scientific inquiry into a new field, just as is the specialist in geriatrics who asks what causes human decay in old age, and how he can arrest or alleviate it. The cabinet-maker, the clock-maker, the bookbinder and other craftsmen may all be concerned with new objects or with maintenance, while the conservator is concerned with preserving something old as much as possible in its original state. It may well make practical sense to replace an old member of a chair with a stronger one of different wood or to strengthen it with chocks and screws; but the first principle of the conservator is to save whatever can be saved and only to replace what must be replaced – and then always in materials identical to those originally used, keeping meticulous records of the work done.

It is up to the Trust to take every advantage of advances in the knowledge of conservation where they can be useful to us, and it is indeed with the generous help of many professional conservators that this Manual has been written. Some of these are full-time employees of the National Trust, most notably the Trust's Deputy Surveyor of Conservation, Hermione Sandwith, and the Trust's Housekeeper, Sheila Stainton, who first conceived the idea of this book and have played a major part in putting it together. Much valuable advice has also been given by the Historic Buildings Secretary, Martin Drury, and his predecessor, St John Gore, and the book has been edited for publication by the Architectural Adviser, Gervase Jackson-Stops. The earliest demonstration of good housekeeping came from Waddesdon Manor where Colonel Waller, the Administrator, and Miss Griffin, the Curator, were kind enough to arrange a demonstration of the de Rothschild methods and traditions in the spring of 1977. Other contributors include James Bellchambers, Jonathan Betts, Stephen Calloway, Pamela Clabburn, Alec Cobbe, Briony Eastman, Andrew Garrett, Paul Giudici, Jean Glover, Mary Goodwin, Roy Hale, Keith Harding, John Hart, John Hartley, Martin Holden, Sheila Landi, Herbert Lank, Judy Larney, John Larson, Paul Levi, Helen Lloyd, Jane McAusland, Jane Mathews, Jim Murrell, Andrew Naylor, Victoria Pelham Burn, Viola Pemberton Pigott, Nicholas Pickwoad, Trevor Proudfoot, James Robinson, Hugh Routh, Francesca Scoones, Phillip Stevens and Muriel Winship. Without help in the early stages from Norman Brommelle and Jonathan Ashley-Smith of the Victoria and Albert Museum, and Garry Thomson of the National Gallery, the Manual would never have got off the ground. Help has also been received from members of staff of the British Library, the British Museum, the Hamilton Kerr Institute, the National Maritime Museum, the Science Museum, the Tate Gallery, the Victoria and Albert Museum and the International Wool Secretariat.

The lists of equipment and suppliers given in the appendices at the end of the book are by no means exhaustive, nor can the National Trust take any responsibility for goods purchased from these firms or guarantee the availability of any items. The lists are given in good faith, based on the information available at the time of going to press, and we hope that it will be possible to widen and update them in future editions of the Manual.

It is very much regretted that the staff of the National Trust cannot give opinions on objects or advice on their conservation. The different departments of the British Museum and the Victoria and Albert Museum in London, and some of the larger provincial museums, can be consulted at certain stated hours during the week, and the names and addresses of bodies concerned with conservation work can be found in the *Conservation Sourcebook*, published by the Crafts Council (1979).

Finally, it remains to be said that *The National Trust Manual of Housekeeping* came into being specifically to answer some of the problems posed by the regular and ever-increasing opening of historic houses to the public. While many of its lessons are applicable to smaller private houses and collections, the mention of druggets and ropes, display cases and room stewards, must be excused by those who have the good fortune not to need them.

Like all textbooks, the Manual may occasionally seem dull and dry but, like all good textbooks, it will repay careful reading. We hope that you will refer to it often, and so help to improve the standard of conservation of the heritage that has been given to each and every one of us.

Second edition, 1991

The Manual has proved its worth by the test of several impressions, and it is now time for a revision because knowledge in the conservation sciences grows apace.

In this new edition every chapter has been carefully scrutinized. Some have only required a few modifications, while others have been radically re-written, and there are also some new chapters.

The preparation of this edition coincided with the tragic fire at Uppark House. This disaster underlined the simple fact that every disaster is a conservation problem. It is very important that the house staff and the fire brigade are properly briefed by conservators, so that they are aware of helpful courses of action in the event of a fire. In the case of Uppark this briefing had taken place and it was thanks to the helpfulness and efficiency of house staff, firemen and volunteers that so much was saved in the first few hours. The prompt action of conservators in carrying out first-aid work and packing and removing the contents to safety avoided further damage. In the aftermath of the fire the vigilance of conservators also saved many fragments of furniture, works of art and architectural decoration that might easily have been lost.

As the now retired Surveyor of Conservation for the National Trust I can say that one lesson learned in my years with the National Trust is that long-term preservation is not a natural activity. As human beings our thoughts tend to stay within the life cycle of birth, maturity, decline and death. We do not want to think beyond our own lifetimes, and much of the present popular interest in the conservation of our heritage is in fact concerned with the present-day enjoyment of it rather than with the restrictions demanded by long-term preservation. An additional problem is that modern life and modern products are concerned with speed and ease of use, whereas good conservation demands slow and patient work and it is always labour intensive. The Bible itself takes a gloomy view of conservation, as, for example, Matthew vi, 19:

Lay up not for yourselves treasures upon earth, Where moth and rust doth corrupt, And where thieves break through and steal: . . .

These are some of the reasons that conservation measures need to be continually thought about rather than treated as actions that can be completed and then forgotten about.

For this new edition of the Manual it is a pleasure to renew our thanks to those who originally helped with it, and to add the names of Fiona Allardyce, Bob Child, Myra Clark, Sandra Davison, Edward Diestelkamp, James Findlay, Alfred Fisher, Miranda Hardie, Rupert Harris, Robert Hayes, Diana Heath, Jock Hopson, Velson Horie, Pat Jackson, Emily Lawlor, Betty Provan, Nigel Seeley, Sarah Staniforth, Peter Thuring and John Williams; and special thanks are due to Maggie Grieve for her patience and skill in preparing the revised text.

The role of the Crafts Council in lending a hand to conservation causes has now been taken over by the Conservation Unit of:

> The Museums and Galleries Commission
> 16 Queen Anne's Gate
> London SW1H 9AA
> Telephone: 071 233 4200

They are able to advise the names and addresses of reliable conservators and they will soon be publishing a Conservation Register.

2. The Saloon at Chirk Castle as normally shown and as 'put to bed' for the winter

INTRODUCTION

BY JOHN CORNFORTH

Get the great dining-room in order as soon as possible. Unpaper the curtains, take the covers off the couch and the chairs, and put the china figures on the mantelpiece immediately. And set them o'nodding as soon as his lordship comes in, d'ye hear, Trusty.

To find such instructions to a servant in a mid-18th-century comedy – the play is George Colman's *The Clandestine Marriage* of 1766 – suggests how widely practices of good housekeeping were understood at the time; the quotation is only unusual in the reference to paper being used to cover curtains. But certainly paper covers for chairs were known, even if none survives. Inevitably, the history of housekeeping with all its fascinating intricacies has been forgotten, because no one bothered to write it down while traditions were maintained by well-established staffs, presided over by a well-upholstered housekeeper. And now we are faced not only by the disappearance of the staff, but by an unprecedented demand to see houses and their contents. It is the combination of the two that has posed such problems for the National Trust.

Despite what one is led to believe, staff problems are not a 20th-century phenomenon, for letters and diaries of earlier generations are full of grumbles about bad servants, servants who would not get up on cold mornings, servants who left, the difficulty of replacing them and their demands for exorbitant wages – which strike us as inhumanly small. In a country house the servants would have waited on the family and on each other, but their care of the house was just as important. In this they were in a kind of unstated partnership with the owner, who was quite likely not to use the front door or the principal rooms every day and would accept that, for normal living, second-best was good enough.

The best was what was wanted in the principal rooms, but it was very expensive, and so it was only used on special occasions and was expected to last for several generations, so as to become part of a family's dignity and evidence of its antiquity. Thus great care was taken to protect objects, particularly against light, and houses were often shut up for lengthy periods while a family was in London for political or social reasons. Indeed many of the houses that are now most noted for their tapestries and materials, like

3. 'The Blue Curtain' by Adriaen van der Spelt, dated 1658. The curtain and rod painted in *trompe l'œil* show what was a common method of protection for pictures and water-colours in the 17th and 18th centuries

Hardwick in Derbyshire, or Boughton (not NT) in Northamptonshire, are those that were least used and so least subjected to light.

Pictures of the 16th and early 17th centuries often had curtains in front of them and tapestries continued to do so as late as 1939 in some exceptionally well-cared-for houses. Fine beds with hangings of damask or needlework also had case curtains and these were often of the same colour as the show material or its lining but of a cheaper, more hard-wearing material. Chairs and settees also had case covers; indeed, as can be seen at Erddig, they often had both everyday covers and a top cover against dust and light as well. Carpets often had druggets to protect them against heavy wear as well as light, and some of these were like heavy damask tablecloths. Chandeliers had bags and mirror frames had covers, while pieces of gilt and veneered or inlaid furniture were sometimes supplied with covers made of leather, or of heavy cotton, carefully lined and cut to fit. Like the case covers of chairs, these would be charged for as part of the original order.

The covers would be taken off the furniture when the family was in residence, but those on the chairs and settees and often the druggets on the carpets would be cheerfully accepted. Also, when the sun came round, blinds would be drawn and shutters closed whether or not there were people about, for it was considered that the protection of the contents of a house should come before the fleeting convenience of a family and its guests.

Opening a house to the public for a long season, year after year, obviously produces the need for a different kind of balance. Visitors must be shown what they have come to see, but if the reason is explained, they will readily appreciate why there are case covers on most of the chairs in a set, why a bed has case curtains, and why blinds are drawn. It can be justified in practical terms – the responsibility of today for tomorrow – and in historical terms too. (Many visitors would surely be intrigued to be told that servants were instructed not to touch gilding.) It can be explained that, in order to show fragile objects in the context of a house, it is necessary to have a code of conduct that includes, for example, reducing the level of light, for otherwise the objects would deteriorate, or even disappear, and that the alternative is to remove them to the neutral but controlled conditions of a museum.

Perhaps we do not always realize what a privilege it is to see so many of our country houses complete with their original contents, a sight that can hardly be paralleled anywhere else in the world, and cannot be re-created. How vital it is, therefore, that the traditions of housekeeping should not just be maintained, or revived where they have slipped, but improved in the light of modern scientific knowledge. It is, without doubt, the only way in which future generations will be able to share our experience to the full.

He had been eight years upon a project for extracting sun-beams out of cucumbers, which were to be
put into vials hermetically sealed, and let out to
warm the air in raw inclement summers . . .

Jonathan Swift, Voyage to Laputa, 1726

. . . The greatest event was that Mrs Jenkyns had
purchased a new carpet for the drawing room. Oh
the busy work Miss Matty and I had in chasing the
sunbeams as they fell in an afternoon right down on
this carpet through the blindless window! We
spread newspapers over the places and sat down to
our book or our work and lo! in a quarter of an
hour the sun had moved and was blazing away on a
fresh spot, and down again we went on our knees to
alter the position of the newspapers.

Mrs Gaskell, Cranford, 1853

Principiis obsta; sero medicina paratur Cum mala
per longas convaluere moras. (Stop it at the start,
it's late for medicine to be prepared when disease
has grown strong through long delays.)

Ovid, Remedia Amoris, 91

CHAPTER ONE

THE RIGHT ENVIRONMENT

Light
21

Environmental Conditions
25

Display Cases
31

4. Window curtains in tatters in the Tapestry Room at Erddig, showing the harmful effects of light

·✤ THE RIGHT ENVIRONMENT ✤·

There are three characteristics of the environment within a house that may be damaging to its contents: excessive exposure to light, the wrong relative humidity and air pollution. It is possible to exercise some control within individual rooms, and ways of doing this are explained in the following chapter. There is also a section on display cases, which may be used in situations where it is impossible to control the environment within a room, but a microclimate is needed for a particularly sensitive object.

LIGHT

Light is extremely harmful to many of the materials from which the contents of houses are made. It causes colour change and weakens materials, and these changes are irreversible. It is important to understand which materials are sensitive, what characteristics of light harm them and to take action to reduce the damaging effects.

The nature of light

Light is a type of radiation, and is a form of energy capable of causing photochemical change. These changes become apparent when a colour change is seen or when organic materials become weak and brittle.

Our eyes are only sensitive to part of the spectrum of radiation filtering through the earth's atmosphere, and we perceive this visible part of the spectrum as the rainbow colours, blue, green, yellow, orange and red. Beyond the blue end of the visible spectrum lies the ultraviolet region. The energy is greatest at this end of the spectrum, and ultraviolet is a particularly potent cause of photochemical damage. This potency decreases through the blue and green regions of the spectrum, and yellow, orange and red light produce little photochemical change. Beyond the red end of the spectrum is the infrared region, which heats objects, and by raising the temperature can cause damaging drying (see Relative humidity, p. 25).

Sensitive materials

Light is very damaging to organic materials, and unfortunately the majority of the contents of historic houses have animal or vegetable origins. Only the inorganic materials (metal, stone, glass and ceramics) are not affected by light. It is most probable that every room contains some organic materials which are very sensitive to light.

5. Sun-curtains in the Long Gallery, Hardwick

The most sensitive artefacts are textiles, water-colours and all works on paper (including wallpaper), miniatures, leather (including leather wall hangings), wood (where the surface colour is important), fur, feathers and other natural history exhibits. Oil paintings and ivory are also sensitive to light but can be exposed to slightly higher light levels (see Appendix 2, p. 307).

Methods of reducing damage by light

There are three basic rules for reducing damage by light:

Elimination of ultraviolet radiation

As ultraviolet radiation does not help us to see, and it is so damaging to organic materials, it should be eliminated from light sources. Daylight contains the highest proportion of ultraviolet and filters should be applied to windows to absorb the radiation. These filters are available as self-adhesive plastic films or as varnishes. They are usually guaranteed for five years, although in many situations they will last considerably longer than this. Their efficacy should be checked twice a year using an ultraviolet monitor (see Appendices 1 and 2).

Fluorescent lamps also emit significant amounts of ultraviolet radiation and should be fitted with ultraviolet absorbing sleeves. Occasionally tungsten-halogen lamps are used by photographers or film and television crews; these also emit ultraviolet but as they are very hot they cannot be fitted with plastic filters. Special types of glass filter are now available that will filter out the ultraviolet radiation.

Limiting time of exposure

Light damage is cumulative: twice as much damage is done by a certain light level in two hours as would be done in one hour. Rooms should be exposed to light for as short a time as possible. For example opening a house seven days a week rather than five increases the deterioration of the contents by exposure to light by 40%. Rooms should be blacked out as soon as the house is closed and not opened up again until just before the house is opened, except when a room is being cleaned.

Reduction of visible light levels

There is no threshold below which photochemical damage will not occur. Even the lowest light levels will cause damage if objects are exposed to them for a long time. A compromise has to be made between the need for visitors' enjoyment and the requirement for most of the contents to be exposed to as low a light level as possible. The recommended light levels (see Appendix 2) are as low as will still allow satisfactory viewing conditions.

Daylight levels must be reduced by the use of sun-blinds or sun-curtains. Sunlight is extremely damaging as it can produce light levels over one thousand times as high as those recommended for sensitive contents. Sunlight should never be allowed to shine directly on to any object; as well as causing photochemical damage the infrared radiation that it contains can heat the object. The level of sun-blinds should be adjusted according to the position of the sun and the weather. It is very difficult to judge light levels by eye, because of the eye's ability to adapt to different light levels, and a light meter (see Appendix 2, p. 307) should be used to make sure that no object is exposed to excessive light levels when the blinds have been set. In some rooms it will be necessary to use dark blinds in addition to the cream-coloured holland blinds (see Appendix 1, p. 301).

When reduced light levels are being used in a house, it is important that there are no bright areas, as they will destroy the eye's adaptation. For this reason it is important that no light source can shine into visitors' eyes. This can be a problem when artificial lighting is used.

Artificial light is much easier to control than daylight; a light meter should be used to ensure that the recommended levels are not exceeded. Once set up, the artificial light levels will not change, unlike daylight.

Some rooms are lit with tungsten incandescent lamps (ordinary electric light bulbs). They produce almost no ultraviolet radiation, but heating can be a problem if the recommended light levels are exceeded. Care should be taken when picture lights are used, as some are positioned too close to the surface of paintings, and the excessive light levels result in heating. Heating may also occur when tungsten lamps are used in display cases; the reduced ventilation may allow heat to build up, resulting in damagingly low levels of relative humidity. In these circumstances it may be advisable to replace the tungsten lamps with fibre optics or fluorescent lamps. Occasionally tungsten or tungsten-halogen spotlights are used. The tungsten-halogen spotlights must be used with glass filters, to absorb most of the ultraviolet radiation. A light meter must be used when they are being installed. Low voltage systems are an advantage as the fittings are smaller and therefore less intrusive than mains voltage systems.

Fibre optic light systems allow light from a projector to be transmitted along a glass fibre light-guide. They are very useful for lighting showcases and, because they are so unobtrusive, for lighting rooms where conventional light fittings or spotlights would be inappropriate. The glass fibre absorbs ultraviolet and infrared radiation, which reduces the risk of damage to objects.

Fluorescent lamps are available in a wide variety of sizes and a range of 'daylight' colours. Some of these may distort colour, and advice should be sought in selecting a lamp with good colour-rendering properties. All fluorescent lamps should be used with ultraviolet absorbing sleeves. If fluorescent lamps are used in display cases, the ballast unit should be installed outside, because it emits heat.

ENVIRONMENTAL CONDITIONS

There are three characteristics of the air in a room which give cause for concern: the temperature, the relative humidity and any air pollutants that may be present. Of these, the relative humidity is the most important to control. The temperature is significant in so far as it affects humidity, and also the rate of deterioration. We are limited in the action that we can take to control air pollutants that enter houses from outside, but we can take care to reduce levels of pollution that may be generated within a house.

Relative humidity

Relative humidity is a measure of the amount of water that the air holds, compared with the maximum that it can hold at that temperature. The higher the temperature, the more water the air can hold. As temperature rises, the relative humidity falls. Air with a low relative humidity is drying and absorbs water from any material with which it is in contact. Organic materials (those with animal or vegetable origins) are moisture-containing: as the relative humidity falls they lose water, resulting in shrinkage. Splits and cracks in furniture stem from periods of time when the relative humidity is low. Conversely, when temperature falls, the relative humidity rises and materials absorb moisture from the air.

Cycles of rising and falling relative humidity are very damaging, particularly when objects are made from many materials which expand and contract by different amounts. The cracks that appear in oil paintings are caused by changing relative humidity. The support (wood or canvas), ground, paint layers and varnish all react differently to changes in moisture content. Extremes of expansion and contraction cause the layers to lose their adhesion; eventually the paint flakes off altogether.

In addition to the great damage caused by fluctuating relative humidity, extremes are also a major cause of deterioration. If the relative humidity rises above 65%, mould may start to grow, and wood-boring insects and moths are more likely to attack organic materials. Below 50% cracking of wood may occur. In the United Kingdom the average outside levels of relative humidity are in the range of 75–85%. In houses we aim to keep the relative humidity as constant as possible within the target band of 50–65%.

In the following chapters a variety of 'ideal' specifications for relative humidity are given, the majority of which fall within the range of 50–65%. It

6. Problems caused by changing humidity: (left) veneer split as a result of dramatic fluctuation in relative humidity; (below) mould growth on the surface of a water-colour caused by high humidity

has to be recognized that, in houses, it is not possible to achieve the level of environmental control that can be achieved in a purpose-built museum. However, a great benefit for the conservation of the contents of houses can be achieved by avoiding the damaging extremes.

In order to control relative humidity, it is first necessary to measure it. Hygrometers are used for this. A selection of suitable hygrometers is described in Appendix 2, p. 308.

Temperature

Unlike humans, most objects are comparatively insensitive to temperature levels. Most organic materials change very little as temperature changes, provided that their moisture content remains constant. Metals undergo significant expansion and contraction on temperature change, and for this reason dramatic changes in temperature should be avoided. Chemical reactions and biological changes, such as mould growth, occur more rapidly at higher temperatures and, for this reason, lower temperatures are preferred in houses. However, by far the most important factor in selecting temperature is its effect on relative humidity. To a large extent, particularly in the winter, temperature can be manipulated to give relative humidity levels within the target band.

During the winter it is inadvisable to allow the temperature to fall below 5°C (41°F). Temperatures above this level should avoid the dangers of frozen pipes and subsequent flooding. In the following chapters a maximum temperature of 15°C (59°F) is specified for many objects, but it has to be recognized that it is impossible to keep below this limit all the time in houses without air conditioning. In the summer, sun-blinds will help to keep solar gain to a minimum.

Condensation will occur on any surface with a temperature below the dew point of the air. Windows are most affected, when outside temperatures are considerably cooler than those indoors. The room air adjacent to the glass cools and its relative humidity rises, until it reaches the saturation point of 100% and the water is deposited on the glass. The condensation that collects on window sills should be wiped off so as to avoid water stains. Artefacts should never be kept in places where there is a danger of condensation.

External walls are another area where there is also the danger of condensation occurring, or local conditions of high relative humidity. Pictures or other objects such as weapons or armour which hang on outside walls should have corks fixed to the back of them, so that air can circulate behind.

Heating

By monitoring relative humidity levels inside and outside National Trust houses over the past ten years, thanks to the efforts of house staff and more recently to the introduction of twenty-four-hour electronic recorders, a clear picture has emerged of the influence of temperature on relative humidity in houses in the United Kingdom. In order to reduce the average relative humidity from levels of 75–85% outside to the target band of 50–65% inside, the inside temperature needs to be raised by about 5°C (10°F) above the outside temperature. In most summers the sun does this for us, although rigorous use of the sun-blinds is important in ensuring that solar gain is not excessive in good summers. During winter, heating can be used to raise the temperature by the required amount.

As National Trust houses are closed during the winter months, they can be heated for the benefit of their contents, rather than for the comfort of visitors. In winter, when the average outside temperature may be below 5°C (41°F) for two or three months, this means heating houses only to temperatures of up to 10°C (50°F). The heating should not raise the temperature in a house to above 15°C (59°F). This is as much for reasons of economy as for the good of the contents, although at higher temperatures processes of deterioration will occur at a greater rate.

As well as being good for the contents, this represents an enormous potential saving in energy costs. Temporary local electrical heating, for example fan heaters, can be provided for staff working in rooms during the winter. It is very important that the heating system should operate for twenty-four hours a day.

The accommodation for families who live in the houses must be treated separately from the rooms containing sensitive contents. In some cases this means making alterations to central-heating circuits, so that hot water does not flow through the showrooms before reaching family apartments, causing dry conditions and wasting energy. The aim is to provide domestic heating where it is needed, and 'conservation' levels elsewhere.

When the house is opened to the public during the winter heating season, this is bound to have a detrimental effect on relative humidity levels. Once the temperature is raised more than 5°C (10°F) or so above that outside, for the comfort of visitors, the relative humidity may fall below the target band of 50–60%. Advice should be sought about the use of the heating before an event; it may be necessary to introduce humidifiers to add water vapour to the air (see below).

Dehumidifiers

It is also possible to reduce relative humidity to within the target band by removing water from the air using dehumidification. This method is preferred in areas which never have to be heated for comfort, as it uses about one third of the energy to achieve the same level of control as heating. However, draughts must be eliminated from the area to be dehumidified, otherwise fresh air replaces the dry air so fast that the dehumidifier becomes inefficient. It is particularly suitable for use in storage areas, where polythene tents can be constructed, and in special exhibition rooms, where a high standard of draught-proofing can be fitted.

There are two types of dehumidifier: desiccant and refrigerant. The desiccant dehumidifier contains a desiccant salt which absorbs water from the air. The water is then removed from the salt by heating and is exhausted from the machine, either as warm, moist air which is vented to the outside by a tube, or as condensed water which can be drained from the machine by a hose. It is efficient at all temperatures, and is therefore more suitable for use in areas where there is no heating in the winter. The refrigerant dehumidifier is cheaper to buy but its efficiency drops off dramatically as the temperature falls, until it becomes incapable of removing any water from the air at temperatures near freezing. It works on the same principle as a domestic refrigerator. Water from the air condenses as ice on the cold coils. Every twenty minutes or so, the machine enters a defrost cycle for a couple of minutes, the water drips off the cold coils and is drained from the machine by a hose.

Dehumidifiers are switched on and off by a humidistat. The humidistat has moisture-sensitive elements similar to those in a hygrometer, and can be set to switch on the dehumidifier when the relative humidity rises above a certain value, usually 65%. Like hygrometers, humidistats require frequent calibration.

Ventilation

In rooms, or sometimes in whole houses, which are known to be damp, and where measures have not been taken to reduce the relative humidity by heating or dehumidification, it is important that there is adequate ventilation. Biological agents of destruction, such as mould and insects, thrive in still air. Air circulation can be improved by opening internal doors, and also windows on days when the weather is fine. Common sense will dictate that windows should not be open in high winds or in unsuitable weather conditions such as rain, snow, fog or mist, or when the temperature within the house is below the dew point of the outside air. If windows are opened when a thaw follows a period of freezing weather, condensation will occur throughout the house.

Humidifiers

Ideally, there should be no need for humidifiers in historic houses. They are necessary only when rooms are over-heated. However, this does sometimes happen, either if rooms are used domestically, or if they are opened for special functions during the winter. If the temperature is raised by more than 5°C (10°F) or so above outside levels, the relative humidity may fall below the target band of 50–65%, and it becomes necessary to add water vapour to the air. The familiar bowls of water left standing by a fire, or reservoirs of water hooked on to radiators, are quite incapable of adding sufficient water vapour to the air. Humidifiers are designed to force water vapour into the air.

There are four types available. Evaporative, steam, ultrasonic and atomizing. Evaporative types are most suitable for use in rooms with precious contents. A hollow rotating drum fitted with a sponge around its circumference picks up water from a reservoir; a fan in the centre of the drum blows the water off the sponge into the air. It can be plumbed in and used with tap water, as any salts remain behind on the sponge. It is very important to keep these machines clean, by using a fungicide in the water and by removing the hard-water salts periodically.

Steam humidifiers work on the electric kettle principle and consume large amounts of energy. Ultrasonic humidifiers contain a plate which vibrates rapidly, so that water droplets on the plate are forced into the air. Atomizing humidifiers contain rapidly rotating blades which disperse water into the air. Both these types will also add any hard-water salts to the air, and therefore must be used with distilled water to prevent a thin film of salts from being deposited around the room.

As with dehumidifiers, humidifiers should be used with humidistats which switch them on when the relative humidity falls below 50%.

Air pollution

There are two types of air pollutant: particulate and gaseous.

Particulate matter, which we usually describe as dust or dirt, has many sources. Grit blown into a house from outside, textile fibres broken off carpets by visitors' feet, soot produced by the burning of fossil fuels, to name but three. We can attempt to reduce the amount of particulate matter entering a house by keeping doors and windows closed on windy days and using good-quality door mats on which visitors can wipe their feet. However, the deposition of some dust on surfaces inside a house is inevitable, and once there it can cause soiling and can attract moisture, biological organisms and acidic pollutant gases. It is therefore very important to remove this particulate pollution by the cleaning methods described in later chapters.

The main sources of atmospheric gaseous air pollutants are the burning of fossil fuels in power stations, and motor vehicles. The acidic gases sulphur dioxide and nitrogen dioxide can cause great damage to stone, metal and organic materials. Ozone is produced naturally in the upper atmosphere, and forms a layer that protects the planet from the very damaging short-wavelength ultraviolet radiation. However, at ground level, where it is generated by the action of sunlight on car exhaust fumes and by certain types of electrical equipment, it is an extremely reactive pollutant which attacks all organic material. It is hard to control levels of gaseous air pollutants without the use of sophisticated air-handling plants. However, it may be a slight advantage that, although air pollution has now spread throughout the world, levels may be marginally lower in houses in country areas which are away from main roads and industrial centres.

It is possible to reduce levels of air pollutants generated within houses. Photocopying machines are a potential source of ozone, and these should not be installed near showrooms. Care should be taken that all fumes from boilers are exhausted up chimneys and not allowed to leak into the house. Display cases can contain dangerously high levels of pollutants from their construction materials, particularly when they are well sealed.

DISPLAY CASES

A microclimate can be provided within a room that would otherwise expose objects to an unsuitable environment by using display cases. In some houses these cases are almost as large as the room, and the visitors walk into a glass enclosure which separates them from the sensitive contents. More commonly, objects are placed in small cases, which may be adapted furniture, or specially constructed boxes. Advice should be sought when the use of display cases is being considered.

Lighting

Ideally, the light source should be outside the case, in a top or side panel. This overcomes the problem of heat build-up, and enables bulbs to be replaced without disturbing the display. If the lamps can only be positioned within the case, less heat will be generated by fluorescent lamps, and no heat generated by fibre optics, provided the fluorescent lamp ballast and the fibre optic projector are outside the case. If the room cannot be blacked out when the house is closed, daylight should be excluded from the case by covering with a thick, dark-coloured material, such as velvet or felt.

Relative humidity

One of the great advantages of using a display case is that relative humidity changes will be considerably less inside the case than outside, because of the buffering effect of moisture-containing materials within the case. A case made of wood and lined with fabric or paper will provide a considerable volume of buffering material. If a case is well sealed, so that changes of air with the room are minimized, it is possible to maintain a higher or lower average relative humidity within a case than the ambient conditions in the room. This can be achieved by using a conditioning material such as silica gel, or by pumping in air of the desired relative humidity. It is essential to seek specialist advice if a microclimate is required. A small dial hygrometer (see Appendix 2, p. 309) should be placed in display cases, and the reading checked daily.

Pollution

In a well-sealed case, designed to provide a stable relative humidity, it is very important that no materials are used in the construction of the case that can give off harmful vapours. Advice should be sought when display cases are being made. Materials such as glass and metal are safe, but wood can produce formic and acetic acids, which attack metals and organic materials. Undyed cotton and linen are safe, but lining materials of silk and wool, or those dyed with certain dyes, can produce dangerous levels of sulphides which tarnish silver and corrode some metals.

New cases, or existing cases which have been lined or relined, should be left open for a few weeks before placing objects in them. This will allow time for resin and adhesive fumes to evaporate. Work on cases must therefore be carried out well ahead of the date on which a house is opened to the public.

If there is no special requirement for relative humidity control, cases can be ventilated to prevent the build-up of pollutants. Ventilation grilles should be positioned near the tops of cases to avoid dust and dirt rising from the floor, and if possible they should be placed at an angle to exclude settling dust. The grilles should be fitted with easily replaceable filters.

Cleaning

If display cases contain objects that might particularly attract the attention of thieves, unbreakable polycarbonate plastic sheets may be used rather than glass. Care should be taken when cleaning these, as they are more susceptible to scratching than glass.

No attempt should be made to clean or dust the objects once they have been arranged in a display case. If the display does appear dusty, or if there is any sign of deterioration in the exhibits, a conservator should be consulted.

Rigidity

Suitably designed supports, covered with cotton or good-quality acid-free paper, should be provided for objects which could move or fall over if the display case were accidentally knocked. The legs of the case should be packed if the floor is uneven. Vibration caused by visitors' feet can shake the cases.

Labels

Labels should be on good-quality acid-free paper or card placed near the object. Small stainless-steel pins may be used to secure the label in position. A label should never be attached to an object, nor should double or single-sided Sellotape, Blu-tack or any other adhesive be used.

Building and decorating work

When building or decorating is to be carried out in or near the room which contains a display case, the objects should be removed to another room which can be kept clean and where the relative humidity can be controlled if necessary. The objects should be transferred carefully with clean hands, and placed on clean white blotting paper on a table or other flat surface. Cover them loosely with acid-free tissue paper and do not return them to the display case until at least two weeks after the redecoration work is completed and the paint fumes have dispersed.

Knowing I lov'd my books, he furnish'd me from mine own library with volumes that I prize above my dukedom.

Shakespeare, *The Tempest*, 1623

Books are not absolutely dead things, but do contain a potency of life in them to be as active as that soul was whose progeny they are . . .

Milton, *Areopagitica*, 1644

CHAPTER TWO

BOOKS AND DOCUMENTS

BOOKS

Introduction
37

Shelf List
37

Cleaning – Routine Care
39

Handling
43

Shelving and Storage Conditions
47

Security
54

Display
55

Books in Need of Repair and Special Cleaning
56

DOCUMENTS

General Remarks
56

Routine Examination
58

7. The library at Dunham Massey

·✤ BOOKS ✤·

INTRODUCTION

It cannot be emphasized too strongly how necessary it is to be careful whenever handling books. A moment's carelessness can ruin a book whose interest and value may well lie in the fact that it has survived undamaged for centuries. A leather binding is not a guaranteed indication of value, and some of the most interesting books may look most unimpressive. A tattered paper wrapper may well be of greater value and almost certainly of greater interest than an ordinary gold-tooled leather binding. So equal care should be taken with every book, however unprepossessing it may appear. Never let the routine nature of much of the work which has to be done to books result in loss of concentration. The too-generous application of the leather dressing can stain leather permanently, and a moment's clumsiness with a duster can cause a lot of damage.

In houses open to the public, there are likely to be books whose condition or value makes it advisable to keep them out of the showrooms. If it is at all possible, shelving should be provided in some part of the house where these special books can be adequately housed. To make it easier to keep a check on the condition of all the library material in a house, and to make it available for use, the material must be protected, accessible and sorted. Sorting will normally involve the relocation of material, and can only be accomplished by the provision not only of extra shelving, but of carefully labelled boxes for some of the more ephemeral material which most houses contain. Such rehousing, in decent conditions, will make the material accessible both for use and periodic examination. It is a case where organization and conservation can be made to serve each other's interests, and where neither is entirely effective without the other. Sorting and classifying material should if possible be carried out under the supervision of a qualified librarian.

SHELF LIST

When cataloguing or carrying out conservation work on the library of a historic house, books should not be moved from the shelves until they have received their shelfmarks. The order in which they are arranged may be of historic interest.

A list of all books, arranged in shelf order, is compiled for every National Trust house for use during routine checks on lost or misplaced volumes. If a system has been used in the library, for historic reasons this should be retained; otherwise a new listing should be made. This is work which can be done by amateurs, and is not to be confused with the cataloguing undertaken by a professional librarian.

To make a shelf list, the bookcases in the library must be divided up into bays, or vertical banks of shelves. There may be two or more bays within a single bookcase, but the width of each bay is defined by the length of the individual shelves, and the bays will be divided one from the other by a vertical member. If a single bookcase contains three bays and there is no existing system of numbering, or lettering, then each bay can be numbered from left to right, 1, 2, 3, or A, B, C.

The books are now ready to receive their shelfmarks, which should be made in pencil on the first plain paper leaf in the book, putting the marks, as far as possible, in the same place in each book. Always write lightly in a book as heavy pressure will mark the leaf below, and may damage some soft papers. Each volume in a multi-volume set should be given a different number.

Any existing shelfmarks must be left undisturbed and not rubbed out. If the new mark might be confused with the old, draw brackets lightly, in pencil, round the old mark.

Starting from the top shelf of a bay, work through the books from left to right on the shelf, writing in each book three separate numbers:

       bay number   shelf number   book number.

The first book taken down from the top shelf would therefore be marked 1.a.1. or A.1.1. The third book from the second shelf down of the second bay would be marked 2.b.3, or B.2.3 and so on. As each book is given its shelfmark, the mark, followed by the title and author of the book (abbreviated if necessary), should be entered in the shelf list.

If a bookcase of three bays has already been given the letter A, the bays can be lettered from left to right A1, A2, A3. This would be followed in the usual way by the shelf number and the book number, A1.a.1 and A2.b.3.

Within each library there may well be a need to adapt any system to suit local peculiarities of library arrangement, but it is important that once each bay has been identified, a neatly drawn plan of the library, with each bay marked on it, be kept with the completed shelf list.

If it should ever prove necessary to move a book after it has received its shelfmark, do not rub out the shelfmark, as this will be the only record of where the book was formerly placed. Instead put brackets round it, and enter the shelfmark of the new location. Remember also to change the shelfmark in the shelf list, and leave a slip of paper or card in the previous location with the title of the book and the new location on it.

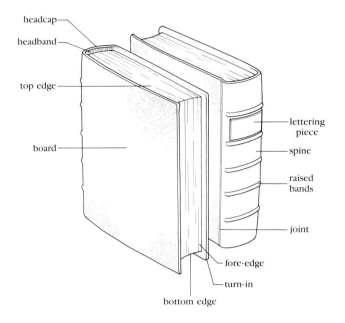

headcap

headband

top edge

board

lettering piece

spine

raised bands

joint

fore-edge

turn-in

bottom edge

Fig. 1

CLEANING – ROUTINE CARE

It is best to take out all the books on a single shelf so that the woodwork can be inspected and dusted. It will make the job easier if there is a strong table near by to put the books on. Make sure that you can see the surface of the shelf when removing the books so that you can notice any signs of insect infestation, such as debris from woodworm, damaged woodwork, etc.

Never attempt to remove dust from the tops of books by banging the books together.

Hold the book firmly by the fore-edge to keep it closed, otherwise you will simply drive the dust into the book. Gently brush along the top edge of the book from spine to fore-edge, using a light, flicking motion with a clean dry hogshair brush – or use a shaving brush (see fig. 2a and Appendix 3, p. 319). Dust trapped in front of the headband should be gently brushed out towards the fore-edge.

Dust which has filtered down the inside of the boards and joints should also be brushed out – but only open the boards to 90°, which is quite far enough, but will not strain the joint.

If it is noticed that dust has got on to the pages of a book, as is often the case when the paper has cockled slightly and opened up the top edge of a book, it

(a)   (b)

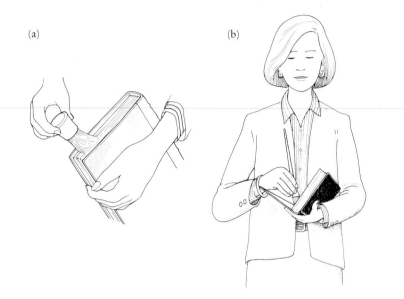

Fig. 2. Dusting a book

may be brushed out very carefully, page by page, with a soft sable or ponyhair brush (see fig. 2b and Appendix 3, p. 319).

Do not attempt to hurry this work; hands must be washed frequently to avoid transferring dirt from one book to another.

As always, particular care should be taken of damaged and fragile books, which should be set aside if they cannot be handled safely.

Dust on the sides of the book or the spine can easily be cleaned off with a duster, making sure that you are holding the loose corners of the duster in your hand so that they cannot catch on the book.

Where books have a thick layer of dust, it is best if they undergo an initial cleaning as they are removed from the shelves and before they are looked at, moved, or receive any other treatment. Use a Hoover Dustette equipped with the brush head. A piece of gauze, nylon net or a similar material should be placed across the tube behind the brush to prevent any small pieces of leather, headbands, etc., being sucked into the vacuum cleaner.

Follow the instructions given above for holding the book closed, but avoid any pressure from the brush on the book.

When doing routine dusting look out for mould, woodworm, silverfish, mice and other pests. Books in boxes or bookshoes (see fig. 14, p. 53) should be taken out for dusting, if only to check on possible infestation or other damage. But be careful – books are usually kept in boxes because they are especially valuable or fragile – or both.

Dog-ears

Dog-eared pages allow dust to penetrate a book, and they should be turned back. The crease left in the page will be evidence of their location. If they are brittle, however, they are better left alone, but comparatively little paper of pre-19th-century date will be brittle. Dog-ears should be distinguished from a turned-in corner that preserves the original dimensions of the sheet of paper, having been turned in before the edges of the book were ploughed or guillotined. These should be left undisturbed, as they provide important evidence of the book's make-up and history.

Maps and documents

These are best left alone folded into a book. They should be examined with great care, and only when necessary, because the paper will frequently tear along the folds, especially where a fold is curved over the opening of a book.

Books with ties

Books which still retain their *silk or linen ties* on the fore-edges should be handled with great care. Do not attempt to tie and untie them as they are usually very fragile. Unless the book is boxed, it is safest to tuck the ties inside the boards before reshelving the book. (See fig. 1 for terminology.)

Loose material

There are two categories of loose material: those items that have become detached from the book, such as headbands, lettering pieces, etc., and those items which have been inserted into the book, in the way of bookmarks, notes, etc. It is important that items in both categories are preserved and not divorced from the books they come from.

Loose boards and spines

Loose or detached boards and spines should be neatly bound with a soft tape to hold them together. This also serves as a warning that they are damaged. When tying the tapes use a bow, as other knots, being hard to untie, will tempt people to force them off over the end of the book, with the consequent likelihood of damaging the leather. *Never* use string or elastic bands to hold books together, for these will damage the books.

Card wrappers can be made to protect damaged books, as shown in fig. 3. Use acid-free lightweight board and tie the wrapper round the book with tape. A fore-edge wrapper can be used to prevent metal fittings from scratching the books on either side of them (see fig. 14, p. 53).

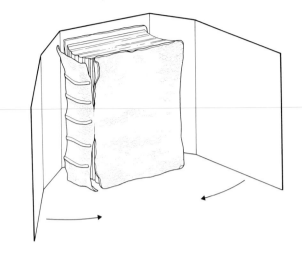

Fig. 3. A protective card wrapper

If, in cleaning and handling books, lettering pieces, headbands, etc., become detached, they should be placed in envelopes clearly marked with the shelf-mark and short title of the book, and these envelopes should be kept together where they can easily be found when books are removed for repair. Attempts should not be made to stick them back unless someone working in the house has been shown how to do this work by a professional book conservator.

No bits of paper inserted into a volume, however apparently unimportant, should be thrown away. They should be kept, as they may have a bearing on the history of the book or the house.

Bookmarks, notes, etc., should be left in the books in the places where they were found. As they may be of significance, record the page number where they are to be found, and the short titles and shelfmarks of the books. (A notebook might usefully be kept in each library for this purpose, and to record other points of interest noticed by those working on the books.) If for any reason such material is removed from books, place it in an envelope with the page number, short title and shelfmark clearly marked on it. This does not apply to metal clips or pins which, if left in the book, may rust and cause damage to the document. Where necessary these may be replaced with stainless-steel pins or clips, but if they have become fixed to the paper by rust, a conservator should be asked to remove them and to repair the paper.

HANDLING

Books are easily damaged by careless handling, especially if they are already in a fragile state. Safe handling is mostly a matter of common sense, but the following guidelines may be helpful.

Removal from shelves

Never pull a book out by putting your fingers over the top of the spine; this may well pull the headband and headcap away from the spine (see fig. 4a). Never pull a book out by gripping the back with your fingernails, as this may scratch it (see fig. 4b). If there is room above the book, reach over the top of the book to the fore-edge and then pull it out (see fig. 5a). If there is no room, push back the books on either side of the one to be removed, to expose enough of its spine to allow you to get a firm grip on it (see fig. 5b).

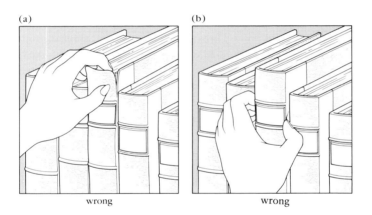

Fig. 4

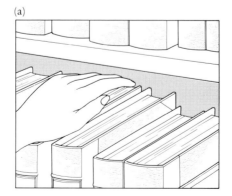

Fig. 5

(b)   (c)

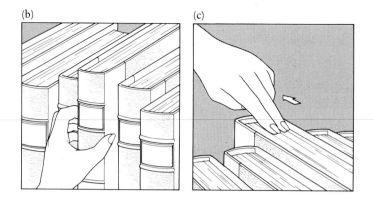

If none of these is possible, use light finger pressure on the top edge of the book to ease it out of the shelf, until enough is exposed to allow it to be grasped firmly (see fig. 5c).

Books must never be so tightly packed in a shelf that it is difficult to move them. When removing a large heavy book from a shelf, grasp its bottom edge as it is pulled out of the shelf so as to be ready to take its weight (see fig. 6).

Fig. 6

It is useful to have two people removing large books from shelves, so that while one is removing individual volumes, the other is holding the remaining books back to prevent them falling over. If shelves have to be left half-filled, heavy smooth-faced blocks or several books on their sides should be used as book-ends to keep the remaining books upright (see fig. 7).

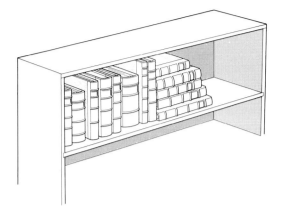

Fig. 7

Carrying books

Never carry more books than you can comfortably hold firmly in both hands (see fig. 8). A small book sliding around on top of a large one is always in danger of falling off. Even when moving large quantities of books, resist the temptation to take on more in weight or size than you can manage easily.

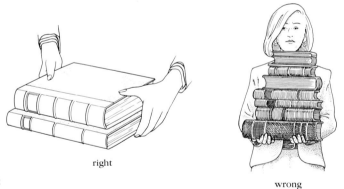

right

Fig. 8   wrong

Should it ever be necessary to move books further than just across the room or into the next-door room, and certainly if stairs have to be negotiated, the books should be moved in tough boxes, with the books lying on their sides. Never force books into the box, and never pack in more than the person who is to carry the box can manage with comfort. Extra large books should not be carried horizontally, like a tray, but upright either under the arm, or, if too large for that, in front of you with both hands (see fig. 9).

Fig. 9

Always treat books which are badly damaged, or bound in fragile materials such as silk or paper, with extreme care, and never pile them up on top of each other. Books covered in dust should not be opened until they have been cleaned, or the dust will get into the book and dirty the pages. (See Cleaning – routine care, p. 39).

Stacking books

Never support books on their fore-edges, as this is likely to damage the structure of a book and loosen the binding (see fig. 10). Keep books well away from liquids, vases of flowers, cups of coffee and so on. Books, especially older books which may well be slightly rounded or wedge-shaped, should not be

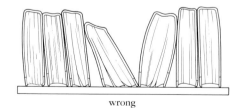

Fig. 10   wrong

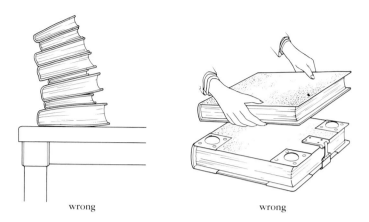

wrong   wrong

Fig. 11

stacked in tall piles, as these are easily knocked over; keep books with metal clasps or bosses separate (see fig. 11).

Transporting books

The books, whether damaged or not, should be wrapped in clean paper and several layers of Bubblewrap and packed in tough cardboard boxes padded with blankets or polystyrene blocks so that they cannot slide around in the box. The box should then be placed in the transporting vehicle in such a position that sudden stops, corners, etc., will not displace it. Putting books loose on the back seat of a car is an invitation to disaster.

If at all possible, books should not be sent by post, nor left in cars or vans overnight, or unattended.

SHELVING AND STORAGE CONDITIONS

If the conditions in which books are kept are inadequate, they will deteriorate on the shelves. A regular check should be kept on the light, temperature and humidity levels in the rooms in which books are kept.

Light

Light will degrade and discolour the organic materials from which books are made. The stronger the light and the longer the exposure to light, the greater the damage. Blinds should be fitted to the windows of libraries, and shutters closed whenever the room is not in use. Ultraviolet-absorbent varnish or film should be applied to the window glass. Fluorescent light fittings in storage rooms should be fitted with UV-absorbent sleeves.

Temperature

As a general rule, the temperature of a room in which books or documents are kept should be as low as practicable, though not as low as to allow condensation to form. At lower temperatures, biological and chemical deterioration processes will occur more slowly. However, the more important consideration is the effect of temperature on relative humidity, and the temperature should be controlled to give relative humidity in the correct range.

Relative humidity

Books, being made almost entirely of organic materials, need a certain amount of moisture. Excessive dryness will lead to the gradual embrittlement of paper, leather and vellum, but excessive moisture will lead to the loosening of starch- and gelatine-based adhesives, and, if there is inadequate ventilation, to mould growth and consequent increase in the incidence of insect attack.

Ideally, the relative humidity of the air around the books should not fall below 55% nor rise above 65%. Fluctuating relative humidity is particularly damaging, and is usually caused by changing temperature. During the winter, heating systems should be kept running twenty-four hours a day, at a temperature that keeps the relative humidity in the recommended range, provided the temperature does not rise above 15°C (59°F) (see The Right Environment, p. 25). Regular temperature and relative humidity readings should be taken and recorded at several places in the room, as conditions may vary between one part and another, especially in large rooms, and particularly behind books against outside walls. Recording thermohygrographs or electronic dataloggers (see Appendix 2, p. 311) are particularly useful for giving detailed information about environmental conditions. The sensors of the electronic recorders are small enough to be placed behind the books on a shelf.

Mould

Whenever mould is detected in books, a professional conservator should be informed immediately, so that appropriate action may be taken. Basically, however, mould can be eliminated only by providing the right environmental conditions. Fungicides provide at best no more than a temporary answer and may even render the books more vulnerable to mould damage.

Pests

Excessive moisture may also provide the right conditions for such pests as silverfish, which will damage both leather and paper.

The creatures which cause the most damage to books are silverfish, book-lice, leather beetles, the larvae of the common furniture beetle (woodworm), the deathwatch beetle and the brown house moth. The first two live on the mould-damaged organic material, and are best controlled by ensuring that damp conditions do not occur. If they are found in any books, or shelving, the source of the moisture giving rise to the mould on which they feed must be located and put right. Silverfish, especially, can cause extensive damage. The other insects do not need damp conditions to thrive, though attack is encouraged by damp-softened papers, and a careful check must be made regularly for signs of infestation. Infestation by wood-boring insects may well have its origin in the woodwork of the shelving or the structure of the house itself, in which case more radical treatment will be required. Infected shelves can be treated with Cuprinol Low Odour Woodworm Killer, but do not replace the books on treated shelves for at least three weeks.

Rats and mice will attack books if they are given the chance. The gelatine glue used on the spines of many books is particularly attractive to them (and dogs), but they will also eat vellum and leather and chew up paper for nesting material. A single mouse can ruin a fine book in a few hours, and the least sign of infestation must receive prompt and efficient attention.

Ventilation

It is important to ensure that not only the rooms where books are kept but also the shelves in which they are kept are properly ventilated.

Inadequate ventilation, coupled with excessive moisture, will result in mould growth. Mould spores will always be present in the air in the houses, but they will only germinate in too damp conditions.

In some cases a fair amount of ingenuity, and possibly expense, will be needed to open up air passages without disturbing the appearance of the shelving. However, the importance of ventilation, especially where there are presses against outside walls, cannot be over-emphasized. Unchecked mould growth can cause hundreds of pounds' worth of damage to a single book, and will eventually destroy the book altogether.

Ventilation is needed in two places – behind the books and behind the bookcases, especially when the bookcase is against an outside wall. Ventilation behind the books can usually be provided quite easily by leaving the shelves 25 mm narrower than the side members by shaving off approximately 25 mm from the back of each shelf. If the shelves are fixed irremovably, then 25 mm diameter holes can be drilled along the back of the shelves at 100 mm intervals. Ventilation behind the bookcases should take the form of an air space at least 25 mm wide between the backing boards of the case and the wall. To be effective, there must be gaps at top and bottom of the case as well, to allow air to move behind the case. The bottom shelf of the case, which is usually immovable, should be ventilated by drilling holes, as described above, and this should have the added effect of opening up ventilation behind the case (see fig. 12).

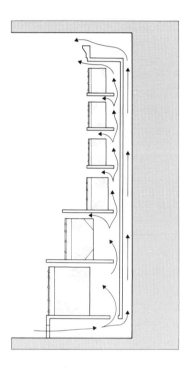

Fig. 12. Cross-section of a bookcase, showing passages for the movement of air

Drawers, cupboards and bookcases with glass doors are potentially danger-ous unless adequately ventilated. In the case of documents and books in drawers and cupboards, removal to better storage elsewhere in the house may be the best answer.

Shelving

Most books are kept on shelves, and the shelving should be designed to provide secure, clean and convenient support for the books in it. Old shelving will frequently need modification to bring it up to standard and new shelving should be designed with the needs of the books in mind.

Unless books can be removed from and replaced on the shelves easily and without obstruction, there is always the likelihood of the books being damaged. The dead spaces formed at the end of some shelves by projecting fascia boards which overlap the front of the shelves should be filled up with wooden blocks. Any projections which are likely to come into contact with books should be removed or otherwise made harmless.

Many old bookcases have grooves cut in the sides to take the shelves at different levels, and these can often mark the books placed against them. This can be avoided by inserting a piece of acid-free mounting board between the book and the side member of the case. Another method of adjustment, the rack and batten system, provides an awkward space at the end of the shelves in which smaller books can become trapped and damaged. This space should be blocked out flush with the thickness of the racks. Where the ends of shelves are obscured by doors or overlapping frames, they too should be blocked out to prevent books becoming stuck at each end of the shelves (see fig. 13).

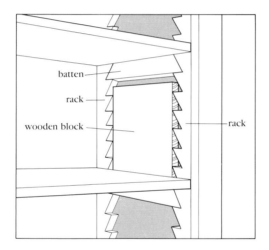

Fig. 13

Any surface that books come into contact with should be kept smooth, if not polished. A rough shelf or side member will wear down a binding very quickly.

Shelves which have sagged and have come into contact with books on the shelf below should be straightened and supported, perhaps by the insertion of a vertical member through the middle of the whole case.

Books must never be crammed tightly into shelves. This will scuff the leather, crush embossed bindings and lead to damage when attempts are made to move the books into or out of the shelves. Equally, books should not be so loosely packed that they will lean over at an angle. This will distort and strain the structures and eventually cause their breakdown. When correctly packed, the books should be easy to move in or out of the shelves, and yet give support to each other on the shelf. If there are not enough books to fill up a shelf, wooden blocks should be used to take up the vacant space. If it is felt to be necessary, these can be given false leather spines, or painted in imitation of leather.

Books of different sizes

Large books should be kept next to large books and small books next to small. A large book with small books on either side will receive no support above the level of the small books, which will put a strain on its structure. But rearrangement of books on the shelves should only take place after the original position of the book has been recorded. Once the books have been arranged in their final positions, a shelf list can be made.

Large books

Many large books should not be stood upright, as they are either too thick or too heavy to support their own weight. Where it can be seen that the fore-edge has begun to sag on to the shelf, it is best that the book is stored horizontally. Do not, however, stack large numbers of books in a pile, as this may damage the books at the bottom. Alternatives include removing the books at risk to extra shelving, or inserting extra shelves in the library bookcase to take several volumes on their sides, or using bookshoes to give the necessary support to books which have to be kept upright.

Books with clasps and bosses

Books with metal furniture, such as clasps, bosses, cornerpieces, etc., make very bad neighbours and will scratch and rip the leather on books on either side of them. As a temporary expedient, a piece of acid-free card should be placed against one board, folded round the fore-edge and on to the other board. This will leave the spine visible while covering the metalwork (see fig. 14).

Bookshoes

The bookshoe is a sort of open-topped slip case which gives support, by means of a textblock packing piece, to heavy and sagging book structures while keeping the book shut under slight pressure and protecting its sides. At the same time, it remains almost invisible on the shelf. It gives more permanent protection than the fore-edge wrapper, but requires special equipment for its manufacture (see fig. 14).

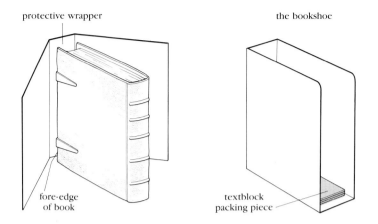

protective wrapper

the bookshoe

fore-edge
of book

textblock
packing piece

Fig. 14. A protective wrapper for books with clasps, ties and delicate tooling, and a bookshoe for large sagging and damaged books. Both leave the tops and spines of the books exposed, but the bookshoe gives more permanent protection

New shelving

Most houses need some new shelving to house books displaced in putting the library shelving in order and to house books stored in inadequate conditions in attics, basements, etc. All such books should be placed on shelves in a dry, clean room where they are seen regularly and are available for use and examination. Books kept in boxes and piles on floors are inaccessible for both purposes. All the shelves apart from the bottom one should be adjustable. This allows for the most flexible and therefore most economical use of the space available. The exact means by which the adjustment is effected can be left to the carpenter, but a simple system of wooden pegs, with holes drilled at 25 mm centres in the vertical members, is quite adequate. Care should be taken to ensure that, whatever system is used, no part of it will be likely to mark or damage the books. The shelves should be at least 20 mm thick, planed smooth, and not more than 760 mm long. They should be at least 230 mm deep for the most part, though shelving up to 460 mm deep will have to be provided for larger books according to the demands of each collection.

If the new shelving is against an outside wall, it should be equipped with a back which must be held at least 25 mm away from the wall. Whether it is against an inside or an outside wall, there should be provision for an air passage behind the books within the bookcase. This is simply achieved by leaving the shelves 25 mm narrower than the side members. A hardwood should be used in preference to a softwood. Metal shelving should not be used, because of the danger of corrosion, nor should glass-fronted shelving or cupboards, unless they are in rooms which are sufficiently dry.

SECURITY

Nylon lines stretched across the front of shelves can act as a deterrent, but care must be taken to ensure that the line does not come into contact with the books. Books should not be tied together in blocks as this is likely to damage the books at each end. A simple system of stringing lines between pieces of wood or hardboard placed between the ends of the shelves and the books at each end is quite effective and does not hamper unnecessarily the normal handling of the books (see fig. 15). Security systems which are inconvenient to use will be abused.

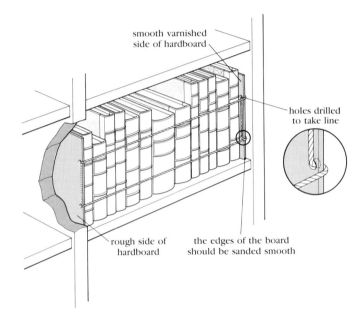

smooth varnished side of hardboard

holes drilled to take line

rough side of hardboard

the edges of the board should be sanded smooth

Fig. 15. Security lines. The line must be taken over the edge of the boards, and the boards should stand slightly proud of the books on the shelf, so that the line does not come into contact with the books. The smooth sides of the boards should be coated with polyurethane varnish to prevent acid migration from the board to the neighbouring book

A shelf full of books, so that a gap would be obvious if one were taken, is also a deterrent. However, books should never be put under pressure in the shelves as this will damage them.

Where valuable books are kept, a steward should always be in the room if it is open to the public, and books on popular subjects, such as gardening, should be kept well out of reach.

Books of exceptional value should, whenever possible, be kept behind locked grilles, or, if this is not possible, removed for safe keeping to another part of the house, but only if the conditions there are satisfactory. Safes and strongrooms, especially those situated in basements, may well be damp and are frequently unventilated.

DISPLAY

The careless and poorly controlled display of books is a major source of damage and deterioration. Books and documents should be displayed only in rooms with proper controls over light levels, temperature and humidity. Display cases should be large enough to take the books comfortably, and must be properly ventilated or otherwise designed to control fluctuations in humidity and temperature. Exhibition in either over-dry or damp rooms should be avoided. Ultraviolet-absorbent filters should be fitted to the glass, unless the windows have already been treated, and the cases should be solidly made so that accidental knocks from visitors do not shake the contents.

Whenever books are selected for display, whether in houses open to the public or on loan to other institutions, however prestigious they may be, the best course is to consult a professional book conservator, who will be able to

8. A cradle made of acid-free board for a book on display

give information on the safest way to exhibit the book. If the minimum conditions laid down are not provided, the book should *not* go on display. Material such as light-sensitive, hand-painted initials and miniatures, and fragile bindings must only be displayed in very carefully controlled conditions, physical and atmospheric. Wherever possible, the use of photographs and facsimiles instead is to be recommended.

In many libraries books are left open in cases at one page throughout the season when the house is open. In many cases this will put a severe strain on the binding if it is not properly cradled and supported. A conservator should be consulted about correct cradling angles and methods of strapping. Overlong exhibition may also result in the fading of pigments and the discoloration of paper. Exhibits should be changed regularly. The National Trust aims to display no single item more than once in every ten years, and then for no more than six months at a time – or less, for sensitive materials. Wherever possible good-quality reproductions should be used to avoid the risk of destroying a binding and spoiling its contents.

BOOKS IN NEED OF REPAIR AND SPECIAL CLEANING

No books should be repaired without the advice of a trained book conservator. There is also little point in embarking on expensive repair work on individual books before the storage conditions to which they will be returned are checked, and, if necessary, put right (see Shelving and storage conditions, p. 47).

A certain amount of cleaning, leather dressing and repair work can be done by amateurs but only under the supervision of a trained book conservator. Serious and permanent damage can be done by using inappropriate methods and materials.

·✣ DOCUMENTS ✣·

GENERAL REMARKS

Light and damp are the greatest causes of damage to documents. Most other damage is caused by careless handling or inadequate protection in storage and transport. The normal practice in the National Trust is for documents to be kept at the appropriate County Record Office, where they can be studied under supervision more easily than in the house.

Handling

All documents should be handled with the greatest care. Never pick up fragile documents with a finger and thumb but support them on a suitable backing sheet. When damage to a document is extensive, it should not be handled or unfolded or unrolled for inspection. The damage should be noted and the advice of a professional paper conservator sought.

If the document has a seal hanging loose, the seal on the document should be supported on thin card if it has to be moved or lifted on to another flat surface. If the seal is to be stored, use acid-free card (see Seals, p. 58).

No attempt should be made to change the sequence of the documents or remove fastening materials, as this may result in the loss of evidence of the original make-up of the documents (see also Routine examination, p. 58).

Loose fragments from documents and maps should be placed in an acid-free envelope and kept with the documents concerned.

Large documents, maps and charts should be unrolled for inspection only if they are strong enough to stand this treatment and then only if a large smooth flat surface is available on which they can be supported. When unrolled, weights will be needed to keep the document flat.

Arrangements should be made to treat large documents, maps and charts so that they can be kept flat, as there is then less chance of damage occurring than when they have to be unrolled for inspection. Vellum documents are particularly unmanageable, especially when they are tightly rolled, as they frequently are.

Light

Strong light, particularly sunlight, causes rapid and irreversible deterioration to paper and also causes inks and pigments to fade. Sunlight should be excluded where documents are displayed and fluorescent tubes should *always* be fitted with ultraviolet-absorbent sleeves.

Ideally, documents should be kept in the dark, stored flat in special acid-free folders or solander cases.

Atmospheric conditions

The temperature and relative humidity conditions required by documents are similar to those recommended for books. Extremes of high and low relative humidity should be avoided, and good ventilation is required in case there are pockets of damp air. Provided the relative humidity is in the recommended range, the temperature should be as low as possible, as high temperatures shorten the life of paper. For this reason, documents should never be stored near radiators or other sources of heat. Attics are suitable for storage only when well insulated.

Mould and mildew

Mould prevention requires that both temperature and humidity be kept within reasonable limits and a good circulation of air maintained.

If mould is discovered in paper documents, immediate action should be taken to improve the environmental conditions so that the mould cannot continue to propagate. The documents should be treated by a professional paper conservator.

Display

Facsimiles of documents can often be exhibited in place of valuable and irreplaceable originals.

When originals are to be shown, display cases should be checked by a professional conservator at the design stage, as slight alterations could make all the difference to the safety of the document. The lighting and ventilation of display cases is particularly important. Documents on display should not be in contact with unsuitable materials.

ROUTINE EXAMINATION

Stored documents

Documents should be checked by a paper conservator and, if necessary, de-acidified before being stored.

Stored documents should be examined at regular intervals, say once a year.

A careful watch should be kept for paper and board that is becoming brown or brittle and for ink that is attacking the paper (see Pictures, p. 229).

Care should be taken to avoid documents being kept in close contact with unsuitable materials. Paper clips, staples and pins made from ferrous metals can rust and cause disfigurement and damage and should be removed, taking care to preserve at all times the original arrangements of the papers. Where necessary they can be replaced with stainless-steel pins or clips, but if they have become fixed to the paper by rust, a conservator should be asked to remove them and to repair the paper.

Paper, vellum and parchment are attractive to rodents and a special watch should be kept for signs of mice.

Seals

Special care is necessary if the document has applied or pendant seals. Pendant seals should be protected by packing with loosely crumpled acid-free tissue paper (see Handling, p. 57). If in doubt, consult a conservator.

Cleaning

Never attempt to remove ingrained dirt from documents and maps. Cleaning should be left to a paper conservator. *Never* attempt to brush away dirt from written, decorated or illuminated areas.

See also Parchment, p. 235.

Then said another – 'Surely not in vain
My Substance from the common Earth was ta'en
That He who subtly wrought me into Shape
Should stamp me back to common Earth again.'

Fitzgerald, *Rubáiyát of Omar Khayyám*, 1859

Whoso teacheth a fool, is as one that gleweth a potsherd together.

Ecclesiasticus xxii, 7

CHAPTER THREE

CERAMICS

Environment
63

Accidents
63

Inspecting for old repairs
63

Handling
65

Cleaning
67

Display
71

Storing
72

9. The State Closet at Beningbrough, showing porcelain displayed on a tiered overmantel of about 1715

·✣ CERAMICS ✣·

Ceramics is a broad term covering porcelain and all types of pottery.

ENVIRONMENT

Ceramics are not so much affected by light, temperature and relative humidity as are organic materials. However, in fluctuating levels of relative humidity, salts which may be present in low-fired earthenwares can repeatedly dissolve and crystallize, eventually causing glazes and bodies to flake. High humidity will affect adhesives and overpaints, causing them to fail more rapidly. Mould may grow on animal glues and natural resins in high humidity where the temperature is high and the ventilation poor.

The drying effect of heat accelerates the breakdown of materials used in ceramic repairs. The most common source of heat is tungsten lighting when it is used in display cases that are not adequately ventilated. Every time the lights are turned on and off the change in temperature will also cause humidity to fluctuate. The intensity of the light will affect the repair materials, causing discoloration. (For suitable lighting, see The Right Environment, p. 21).

ACCIDENTS

Ceramics will not deteriorate while awaiting repair, so do not attempt to stick things together in the house, but consult a conservator.

If an object is dropped, never try to fit pieces together to see if they join, as more damage is done to the broken edges through being grated together.

Wrap each piece separately in tissue paper and put away safely in a strong box, clearly labelled. Be sure to pick up all the tiniest chips, which may have fallen over a wide area.

INSPECTING FOR OLD REPAIRS

Before attempting to move or clean a ceramic, inspect it carefully to see where it may be weak or badly repaired. In particular look out for:

Rivets

Iron or brass staples used in the past to clamp broken edges together, set in holes drilled in the ceramic and packed in with plaster. Whenever possible these should be removed by a conservator and the ceramic properly repaired. If stored in damp conditions, rivets can corrode and stain the ceramic. They may also work loose and exert an uneven pressure, causing further cracks and damage.

Adhesives

Until the 1950s, these were often based on animal or vegetable matter, and are readily soluble in water. They are also liable to fail suddenly and without warning. Often the adhesive has discoloured brown; the more discoloured it is, the weaker the join may be. Large quantities of adhesive do not indicate a stronger joint, as the break edges will not be tightly bonded. More recently, epoxy resins have been used, but even these are not all water-resistant.

Overpaint

A synthetic varnish used to simulate ceramic glaze and hide repair. Over the years, with exposure to heat and light, this discolours and becomes rather yellow. Often it conceals areas of undamaged ceramic. If it appears to be flaking, this may indicate that the repair underneath is deteriorating. Never be tempted to pick off the overpaint, as it is easy to scratch the ceramic underneath. Consult a conservator and have the ceramic repaired again.

Fillings

Before 1950, plaster was commonly used to fill missing areas. Allowed to become damp or wet, the plaster will deteriorate and dissolve. Nowadays fillings are made of epoxy putty, acrylic or polyester resin. Often they are tinted to match the body of the ceramic, obviating the need for any overpaint, and providing a more discreet and long-lasting repair.

Hairline or travelling cracks

These occur when a ceramic has been knocked against a hard surface, causing a crack to run from the edge of the vessel towards the centre. Cracks most often appear in ceramics which shrank unevenly during the firing process, creating a stress in the body. If the ceramic is handled carelessly and knocked again the crack will 'travel' further, eventually breaking the ceramic. Cracked ceramics are not safe for display and must be consolidated by a conservator.

HANDLING

Ceramics should be handled as little as possible.

Always look carefully at the object before attempting to lift it to see if there are any repairs that could part or bits that could be knocked off.

Always use both hands when picking up an object and make sure you have plenty of elbow room and are not liable to knock another object. *Never* reach over one object to pick up another. Always handle one piece at a time.

Hairline cracks are difficult to detect by eye, so as well as taking care when picking objects up, be equally careful when putting them down again. Take extra care when putting ceramics down on very hard surfaces, such as marble.

It really is necessary to concentrate when handling objects; do not turn round to talk to someone, particularly when putting something down. The distance above the table surface can easily be misjudged and too heavy an impact will cause breakage.

If objects are to be left out on a table for any length of time, make sure that they are placed well away from the edges so that they do not get accidentally knocked over by people passing by.

Always put an object down safely before answering the telephone or opening a door; it is advisable to have two people available for carrying whenever doors need to be opened, as this saves putting the object down and picking it up again.

Lids

Test carefully any object with a lid to see if it is fixed or loose and do not pick it up by the knob or handle. If the lid is loose, remove it and place it somewhere safe before picking up the rest of the object. Even if it appears to be stuck or attached in some way, always support the lid with one hand when turning the object upside down.

Handles and rims

Never pick any object up by the knob or handle. Knobs or handles may have been broken and repaired. Use both hands cradled under the base when lifting a jug or cup. *Never* pick up a plate or bowl by the rim alone, but support it under the base, using both hands.

Figurines: bocage

Objects with bocage or pieces sticking out should be picked up by supporting the base with both hands. Flowers, leaves, etc., particularly on Chelsea- or Derby-type figurines, are extremely delicate and pieces can snap off quite easily if gripped.

10. A Delft vase from Dyrham before and after repair. The fragments should never be placed in contact, as in the top photograph

Carrying objects

A basket, wicker if possible, is best for carrying objects, but baskets are expensive, bulky and difficult to store, so plastic-coated wire trays sold for storing vegetables or as freezer baskets can be used instead. Line them with felt and use plenty of tissue paper for padding.

Whether using a basket or tray, when carrying several articles at once make sure that the weight is evenly distributed so that it can be carried level and that there is enough packing between each item to prevent them rolling against each other should the basket be tipped or jolted.

Never try and squeeze in that one extra object to save a trip.

When dealing with an object of awkward size, or one which is very heavy or extensively repaired, be sure to have enough padding and, if necessary, have another person to assist. Do not have odd pieces hanging over the edges of the tray or basket.

CLEANING

Dusting

It is better to dust infrequently but thoroughly than to attempt to dust every object daily in a hurry. In houses that are open to the public, try to dust ceramics on a closed day when there is more time. One of the several advantages of closed days is to allow the necessary time for careful cleaning.

Large ceramics with smooth surfaces can be dusted with a soft duster, making sure that it has no loose threads or dragging corners that could catch or snag. Steady the object with one hand, and wipe gently with the other, avoiding gilded areas which may gradually be worn away.

Smaller ceramics with knobs and handles, figurines and objects with raised or encrusted decoration are best dusted with the tips of a hogshair brush (see Appendix 3, p. 318). Wrap the metal ferrule of the brush in insulating tape to prevent the metal from scratching or knocking the ceramic. Steady the item with one hand while brushing with the other.

Spring-cleaning

Ceramics should be handled as little as possible. Every time an object is dusted it is at risk, so during the winter, when houses normally opened to the public are closed and where space is available, move all ornaments except clocks on to one table and cover them individually with paper hats made of acid-free tissue paper and pins, and marked with the inventory number. This avoids the need to dust and so considerably reduces the possibility of an accident. Another advantage is that the chimneypieces, shelves and occasional tables, etc., are clear, ready for the room to be spring-cleaned. Also, covering the objects for five months of the year when the house is closed may postpone the need for special cleaning for several years.

As with furniture, if the object looks clean and fresh no special cleaning is necessary. A careful dust with a soft duster or a hogshair brush should be enough. Occasionally, if builders have been working in the house or objects have come from a store, ceramics have to be washed. First try to identify the type of ceramic.

Ceramics can be roughly divided into the following four categories:

Low-fired pottery or earthenwares (soft, porous)
For example, Neolithic, Greek, Roman and Chinese potteries; (tin-glazed) Islamic and Hispano-Moresque potteries, Italian majolica, French faience, Dutch delft and English delftwares; (lead-glazed) Islamic potteries, slipwares, Staffordshire potteries.

High-fired pottery or stonewares (non-porous)
Chinese Yueh ware and celadons; (salt-glazed) Rhenish and English stone-wares; (lead-glazed) Staffordshire stonewares and creamwares; (unglazed) Wedgwood basalt and jasper wares.

Soft-paste 'imitation' porcelain (porous)
Medici, Capodimonte, Rouen, St Cloud, Mennecy, Vincennes, Sèvres, Bow, Chelsea, Derby, Worcester; bone china; (unglazed) Parian wares.

Hard-paste 'true' porcelain (non-porous)
Chinese and Japanese porcelains, Meissen, Vienna, Plymouth, Bristol; (un-glazed) biscuit wares.

Low-fired potteries and soft-paste porcelains tend to be more fragile and porous; high-fired stonewares and hard-paste porcelains are generally more durable and non-porous.

Preliminary examination

Always examine the object very carefully before washing, as many old repairs were done with water-soluble adhesives which part relatively easily in warm water. Also consult a ceramics conservator before cleaning very dirty pieces, as over-painted areas may not be so obvious when the rest of the object is dirty, but could show up and be visually disturbing against a cleaner surrounding, making further restoration necessary.

Ceramics which should be cleaned with special care and attention

Unglazed ceramics

Terracottas, Wedgwood stonewares, earthenwares, Greek and Roman pot-teries are extremely difficult to clean without driving dirt further into the porous body. A conservator can use sophisticated techniques to remove the dirt without causing further damage.

Porous and soft-paste ceramics

Porous and soft-paste ceramics should not be immersed, as dirty water absorbed through the base can cause staining. They also take a considerable time to dry out thoroughly, but they can be stood on a flat surface and cleaned using swabs of damp cotton wool.

Parian and biscuit ware

Parian and biscuit ware, which are usually white, are unglazed. The dirt is often ingrained in the surface, which makes it harder to clean. If the dirt does not respond to water and Synperonic N, consult a conservator.

Gold decoration

Never immerse an object which has gold decoration. Gold sometimes comes away even when dusted, so, with any form of cleaning, stop if the gold appears to be unstable.

Metal and ormolu mounts

Metal, especially ormolu, must not get wet. Ceramics which have ormolu mounts should be dusted and, if very dirty, the ceramics only cleaned with a slightly damp swab of cotton wool and dried immediately.

Damaged glazes

Glazes make the porous bodies of ceramics watertight. If the glaze is chipped, cracked, crazed, flaking or otherwise affected by iridescence, stains or emerg-ing salts, it should not be washed, as water penetrating the glaze will aggravate the problem. The body will also be difficult to dry out, and further staining may occur underneath the glaze. Consult a conservator who will be able to treat the problem and clean the ceramic safely.

Equipment needed for washing ceramics

It is not necessary to wash ceramics near running water. A sink with its taps and other projections is often the most dangerous place. It is often better to set up a trestle table in the room rather than carry the objects a great distance.

Cover the working area of the table top with a piece of thin foam plastic (5–10 mm) to soften the surface and cover the foam with a tea towel. Protect the floor with dust-sheets. Do not use polythene sheeting on the floor as it is very slippery. Place a plastic bucket half-full of clean, tepid water under the table cn the dust-sheet. Half fill a small bowl from the bucket and add one drop of Synperonic N (see Appendix 3, p. 321) to the water. *Never* use ordinary household detergents, which may contain harmful additives such as bleach. If Synperonic N is not available, Fairy Liquid, a mild commercial detergent, is a suitable alternative. *Never* use soap, as it will leave the object smeary.

Washing

As it is often very difficult to see old repairs, do not immerse the object but stand it on the table and wash it with cotton-wool swabs, damp rather than wet, held in the hand. A hogshair brush will usually deal with the more intricate parts that are difficult to get at.

Always keep one hand on the object when washing, as a support. Work from the top down, rinsing off as you go with a cotton-wool swab squeezed out in clean water. The swab must be kept clean, which means changing it frequently. Use a tiny cotton bud (made by twisting cotton wool on to a wooden toothpick) to clean soapy water out of small crevices.

Allow each piece to dry naturally, standing on a soft linen tea towel or white kitchen paper towels.

If washing the piece on the table top is too worrying, have a plastic bowl available. Stand the object in the empty bowl and then, still supporting the item with one hand, clean it in the bowl (see Washing, above). Figurines are better washed in a round bowl, as allowance must be made, for example, for outstretched arms, branches and foliage, which could easily be knocked.

Accidents while washing

Should any object come apart, or an accident occur, allow the pieces to dry naturally and then wrap each piece separately in tissue paper or soft paper towel. *Never* attempt to fit the bits together again, as you may damage the edges, making the object difficult for a conservator to repair.

Very dirty objects

If the object is exceptionally dirty it may be better to take it to a sink so that the dirty water can drain away. The less the object is handled the better. Make absolutely sure that the object is well clear of the taps, which can easily get in the way of taller objects. Wrap the taps round with old rags or dusters as a safeguard against an accidental knock. Line the bottom of the sink with foam plastic. Make sure that the water is lukewarm.

Greasy dirt on glazed surfaces

A mixture of 300 ml white spirit, 300 ml water, with half a teaspoonful of Synperonic N, makes a good cleaner for greasy dirt on glazed surfaces. (If Synperonic N is not available, use Fairy Liquid.) Shake well before use and apply with a swab of cotton wool. Rinse well in clean water, using a damp cotton-wool swab. Use this treatment on rare occasions and only on glazed surfaces. Always try lukewarm water with a very little Synperonic N first, and if in doubt ask a specialist conservator.

Stains

Never use household detergents or bleaches on ceramics to try to remove stains.

DISPLAY

Mats

Most ceramics have rough bases which can scratch polished surfaces. Mats made out of chamois leather or suitably coloured felt can give protection. Use craft felt for small objects and thick felt (Feltlux) for heavy pieces. Large mats should be cut at least 30 mm larger than the diameter of the foot-rim, as felt often shrinks. Where smaller objects need to be moved frequently for dusting, it is sometimes possible to stick felt on to the foot-rim. Cut a series of 10 mm wide strips of craft felt on a curve and stick them carefully to the foot-rim using a water-soluble adhesive or PVA emulsion (such as Evostick Resin W). This method leaves the manufacturer's mark and the inventory number still visible on the base of the ceramic.

All flower vases should stand on glass mats, even if placed on marble or stone-topped surfaces. Water can so easily spill and not be noticed, leaving marks on all types of surface (see Furniture, p. 109).

Plate stands

The size and weight of the plate stand must be adequate to counterbalance the plate. The height of the back support should measure at least three quarters of the diameter of the plate. The plate should incline backwards at an angle of about 20°. A plate stand of polished wood with a rectangular base lined with felt is appropriate but is hard to find and may need to be made by a cabinet-maker or furniture conservator. Perspex stands (one type for plates and another for bowls) are available by mail order from a number of firms (see Appendix 4).

Hanging plates

Plastic-coated metal hangers, with four arms and two springs, are safe to use for hanging plates provided the plate has no hairline or travelling cracks.

It is important to make sure that the hanger is the correct size for the plate; if too small the plate will be put under stress. The arms should be long enough to reach from rim to footrim, so that the springs lie flat within the footrim and are not stretched over it.

At present it is not possible to buy these hangers for plates larger then 350 mm diameter, so display larger plates on plate stands or commission a special perspex mount.

As a temporary measure, protect ceramic glaze from metal clip hangers with strips of chamois leather or polythene tubing until replaced with plastic-coated metal hangers.

When removing or fitting a plate hanger, one person should steady the plate while the other stretches the springs. Existing plate hangers without springs need to be removed carefully by using a hacksaw blade. While cutting, protect the back of the plate from accidental scratching with a strip of thin card under the line of the cutting blade.

STORING

Do not overcrowd shelves or cupboards and, wherever possible, place smaller objects in front of larger ones.

Make sure an object is dry before it is put away in a cupboard.

Before closing cupboard doors, check that there is plenty of clearance and that the object will not get damaged.

Cups and bowls

Never stack cups and bowls one inside another. It is worth the expense to fit extra shelves, narrow and shallow, between existing ones, for accommodating smaller objects. It will save time as well as being safer for them. Do not hang cups on hooks by their handles and do not turn them upside down as this may damage thin or gilded rims.

Plates

Never stack more than ten plates in a pile and make sure that the plates in a pile are of the same shape and size. Never put a larger plate on top of a smaller one and always place damaged or repaired plates on the top of the pile.

Interleave a pile of plates with white kitchen paper towel or with folded pieces of tissue paper to protect the surface of each plate from the foot-rim of the plate above and to stop one plate wobbling on another. Deep soup plates often need thicker padding than tissue paper to give the necessary support.

Make sure that any metal hangers on plates are removed before storing.

Figurines

Space out well and take particular care that there is plenty of clearance before closing cupboard doors. Cover each item with an individual paper hat and label each cover clearly.

Transporting ceramics by car

When packing ceramics for transport by car, take particular care to pad rims and handles of vessels, and the heads and limbs of figurines. Use rolled-up pads of acid-free tissue paper to wrap the ceramics and secure with masking tape. Pack each part separately, e.g. lids and jars. If the ceramic is broken, state clearly the number of fragments on the outside of the package.

Further protect the package with a double layer of Bubblewrap, secured with masking tape. Place the bundle in a strong cardboard box, lined with a 50 mm layer of foam plastic, with extra layers between bundles and inside the lid.

Be sure to wedge the box in the car in such a way that it will not fall if the car stops or swerves suddenly. A seat-belt is often useful to restrain boxes on the seat of a car.

'Pray my dear', quoth my mother, 'have you not forgot to wind up the clock?' – 'Good G—!' cried my father, making an exclamation, but taking care to moderate his voice at the same time, – 'Did ever woman, since the creation of the world, interrupt a man with such a silly question?'

Laurence Sterne, *Tristram Shandy*, 1759–67

CHAPTER FOUR

CLOCKS AND WATCHES

Display
77

Care and Maintenance
77

Handling, Taking Down and Setting Up
80

Storing
87

11. At Anglesey Abbey, a fine ormolu musical automaton clock by Henry Borrell of London, c. 1800. Every four hours the clock plays one of four tunes on ten bells as the plants slowly revolve and unfold their leaves

Clocks and watches should be kept out of extremes of temperature, humidity and airborne dust, which means away from direct sunlight, radiators, central-heating vents and positions near open fires. Windowsills, which are exposed to extreme changes of temperatures and where condensation might form, should also be avoided.

The ideal conditions for the wooden cases of clocks conflict with the needs of the metal mechanism, but a good compromise would be 50–65% relative humidity, in a temperature not exceeding 15°C (59°F). The atmosphere should, of course, be as clean as possible.

As well as avoiding sudden changes in temperature and humidity, try to choose a position where the clock is least likely to have to be moved, and where it will be on a solid, stable base.

CARE AND MAINTENANCE

Clocks in good working order should be kept wound and running. If clocks are stopped for long periods, e.g. during the winter months, the lubrication can sometimes solidify or spread. They should be inspected by a conservator before being started again to ensure the lubrication is sound. While watches should be kept in good working order, it is not recommended that any watch not in everyday use be wound and run.

If a clock does not work, or begins to behave erratically, it should be *left stopped* until it can be inspected by a properly qualified clock-maker. There are very few capable of properly restoring and recording a rare clock; never trust the 'little man round the corner'.

Day-to-day care

Never try to repair, clean or oil clock or watch mechanisms or to clean the dials or brass case mounts in any way.

Dust the case with a clean, soft duster and avoid using proprietary glass cleaners which may contain ammonia.

If the case is of wood and needs polishing, use the recommended wax furniture polish (see Furniture, p. 109), making sure the case is steady and that there are no loose or projecting veneers or mouldings that could be 'snatched' by the cloth. Should parts become detached, put them in an envelope, marked with the inventory number, in the furniture 'bit box' so that they can be re-attached on the next visit of a furniture conservator.

Pieces removed from clocks and returned by the clock conservator should also be labelled and preserved for possible future reference.

Watch cases should be dusted but not polished, as this would wear the surface. An occasional 'dusting' with a silver cloth is acceptable.

All clock cases should be kept locked and case keys, as well as those for winding, should be kept labelled and in one safe place. A board on a wall would be ideal.

Tower and stable clocks should be maintained only by a recommended specialist company, on a contract basis.

Winding and setting

Each clock should have its own winding key, which should fit the squares in the clock snugly to avoid damage.

When winding, keep the clock case steady with one hand and wind with care, especially towards the end. It is useful to note or remember the direction of winding and the number of turns needed for each clock. Also, it is a good idea, if there are several eight-day clocks in the house, to choose one set day of the week on which to wind them all.

If there are a number of clocks requiring winding it is a good idea to use a portable keyboard to carry the keys (see plate 12). With the keys organized in the order of winding, finding each key is much easier and missing keys can be spotted readily. The appropriate winding keys can also be carried, on the reverse side of this board. The board shown has a compartment at the base, useful for dusters, etc., and the reverse side has a slot for keeping a notebook, should the going of the clocks need to be recorded. The board can be stood upright on the floor. After use hang the board on a wall out of the way.

When setting the hands always move them clockwise, *never* anti-clockwise.

On striking clocks, wait for the clock to finish striking before moving on; for example, if the clock is quarter striking, you should wait at each quarter hour until it has completed striking.

If for any reason the hands should jam, do not force them. This applies to all movable parts.

The calendar indication in an aperture on the dial of some long-case clocks is often difficult to advance at the end of short months. This is best done by pushing the calendar forward (usually from left to right) with an 'eraser pencil' (a pencil with eraser rubber instead of lead), but avoid those containing abrasives. Venus 'Type-e-Rase' is one good make.

When winding a tower or stable clock always use the 'maintaining power' device, if present, to avoid damage to the escapement (see fig. 16).

12. Portable clock keyboard

If hand setting on a tower or stable clock can only be achieved by disengaging the pallets of the escapement and letting the clock run freely, always keep the speed low, and *never* re-engage the pallets until the escape wheel is stationary.

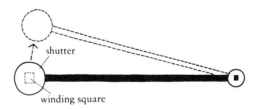

Fig. 16. 'Maintaining power' device

Regulating

With pendulum-controlled clocks, the pendulum bob must be lowered if running too fast and raised if running too slow.

79

Find the rating nut, usually below the bob, which, if turned clockwise (when looking down on the nut from above), lowers the bob to make the clock go slower and vice versa (fig. 17). Only a very small adjustment is usually necessary. For example, on a typical English long-case clock, one complete turn of the nut is usually about 30 seconds per day.

Some French pendulum clocks have a small square above the twelve on the dial, for fine regulating. This is useful as it saves having to move these often very cumbersome clocks. Use a small watch key, normally turning the square anti-clockwise to slow the clock down, and vice versa. If it is necessary to adjust the pendulum of a 19th-century French clock, the nut is often positioned in the *centre* of the bob (see fig. 17). With these pendulums it is usually necessary to slacken a screw on the back of the bob before adjustment. The pendulum will have to be taken off for this operation.

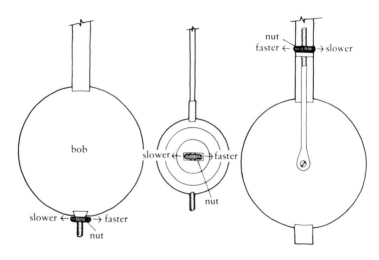

Fig. 17

Clocks with platform escapements instead of a pendulum normally have a small lever to regulate the rate of the balance, but this adjustment is better left to a qualified clock-maker.

HANDLING, TAKING DOWN AND SETTING UP

Avoid the handling, taking down and setting up of clocks. Consult an expert first; if handling is unavoidable, the advice given below must be followed.

Spring-driven clocks

Never pick up a clock by its carrying handle alone. Support it underneath as well in case the handle fails.

Platform escapement clocks, with balance wheels, may be moved carefully without fear of damage to the mechanism.

There is sometimes a pendulum-securing device on English pendulum spring clocks. It might take the form of a brass threaded knob (normally stored screwed into one of the case brackets) which should be unscrewed and screwed over the pendulum rod into a central brass block (fig. 18) or there may be a similar device with a clip instead of a brass knob (see fig. 19). Sometimes, on earlier spring clocks with verge escapement, there is a C-shaped hook on one side of the plate, into which the pendulum rod can be placed (fig. 20).

Even without such devices, pendulum spring clocks with a crutch can be moved short distances if the dial of the clock is leant towards the carrier so that the pendulum is resting on the backplate of the movement.

If the pendulum is removed the clock might 'trip' (run faster than usual). This does no harm. Beware of damaging the very delicate suspension spring of the pendulum, usually attached to the top of the pendulum rod in English clocks, but often attached to the movement in French clocks. It is not possible to remove the pendulum on verge clocks (see fig. 20).

Sometimes, especially in French clocks, it is necessary to remove the bell, if on the backplate, before the pendulum can be removed.

Setting up again involves procedures very similar to those for weight-driven clocks.

Weight-driven clocks (long-case, lantern clocks, etc.)

Proceed as follows if a weight-driven clock has to be moved, or if it is to be taken away for repair. Cotton gloves should be worn when stabilizing the movement so as to avoid leaving fingerprints on the metalwork (see Handling, p. 109).

Wait until the clock has completely wound down.

With the clock stopped, remove the hood (on hooded wall clocks and long-case clocks). Sometimes, up inside the case, just below the bottom of the hood, a hidden swivelling catch or a vertical bolt locks the hood. Once this is undone the hood should slide forward; or sometimes on early English clocks the hood rises and may be lifted right off. (The catch on the backboard of these clocks cannot normally be relied upon.)

Lift the weights off their pulleys.

Stabilize the movement, with one hand on the edge of the dial, as it may not be secured in the case, and lift the pendulum up and back, off the suspension block, allowing the thin, delicate suspension spring to pass down through the

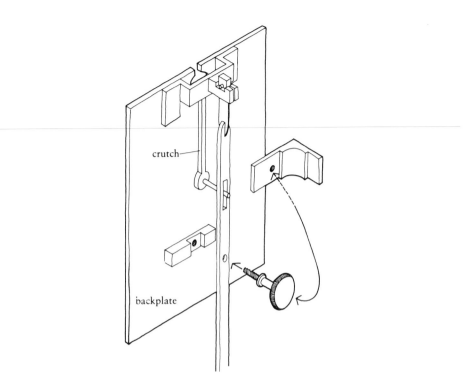

crutch

backplate

Fig. 18

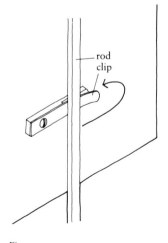

rod
clip

Fig. 19

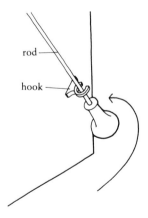

rod

hook

Fig. 20

crutch while lowering the pendulum (fig. 21). This operation is more easily performed with a helper (also wearing cotton gloves) at hand to stabilize the movement.

While the pendulum is out, be careful not to damage the suspension spring.

The movements of wooden-cased clocks can now be removed from the case. With 'tavern' clocks and the like, the movement can be left in.

The movements of eight-day and month-going clocks should be removed from the case with the seat-board, at the same time guiding the weight lines out of the case. This might mean unscrewing the seat-board, if it is not loose, or, if it is firmly secured to the case with nails, seek the advice of a recommended clock-maker as the lines will have to be cut.

On thirty-hour clocks it is often possible simply to lift the movement out, guiding its rope or chain without having to remove the seat-board.

Clocks without cases, such as lantern clocks, can, of course, just be lifted down from the wall at this stage.

When the movement is down, the lines should be carefully wrapped around the seat-board, or coiled up neatly, to prevent them from becoming tangled with the movement or each other. Then it should be stored in a box padded with acid-free tissue paper.

The case can now be moved.

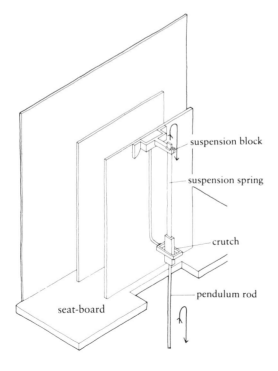

suspension block

suspension spring

crutch

pendulum rod

seat-board

Fig. 21

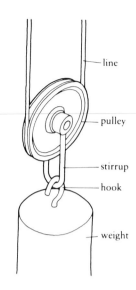

line

pulley

stirrup

hook

weight

Fig. 22

Setting up

To set up again, weight-driven clocks like long-case and hooded wall clocks should be screwed on to the wall, and this should be done only in consultation with the qualified clock-maker. Make sure that the case is vertical, not tilting forward or backward, so that the pendulum will be free to swing in the case.

Unwind the lines/rope/chain, and feed them into the case as you replace the movement. Here again, a helping hand is an advantage. Stabilize the movement until the weights are replaced.

Make sure the movement is central in the case; if it is too far back the crutch will touch the backboard. Rescrew the seat-board if applicable.

Find the bottom of each line with its pulley and hang the weight on the pulley stirrup or hook, at the same time making sure that the line is on the pulley wheel (fig. 22). Once this is done the timekeeping side of the clock might start to 'trip' – run faster than usual. This is quite normal.

Hang the pendulum on by carefully feeding the suspension spring up through the crutch and sliding the spring forwards through the fine slot in the middle of the suspension block (fig. 21).

Ideally the clock should be 'in beat', which means that the times between 'tick' and 'tock' should be equal. If necessary, this can be achieved by gently bending the crutch in the middle, but this is a delicate operation and if in any doubt (and the adjustment is only very slight), it is probably better to tilt the case very slightly. With long-case clocks, if the case is screwed to the wall it is

13. The giant long-case clock by George Graham in the hall at Dunham Massey

14. The rare wooden mechanism from the long-case clock by John Harrison of Barrow, dated 1717, at Nostell Priory

often possible to shift the base of the clock sideways a little to bring the clock into beat.

These notes on handling are by necessity very brief, and there will inevitably be many exceptions to all these general rules. Therefore, if in any doubt always seek the advice of the recommended clock-maker.

STORING

Clocks in store must have their pendulums, weights, keys and other appendages clearly labelled and boxed, or attached to the clock in some way.

Watches not on display should be kept together, wrapped in acid-free tissue paper and locked up in a safe place.

Storage conditions, like display conditions, should avoid extremes of temperature and humidity, so areas such as cellars and attics should not normally be used.

A servant with this clause
Makes drudgery divine;
Who sweeps a room as for Thy laws
Makes that and th'action fine

George Herbert, 'The Elixir'
from *The Temple*, 1633

He [the Rubber] is under the Direction of the Housekeeper to Dry rub the Floors in the House . . . and assist upon the Ladders in Washing the wainscot and cornishes . . .

Any fee given by any Person or Persons who come out of curiosity to see ye house shall be divided viz.

To the housekeeper 1/5
To the rubber 1/5
To the housemaids 3/5

From the servants' instructions at
Boughton House, Northamptonshire,
in the time of John, 2nd Duke of Montagu
(*c.* 1730)

CHAPTER FIVE

FLOORS

Introduction
91

Protecting Floors
91

Dust Prevention
92

Cleaning
94

Sealing Floors
97

Rush Matting
97

Woven Coir Matting
98

Early Floor Coverings
98

15. Hoogstraeten's *trompe-l'œil* painting at Dyrham, dated 1662, showing a newly swept floor

·✤ FLOORS ✤·

In the 17th and 18th centuries, floors seem to have been seldom polished. An American visitor to England in 1772 described them being 'washed and rubbed almost daily', so that they 'have a whitish appearance, and an air of freshness and cleanliness, which the finest inlaid floor has not always'. Small beer was sometimes used to scrub floors, and so was vinegar. But washing, because it made a room damp and could damage pieces of furniture and skirtings, was not as popular in practice as 'dry scrubbing'. Susannah What-man's manuscript housekeeping book of 1776 advises the use of 'as little soap as possible (if any) in scowring rooms, Fuller's earth and fine sand preserves the colour of the boards, and does not leave a white appearance as soap does. All the rooms to be dry scrubbed with white sand.'

Hannah Glasse in her *Servants Directory*, published in 1760, also recommends this method: 'take some sand, pretty damp, but not too wet, and strew all over the Room, throwing it out of your Hand hard, and it will fly about the Floor and lick up all the Dust and Flew . . . Sope is not proper for boards, and sand and water shews the grain, which is the beauty of a Board.' An alternative was to sweep the floor with herbs: 'Take tanzy, mint, and Balm; first sweep the Room, then strew the Herbs on the Floor, and with a long hard Brush rub them well all over the Boards, till you have scrubb'd the Floor clean. When the Boards are quite dry, sweep off the greens, and with a dry Rubbing brush dry-rub them well, and they will look like mahogany, of a fine brown, and never want any other washing, and give a sweet smell to the Room.'

Without a large labour-force at hand to clear a room of furniture and to wash or dry-rub floors almost daily, it is hardly practicable to employ such methods today, particularly in houses open to the public, where floors generally need the protection of polish. On the other hand, it should never be forgotten that the dry, silvery look of old boards (in a room like the Saloon at Uppark) is infinitely preferable to the high polish too often seen in 18th-century interiors today.

PROTECTING FLOORS

Housekeeping starts at floor level. Floors suffer. Think of the number of feet walking across an entrance hall on a busy day. Floors also have to support the weight not only of visitors but of sculpture and heavy furniture.

Moving heavy objects

Before moving heavy objects across a floor, consider its construction. It is easy to see what a floor is made of, but how it is put together and what lies beneath it is a different matter. A paving stone, for example, may be too large for its thickness, particularly where there has been some settlement of the ground or brickwork on which it has been set, so that it is no longer well supported.

It is therefore better to assume the worst and to avoid a concentration of weight by laying down planks or chipboards, so as to spread the load when moving a heavy object across a floor.

Such a precaution also prevents scratching or crushing of an aged surface by such things as piano wheels, scaffolding poles or heavy table legs.

Stone or marble floors

The pavings of a stone floor are kept apart by lime mortar to prevent them from moving, which would result in the pinching and breaking of the edges of the pavings. Stone floors should therefore be kept well pointed with lime mortar that is weaker than the stone or marble paving. A well-pointed floor will also prevent the joints harbouring dirt and dust.

DUST PREVENTION

All floors take an incredible amount of wear and must be given protection from dust and grit. Experiments by the International Wool Secretariat prove that people's shoes are only cleaned of normal dirt after walking over three metres of absorbent matting.

Grids

Many paths and drives are surfaced with gravel which can scratch and cut into all types of floors. Metal or rubber grids set outside the entrance door can help clear stones from shoes. If alluvial pebbles, worn round by water, are laid as 'hoggin' on paths and drives, this problem will be much reduced.

Coconut matting

The lowly doormat is very important. In fact it is the first line of defence in keeping dust out of the house. Mats intended to clean visitors' feet should be at least large enough for both feet to fall on the mat when taking a normal stride. Large mats are heavy and difficult to handle so it is better to place two smaller mats together. Local ironmongers or builders' merchants will normally order special sizes from suppliers.

Coconut matting *must* be kept clean. It is so effective that, if not kept clean, it will simply get choked up with dust and start recycling dirt round the house instead of collecting it.

Vacuum daily with the strongest suction and at least once a week take the mat outside, turn it upside-down and beat it. Even more effective, occasionally take it outside, roll it up top side out and tie it before beating it with a stick. Rolling it up forces the fibres apart and lets the dirt out. When there is no time to take the mat outside, turn it upside-down and let people walk over it for a day. It is surprising how much dirt falls out. Only do this on the least busy day, as the mat moves easily when upside-down and so could be a hazard. Do *not* beat the mat against a wall, as this damages the edges.

Dust mats

There are many types of dust mat on the market and some are very effective. They are not pretty and are therefore difficult to fit into the setting of a historic house, but they collect dust and absorb moisture and are good in passages. Runners put down on really wet days give such good protection to the house that the utilitarian look can be accepted (see Appendix 4).

Druggets

Old stone or brick floors get very worn and can create a lot of dust. Use druggets of woven coir or jute to lessen the dust and protect the floor. If the floor is likely to be damp it is better not to have a rubber backing to the matting as it will trap any moisture.

Fragile and delicate floors, for example rare marble or painted or inlaid wood, should have a drugget of carpet or felt. If woven coir is chosen, carpet paper or underfelt must be used for the roughness of the matting can damage the floor surface (see also Textiles, p. 258, and Appendix 3, p. 312).

Plastic slippers

No visitor should walk round a house in unsuitable footwear, such as walking boots or gumboots. Sharp-heeled shoes do irreversible damage. They pockmark wooden floors, break up stone and can cut a carpet to ribbons. Plastic slippers that stretch to fit most feet are now available at such minimal cost that they can be given away (see Appendices 2 & 4).

16. Plastic protective throw-away overshoes and socks

CLEANING

Dusting floors

Old stone floors which are beginning to break up are particularly dusty. To prevent dust from flying about, vacuum wood, stone, marble or tiled floors with a domestic cylinder vacuum cleaner, or, in large houses, with an industrial vacuum cleaner, on low power. A dry mop picks up dust, but care must be taken to keep it clean.

Protect furniture from knocks by sticking a piece of thick art felt round the edges of the vacuum head.

Take great care that fringes on carpets, hangings and furniture are not sucked into the machine (see Textiles, p. 263).

Scrubbing floors

Wash and scrub floors only when necessary. Add a little Synperonic N (see Appendix 3, p. 321) to warm water. Always use as little water as possible, rinse in clean water and dry quickly. Two buckets are needed.

All curtains and hangings should be lifted on to a windowsill or chair before any scrubbing or polishing is started.

17. The Saloon at Uppark. Wooden floors were often scrubbed or 'dry-rubbed' in the 18th century, rather than being polished. This floor survived the disastrous fire of 1989

Unpolished wood floors

Mop occasionally in clean water and dry off with a dry mop. If the floor has to be scrubbed, the scrubbing brush should not be too wet as water softens the wood. Scrub in the direction of the grain of the wood and not too vigorously.

Stone, marble or tiled floors

If soaked or left wet too long, harmful salts are activated, particularly in stone and marble, and the surface is damaged.

Furniture on stone, marble or tile floors often has a white tide-mark on the feet or base. This usually happens when too much water is used on the floor and it is left wet.

A scrubbing machine splashes, so place a piece of hardboard or 3-ply 450–600 mm high and 1–1.5 m long against the skirting board. This prevents the walls from being marked. The more water used, the more the machine will splash. When scrubbing large areas a wet suction machine is almost essential for drying the floor quickly. Scrubbing and suction machines are very powerful and can cause damage to old stone and grouting, so use with care.

If the floor is of rough stone, a stiff brush can be used. First sprinkle damp sawdust to lay the dust.

Any black marks made by rubber heels on marble floors can be removed with a mixture of 300 ml white spirit, 300 ml water and a teaspoonful of Fairy Liquid. Shake well before and during use. Apply with small swabs of cotton wool, well squeezed out, and then rinse off in clean water before drying.

Polishing floors

Lift all curtains and hangings on to a windowsill or chair before any polishing is started. Also protect all edges of carpets.

Wood

A dry polish with the polisher is generally all that is needed, but make sure the brushes or felt pads are clean. Never let a brush become impregnated with polish so that the bristles appear to have match-stick ends, because the brushes are then useless. To clean the brushes, soak the bristles in white spirit to soften the hardened polish and then wash and dry thoroughly before use.

A cloth impregnated with paraffin (kerosene) and vinegar is excellent since it collects the dust effectively and leaves the polished floor shiny. Tie the cloth round the head of a dry mop. To prepare impregnated cloths for floors, cut old woollen blankets into 600 mm squares; soak in a 50/50 mixture of paraffin (kerosene) and malt vinegar; hang them out to dry and keep, when not in use, in screw-top jars or airtight plastic bags; 300 ml each of vinegar and paraffin (kerosene) is enough mixture for six cloths. Do not use man-made material as this dries out completely and is useless.

Very occasionally apply a little Johnson's Traffic Wax. The liquid form is easy to use. Do not apply it more than two or three times a year or you will give yourself a lot of unnecessary work, and the polish will build up and become smeary so that every footmark and scuff will show. Too much polish will also darken the floor. It may be necessary to apply wax more often in doorways and areas of heavy wear. The shine of the rest of the floor can be maintained by buffing with clean felt pads without adding any more polish. Use a piece of hardboard to protect the skirting board from polish and marks from the polisher.

Apply the liquid wax sparingly on a cloth tied round a mop end. Then, using an electric floor polisher, work the polish in with the nylon pads; buff up with the brushes and, finally, finish off with the felt pads.

Stone and marble

Some houses have a tradition of polishing stone floors. But polish can radically change the colour and character of the floor and is difficult to remove. It is better to use dry mops, or dry polish with the polisher, using clean felt pads.

Chewing-gum

Rub chewing-gum with a block of ice until it gets so cold that it will just chip off.

SEALING FLOORS

All seals change the character and colouring of the floor. Do not use them unless the dust problem is insupportable, and then try small sample areas before any seal is applied to the floor generally.

RUSH MATTING

To give this type of floor-covering some resilience it should be watered occasionally. Use a watering can fitted with a 450 mm weedkiller bar (fine spray) to give a light covering; 5 l damps about 165 sq m. When the rush matting is on wood floors in dry houses, this can be done once or twice a week. On stone floors and in damp conditions the matting should be watered less often, for there is danger that mould may grow under the matting.

If possible roll the matting up and vacuum the dust from underneath two or three times a year.

WOVEN COIR MATTING

This is very coarse and can mark wooden floors, which must therefore always be protected with carpet paper. When in use, the matting will stretch, but it can be shrunk back to size with a light watering (see above, Rush matting). Woven coir matting needs vacuuming very frequently.

EARLY FLOOR COVERINGS

In old houses be careful to check the floor covering of remote attic passages where some early floor covering may have lain undisturbed.

Printed canvas, oilcloth or waxcloth

Printed canvas was used as a floor covering in the 18th century. The canvas was woven of flax with a design printed on the surface. A cheaper fibre, jute, was imported from India in the 19th century. The floorcloth, oilcloth or

18. Watering the rush matting in the Long Gallery at Montacute

waxcloth of this period was coated with several layers of paint before the pattern was handblocked on to the surface, before varnishing. It was thicker and heavier than the painted canvas of earlier days. It wore well and became popular.

Linoleum

About 1860, Frederick Walton used oxidized linseed oil which formed a rubbery surface and gave the resilience which the earlier floorcloth had lacked. He combined oxidized linseed oil, ground cork, woodflour and other ingredients, rolled out on to jute hessian backing, to produce the new material he called 'Linoleum' from the Latin for flax, *linum*, and oil, *oleum*. The methods of making Linoleum have changed very little. At first Linoleum was decorated, then plain brown became available before other pigments were added to create a whole range of plain colours.

Decoration painted on the surface wears off in time. To overcome this, between 1870 and 1880, inlaid pattern Linoleum became available where the coloured mix was poured into stencils or moulds and extended right through to the jute hessian backing. Finally, in 1895, Walton designed a machine to build up inlaid pattern Linoleum in pieces, like a jigsaw puzzle.

Feltback floorcloth

This was sold between the wars. It was made of paperfelt saturated with a hot bituminous mixture and coated on both sides with a colour wash to seal off the bitumen before being printed with paint like Linoleum.

Vinyls

Since the Second World War, the introduction of vinyls has had the greatest impact on composite floor coverings. The capital outlay for its manufacture is only a fraction of the cost of setting up a Linoleum plant.

Treatment

Cleaning of all composite floor coverings

Use a mop slightly dampened with water to which a little Synperonic N has been added. Rinse before drying. Do not soak the floor as this may cause the covering to swell, lift and curl at the edges.

Cork-based Linoleum

Use a spirit-based wax such as Traffic Wax. To apply and polish see Polished wooden floors, p. 96.

The wax will help keep the Linoleum supple. Do not use a water-based wax (see vinyl, below), which would make the Linoleum more brittle.

To remove excess wax polish

Using clean pads or brushes and without adding any more wax, polish the floor with the electric polisher until the smeary surface has been removed. By this method it is sometimes possible to redistribute excess polish to heavily worn areas, such as doorways.

Modern vinyl and thermoplastic floor coverings

A water-based polish must be used, such as Klear or Carefree Life. Apply according to instructions on the tin. It will dry to a shine and only needs buffing up to maintain. When the surface becomes worn consult the manufacturer of the polish, as a build-up of wax is difficult to get off. Do not use a spirit-based wax (see Linoleum, above) as it would make vinyl floors too slippery and the spirit can cause the vinyl to crack.

Joint-stools were then created; on three legs
Upborne they stood. Three legs upholding firm
A massy slab, in fashion square or round.
On such a stool immortal Alfred sat,
And sway'd the sceptre of his infant realms:
And such in ancient halls and mansions drear
May still be seen; but perforated sore,
And drill'd in holes, the solid oak is found,
By worms voracious eating through and through.

William Cowper, from *The Task*, Book I,
'The Sofa', 1785

CHAPTER SIX

FURNITURE

Environment
105

Handling
105

Cleaning
108

Furniture in Need of Repair
113

Woodworm or Furniture Beetle
114

Storage
116

Security
116

19. The Cartoon Gallery at Knole, with its 17th-century seat furniture and (below) the famous Knole settee in the Leicester Gallery. Handling pieces of such rarity requires considerable expertise

Furniture may be made up of several types of timber, the carcase wood differing from those used for veneers and marquetry. Gesso, gilding, lacquer, paint and polishes may be added as surface decoration. As the relative humidity changes, these woods and materials expand and contract at different rates, causing splits, cracks and flaking to occur. Furniture made only of one type of wood will also be affected, as expansion and contraction are different along and across the grain. Furniture should therefore be kept in a stable environment of 50–65% relative humidity, with daily fluctuations of less than 10% (see The Right Environment, p. 25).

Heat lowers the relative humidity. Radiators and heaters may cause local areas of low humidity, so avoid placing furniture near such sources of heat. The heat generated by spotlights and lamps may similarly affect both timber and surface decoration.

Light

Light affects the colour of wood and the polishes and varnishes used to protect it. Light wood tends to get darker and dark wood tends to get lighter. Where the surface is made up of more than one wood, contrast can be lost, and thus the design. Damage caused by light cannot be reversed without removing some of the surface.

If daylight falls unevenly or only on part of a piece of furniture, the surface will acquire a patchy appearance. Move objects on a wood surface from time to time to prevent dark unfaded patches occurring.

Where textiles are part of the furniture, they will deteriorate rapidly if exposed to strong light (see The Right Environment, p. 19).

As a general rule, antique furniture should be moved and handled as little as possible.

It should always be carried using the lowest load-bearing member as a purchase. Moving even quite a small piece in this way usually needs two people. Even if it is fitted with castors, never drag a piece of furniture, however smooth the floor; it always puts a strain on the carcase and this can loosen the joints or even snap off a leg. It can also mark the floors badly.

Separate the object into smaller units where practicable before moving it, but if drawers are left in, lock them, and shut doors firmly so that they cannot fall open and be damaged while the object is being moved. If there is no key, tie wide tape right round the piece.

Before lifting the object, make sure that all parts to be handled are in sound condition. If furniture has to be turned over, it should be lifted up, turned in the air and put down squarely – if it is just tipped back, more weight is put on the back supports than they were intended to carry and they may well break under the strain.

All the legs and/or supports of furniture should share its weight; it is sometimes necessary to use wedges to compensate for an uneven floor or in cases where some legs are on a carpet and some are not.

Keep an eye on heavily loaded furniture and pieces with marble tops: if the stand is not in a sound condition it could be dangerous. The weight on top often makes an object appear more stable than it is. If a lot of furniture needs to be moved it is better to use trained furniture removers. Untrained helpers, however willing, are unlikely to know how to handle old furniture and film crews in particular rarely have experience of handling fragile objects.

Some awkward pieces may be manoeuvred by using lengths of webbing as slings. This may be particularly useful for picture and mirror frames and marble table tops. Upholsterers' or car seat-belt webbing may be used. Always have enough helpers to handle awkward pieces.

Gilt wood, and objects with ormolu or other metal decoration, should be handled only while wearing clean cotton gloves.

Seat furniture

Never touch original upholstery, where it survives, in the course of moving the piece of furniture. Deep fringes on 17th-century stools and chairs have suffered badly because the piece has been lifted by the seat rail.

Stools and chairs should be carried by the legs, particularly if the seats are covered in textiles or have fringes. This means that most chairs will need to be carried by two people.

Upholstered drop-in seats are often numbered to match a particular chair and should be kept together. They can break the seat rail joints when forced in. This is usually because a new cover has been put on top of the old one, making the seat too big.

In houses open to the public, no chairs of any historical value (particularly those belonging to sets) should be used by room attendants.

Drawers

Check that the drawers are not overloaded, and if a drawer is sticking, do not force it. Rubbing a white candle along the runners of the drawer will help it run smoothly.

Always pull on both drawer handles, where they exist. Do not force a drawer inwards, as it may knock off the backboard of the chest or damage lip-mouldings on the drawer face.

Door catches

On bookcases, wardrobes and presses, ensure that interior catches are locked before closing the second door.

Mirrors

Glass is very heavy. If an elaborately carved frame has to be moved from the wall, a frame conservator can screw a sheet of plywood to the back large enough to project beyond the carving on all sides. This strengthens the frame while providing a base of plywood on which the mirror can be stood vertically. If the mirror needs to be moved any distance, place webbing upholstery straps under the projecting plywood board. Keep the mirror upright.

Two lengths of batten screwed to the back, like legs, so that the mirror can be stood vertically, without the frame touching the ground, can be fixed by the conservator instead of plywood when dealing with stronger and lighter mirror frames (see also Glass, p. 119).

Marble and glass tops

Never carry marble and glass tops flat, as they can break under their own weight. They should be raised into a vertical position and then lifted and carried vertically.

Handles

It is unwise ever to trust a handle, even if it has apparently been provided for the purpose of lifting.

Keys

In houses open to the public, keys should not be left in locks, since they may be pilfered. It is best to leave most pieces of furniture unlocked, since a determined thief will use a lever or hammer and damage a locked drawer or door. However, all drawers and doors along the visitors' route should be locked as constant opening and shutting of drawers by the inquisitive puts a strain on handles, catches and hinges.

CLEANING

Polished wood surfaces – day-to-day care

The surface finish given to a piece of furniture when it was made was intended to be permanent; in normal circumstances it only needs a light dusting with a clean, dry duster to keep it clean and free of dust. Occasionally buff up the polished surface with a duster or chamois leather, which should be soft, clean and dry. Wax polish should be used only once or at most twice a year.

Care should be taken to collect the dust and not just to move it on. *Always* use a clean duster, which must be shaken out and washed regularly. (This obviously means that a good supply of dusters is needed.) Chamois leathers must also be kept very clean (see Appendix 3, p. 320).

Never use dusters with raw edges and dangling threads, which can catch on the furniture, leaving tufts, and even pull pieces off.

Never use feather dusters, as they cannot be washed and the feathers break and scratch the surface.

Be particularly careful when dusting furniture which has pieces of moulding or veneer missing because the pieces next to the gap are nearly always loose and could be knocked off.

Care should be taken that furniture, after day-to-day dusting, is put back in the right position. It is very easy for chairs to get pushed against walls, hangings and tapestries. Tables should stand clear of upholstered furniture and not, for example, rub against the backs of sofas.

Furniture in rooms with stone floors

Avoid the legs and bases of furniture when mopping stone floors. Furniture in rooms with stone floors needs very careful dusting to prevent white cement-like dust accumulating in the crevices. Some stone floors can be very damp. In such cases the furniture may stand on pads of sheet lead.

Ornaments, flowers and jardinières

Put a piece of brown felt or chamois leather under ornaments to prevent their scratching the polished surface. Avoid brightly coloured felt because the colour could migrate on to the objects.

Flowers or plants standing on furniture must be very carefully watered, using a long-nosed can, not an ordinary jug, so as to avoid spillage and subsequent water stains. Keep flowers well away from gilded surfaces, which can be irreparably damaged by water. All vases must stand on a glass mat. Stick circles of felt (30 mm diameter) on the lower side. These will take up the unevenness of the wood surface.

Avoid flowering plants which drip nectar on to polished surfaces. Take care that the wet leaves of plants do not touch the wood, because this results in water marks which cause staining, and damp can loosen the veneer.

Some attractive vases are slightly porous. Watertight ones should be selected or a watertight plastic food container may be carefully inserted.

Polished wood surfaces – spring-cleaning

Dusting

The result of spring-cleaning should be that objects look cared for without any obvious changes in their appearance; an object in a room may look shabby but it should look clean.

Time saved in not polishing unless really necessary should be spent in dusting thoroughly all the hidden places which there is not time to reach in day-to-day cleaning.

Thorough dusting, underneath a piece of furniture, round the back, inside and outside the drawers, so that every surface which can be reached is free of dust, is the greatest aid to conservation and the most important part of spring-cleaning. Wherever possible, all furniture should be moved once a year so that dust does not become trapped underneath and behind it and become a haven for moth and beetle.

Polishing

Never polish too near any pieces of wood that are cracking or lifting; if wax gets under them, it will make it more difficult to repair the furniture and glue back the bits.

Polish does not penetrate the surface and feed the wood, as is generally supposed; it gives the surface protection, an attractive appearance and a shiny finish, which is easier to dust than a dull one.

It is because wax polish builds up a protective surface over many years that it should always be applied very sparingly and evenly, and rubbed well until a good shine has been built up. If the wax polish is put on too thickly the solvent in the polish evaporates before you have finished polishing, leaving the surface smeary and you will give yourself unnecessarily hard work trying to remove the smears on the surface with elbow grease.

Use only the recommended wax polish (see Appendix 4, p. 327). If the dye in the wax polish is darker than the object being treated it will darken the wood. If using lighter coloured polish on dark furniture, take care that no residue is left in the crevices, because it will show up when the wax dries out.

Furniture cream is not recommended because in order to keep the wax and solvent in suspension an emulsifying agent has to be used. Although many of these agents are harmless it is unfortunately impossible to check all the many cream polishes on the market, so it is better not to use them.

Never be tempted to use an aerosol polish, or any polish with silicone in it. These modern patent furniture polishes give an instant shine but there are several objections to their use: the film does not fill scratches and other surface blemishes, as wax does; with aerosol sprays the solvent comes out with such force that it can damage the polished surface; it can also make the surface slippery.

Where an aerosol is sprayed on frequently, the surface can acquire a slight milky look. No remedy has yet been found. It is *impossible* to remove this aesthetically objectionable film without first stripping and then resurfacing the object.

Polished carved furniture

Occasionally it may be necessary to go over polished carved furniture with a soft bristle brush to remove dust trapped in the carving. Use a hogshair brush (see Appendix 3, p. 318). Wrap insulating tape round the metal ferrule. Keep this brush for polished wood only, otherwise wax may get on to other surfaces, such as stone or marble. (See also Gilded furniture, below.)

On carved polished furniture, wax polish may be more easily applied and burnished with a soft bristle furniture brush (see Appendix 3, p. 318).

Textiles

When polishing furniture, great care must be taken not to touch any of the textiles. Squab cushions and drop-in seats should be removed before polishing the woodwork. Take special care not to touch fringes.

Leather

Historically important leather should be treated only by a conservator.

To spring-clean plain leather upholstery which is in good condition, dust carefully and then apply Connolly's Hide Food with swabs of cotton wool. Use sparingly. Leave for twenty-four hours so that it will be absorbed well. Polish with a soft clean duster. If the leather upholstery has a badly damaged surface, do not treat it, but seek advice from an expert conservator.

Leather on desk-tops and bureau-falls can be similarly treated, avoiding any embossed gilding and taking care not to touch the surrounding wood.

Special cleaning of neglected polished woods

This is best undertaken with the advice of a furniture conservator, since these objects may well be in need of repair.

Where the piece is polished and the surface is sound, it is possible for the dirty surface to be washed, but attempt only small manageable areas at any one time. Reviving or resurfacing can only be carried out by the conservator. It may be necessary to wash furniture during spring-cleaning, especially if the house is very dusty or where visitors unavoidably touch certain pieces. You will need at least three cloths and two bowls. Put warm water in both bowls. Add a very little Synperonic N (see Appendix 3, p. 321) to one of the bowls of water. *Never* use commercial detergents, whether in powder or liquid form; they may contain impurities, such as bleach, which can damage the surface. Use one cloth, well wrung out, for wiping the surface with the detergent; rinse off with water with the second cloth, well squeezed out. Then dry the surface immediately with the third cloth, which will have to be changed as soon as it gets at all damp. Leave the object overnight, until thoroughly dry, before applying a thin coat of wax polish in the usual way.

Never let water get near any gilded or painted gesso surface.

Brass fittings

When the furniture was made, the wood was bright and unfaded so that bright, brass handles (sometimes gilded) acted as a complement to it. Now the wood has faded, the brass should be allowed to tone down with it. This also applies to metal inlays.

Where there are brass fittings on furniture, such as handles or knobs, the patina on the surface of the brass should *never* be removed. The brass should look cared for but not gleaming or shiny. To get this effect, brass should only be polished at the same time as the wood, using the same wax furniture polish.

Never use a patent brass cleaner on brass fittings on furniture. As well as making the brass too bright, it also often leaves a smear and white marks on the wood round the brass. Removal of smears on the wood around handles and mounts where a patent metal cleaner has been used in the past is best left to a furniture conservator.

Day-to-day cleaning should be exactly the same as for the rest of the piece of furniture: ordinary dusting, and an occasional buff-up with a clean, dry chamois leather or duster.

20. Detail of a Boulle bureau at Erddig, showing the lifting of the brass and tortoiseshell marquetry

Boulle, tortoiseshell, lacquered, japanned and papier mâché surfaces, painted furniture

The metal marquetry of Boulle is nearly always slightly loose and higher than the tortoiseshell, so rubbing over the surface with a cloth or chamois would catch in the metal and pull it out.

Never use a duster. If the surface is sound, brush Boulle with a soft banister brush (see Appendix 3, p. 318). Boulle should never be polished.

If lacquer is flaking or crumbling, it should be left alone, because this indicates deep-seated disturbance for which treatment is difficult. A furniture conservator will advise on day-to-day maintenance of damaged pieces as this will vary according to the extent of the damage. This also applies to the other categories mentioned above.

Gilded furniture

If any piece of gilt or gesso seems to be flaking, the object should not be cleaned; advice should be sought from a furniture conservator who specializes in gilding.

Never rub gilding; if it is necessary to brush the dust out of the carving on gilded furniture use a ponyhair brush (see Appendix 3, p. 318), and brush off the dust into a Hoover Dustette held in the other hand. Take care not to knock the gilded surface. Ingrained surface dirt can be safely treated only by a conservator who specializes in gilding.

Never let water get on any gilded surface, as it could ruin it. If there is an accidental spillage of water on gilding, do not wipe the surface. Let it run off and dry naturally. Contact a gilding conservator without delay. This also applies to painted furniture and any gessoed surface (see also Pictures, p. 216).

Never touch in gilding with any form of gold paint because it gives a totally different effect and will discolour anyway.

Gilded pieces should always be handled while wearing clean, dry cotton gloves.

Glazing

If the glass is not very dirty, just buff it up with a dry chamois leather or soft lintless duster, taking care not to rub any gilded edges round the glass.

If the panes of glass on a piece of furniture such as a glazed bookcase are very dirty, dust them and then wipe the glass over with methylated spirits on cotton-wool swabs. Use the swabs when they are almost dry and with a circular motion so as to avoid leaving streaks. Keep changing the swabs as soon as they are dirty.

The swabs must not be allowed to touch polished wood surfaces or gilding. Hold a postcard against the inside edge so that the swab is kept away from the surrounding wood.

Card tables

The felt on card tables can become a haven for moths, so vacuum carefully with the Hoover Dustette at least once a year.

FURNITURE IN NEED OF REPAIR

While cleaning look out for damage such as lifting veneers or brass inlay and flaking lacquer, or structural defects such as rickety legs.

Never attempt to stick bits back on the furniture. Any bits should be carefully stored in a 'bit box' and left to the furniture conservator to replace. The sealed plastic bags in which bits are kept should be clearly marked to identify the piece of furniture, its inventory number, location in the house and, if possible, the position of the damage and the date the damage was discovered.

21. Woodworm damage on the frame of a walnut chair from Canons Ashby

WOODWORM OR FURNITURE BEETLE

Woodworm is a widespread and potentially very serious problem; it has been found to be active in practically every National Trust house.

Woodworm infestation is usually found in glue blocks inside furniture, inside seat rails, in the blocks of tip-up tables, in hinged brackets under table flaps, in drawer linings, and generally in parts of furniture which are more functional than decorative. It is also found in old oak furniture or the sapwood of oak, and anywhere in furniture made of walnut, pine, beech, ash and various other woods.

Life cycle

The eggs are laid in crevices and on rough surfaces of the wood, and hatch within four weeks. The grubs immediately begin to bore into the wood and will remain there for between one and five years. During this time the wood is being tunnelled and consequently weakened.

Inspection

A look-out must be kept at all times for signs of active woodworm, and a thorough inspection made once a year.

A torch should be used; if it is shone across a board of wood, any new flight-holes will be shown up quite clearly by the clean wood inside the hole and its sharp, freshly cut edge. This is more effective than looking for the little piles of frass or wood dust which appear on the surface of the wood or on the floor underneath, since these are often swept up before enough has accumulated to be noticed.

Always inspect a new piece of furniture for woodworm and treat it if necessary before admitting it to a house.

See also Pests, Moulds and Insects, p. 192.

Treatment

Late spring and summer are the most effective times for treatment, when the beetles are emerging or eggs and newly hatched grubs are near the wood surface. Treatment should be given immediately signs of attack are noticed, but it may be impractical to treat the furniture while a house is open to the public, in which case it should be dealt with as soon as possible after the house closes in the autumn.

Work in a well-ventilated room or near an open window if possible, and wear rubber gloves, goggles or glasses and a mask. If necessary, protect the floor with a polythene sheet.

Use a plastic injector bottle with an applicator or a special syringe (see Appendix 4) to inject Cuprinol Low Odour Woodworm Killer into holes every 50 mm or so. The fluid sometimes comes straight back out of another hole, hence the need to protect the eyes. Then use a paint-brush to apply fluid liberally to all unfinished surfaces (e.g. insides, backs, and undersides). If any fluid gets on to a 'finished' surface, it must be wiped off quickly and carefully.

If possible, treat an object in this way and then top up with fluid a couple more times within the next month to get really good penetration. Make a note of the piece of furniture. Repeat this treatment for at least two years running, and even after really thorough treatment do not give up the annual inspection. This is because woodworm infestation is often very persistent and it is rarely eradicated completely.

For the treatment to be effective, it may be necessary to separate furniture into its component parts and/or turn it upside-down (see Handling, p. 105). Take the opportunity to clean inside, underneath, etc. (see Dusting, p. 108).

Great care should be taken not to contaminate textiles with insecticide fluid when treating furniture for woodworm; where there is danger of this, it would be better to get an expert to treat the area.

Gilded wood should only be treated by a furniture conservator.

STORAGE

Store-rooms should be kept clean as the contents are very vulnerable to attack by woodworm, moth, mould, etc.

A complete list of objects in store should be available and stored pieces should be inspected once a year and checked off on the list.

To avoid damage from rising damp and condensation, furniture should not be stored directly on a stone or brick floor, and also not too near outside walls. Proximity to damp walls can also affect furniture in rooms that are lived in, or open to the public; a 50 mm gap behind every piece will allow the air to circulate freely. Basements are therefore unlikely to make suitable store-rooms.

Exclude light as far as possible by closing shutters or blacking out the windows, but remember that it is important to have adequate ventilation. Avoid sudden changes in temperature and humidity. Attics are suitable only if the roof is well insulated.

Cover stored objects with a dust-sheet to protect them from light and dirt (see Appendix 3, p. 320). Objects in store get scratched and damaged easily. Do not stack anything on top of a polished surface.

Dust-sheets must be washed so that dirty dust-sheets are not put on to the clean furniture. Covering the furniture with dust-sheets is particularly important when builders are working in the house. Care should be taken in placing and removing dust-sheets to avoid tearing off loose gilding and veneer.

SECURITY

Use nylon fishing line if, for security, small objects have to be tied down. Metal wire can damage both the object and the piece of furniture it is tied to. *Never* try to stick objects to the surface of any piece of furniture.

John Vavassour de Quentin Jones
Was very fond of throwing stones . . .
Like many of the Upper Class
He liked the Sound of Broken Glass*
It bucked him up and made him gay
It was his favourite form of Play.

(*A line I stole with subtle daring
From Wing-Commander Maurice Baring.)

Hilaire Belloc,
Cautionary Tales for Children, 1907

CHAPTER SEVEN

GLASS

Glass
121

Enamels
123

Chandeliers
123

Mirrors
129

22. A late-17th-century Bohemian glass goblet and cover at Waddesdon Manor

GLASS

Handling

Glass is light and is easily knocked over. When glass has to be moved out of the way to reach something, place it on another surface near by and do not just push it to one side.

Glass is less easily seen than ceramics, so do not leave glass near the edge of a table – it is liable to be brushed against or knocked over.

Never pick up a glass by using finger and thumb on the rim. Cup the bowl in one hand and where possible support the base with the other hand so as to cradle the glass from knocks.

When moving glass within the house, never try and carry more than one glass at a time unless you use a deep wire tray, strong box or basket, padded with plenty of acid-free tissue paper or Bubblewrap to prevent individual pieces touching. Lids or stoppers should be packed separately (and identified) or bound in place with cotton thread so that they cannot fall when the glass vessel is lifted. Carry heavier objects separately. Packing glass for transport is a job for an expert.

As with ceramics, never turn to talk to someone while putting a piece of glass down as it is easy to misjudge the distance of the base of the object from the table top. Set the base of the glass down flat and not heavily or at an angle.

Accidents and repairs

Broken pieces should be carefully wrapped in acid-free tissue paper, clearly labelled and put away safely. Stick a piece of gummed paper tape across a hairline crack before packing it away to minimize the risk of further damage.

Old repairs

Mould may appear on old repairs made with animal glue. This can be wiped off with small swabs of damp cotton wool. A glass conservator would be able to take such old repairs apart and rejoin them with a more suitable adhesive. This also applies to ceramics.

Cleaning

Glass which has painted or gilded decoration or early glass (pre-1700) should not be touched. Decoration often adheres lightly and should be handled as little as possible. Consult a glass conservator when necessary.

Larger pieces can be wiped lightly with a lint-free duster or soft dry chamois leather. Steady the glass with one hand. For smaller and more intricate pieces remove the dust with a ponyhair brush (see Appendix 3, p. 318). Wrap insulating tape round the metal ferrule.

Metal and ormolu mounts

Metal, especially ormolu, must not get wet. Glass which has metal mounts should only be dusted or, if very dirty, the glass only cleaned with slightly damp swabs of cotton wool and dried immediately.

Washing

Examine the object carefully before washing (see above).

Never immerse glass which has been repaired. A water-soluble adhesive was commonly used to bond glass and the pieces will part company very easily. Repairs to the stem are often difficult to see. To clean repaired glass wipe cautiously with swabs of cotton wool, which should be damp rather than wet.

Use lukewarm water in a plastic bowl with a few drops of Synperonic N (see Appendix 3, p. 321). If you use too much, you will not be able to see the glass in the bowl because of the suds.

Never put in more than one glass object at a time and never leave anything in the bowl if you are called away. Someone could easily come along and drop something in which would cause a breakage. Be careful not to put pressure on the rim of the bowl of the glass either from the inside or outside.

Rinse thoroughly in clean lukewarm water.

Draining and drying

Never put glass straight down on to a wet, smooth surface to drain. It could easily skid, especially if put down on its rim. Paper towels laid down on the surface are a good idea, as they prevent slipping and also absorb the excess water as the glass drains.

The slightest impact is enough to break glass, so do not overcrowd the working surface. Because glass is transparent it is sometimes difficult to judge how much space there is between objects.

Use a soft cloth or soft white kitchen paper towel for drying, taking care not to put excess pressure on any one area, particularly the rim or bowl. Never hold a glass by the stem when drying as it could snap under pressure – support it by cupping one hand under the bowl.

Storing

As with ceramics, make sure the objects are thoroughly dry before they are put away.

Do not overcrowd shelves and *never* let glass objects touch each other. Place smaller items at the front so that they can be seen.

Never put glass objects one inside another.

Make sure there is sufficient clearance from the front of the shelves, so that the glass will not be crushed and broken when the doors are closed.

Display

Glass is probably best displayed on glass shelves in glass-fronted cabinets. Make sure that the cabinet is steady and the shelves are level. The vibration caused by visitors' feet may make it necessary to use acrylic mounts to support glass which might otherwise wobble and also for such objects as Nailsea glass bottles which do not have a flat base.

Lighting

Do not spot-light glass vessels for dramatic effect: the build-up of heat on glass with painted surfaces can be very serious. Where it is possible use mirror glass shelves to reflect light upwards (see The Right Environment, p. 31).

ENAMELS

Enamels are complex multi-layer works of art and should be handled with extreme care. Dust only occasionally with a ponyhair brush and *never* use water, which would penetrate between the layers and set up corrosion, leading to surface losses. Variations in temperature could cause differential expansion between the glass and the metal and enamel would become unstable. The metal base will corrode if kept too damp.

CHANDELIERS

Chandeliers get knocked all too frequently by builders, window cleaners, photographers and occasionally even house staff, working with ladders, tower scaffolding and other equipment. All need to be reminded that there is a chandelier in the room.

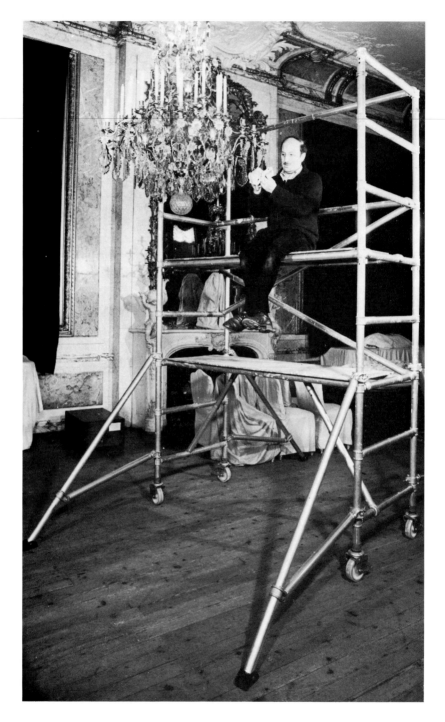

23. A steward at Waddesdon cleaning one of the chandeliers from a portable scaffold

Inspection

Suspension

The best time to check the main chain, safety hauser and ceiling fixings for any signs of weakness or corrosion is when the chandelier is dismantled for cleaning (see below). At the same time inspect the electric wiring and earthing. Chandeliers should in any case be thoroughly checked by a specialist once every ten years.

To reduce the risk of damage when cleaning and also to make it easier to change the electric light bulbs, it may be possible to install a rise-and-fall mechanism so that the chandelier can be lowered. The limiting device would hold it at a point some feet above the floor.

Metal sections

When rotating any chandelier during inspection or cleaning, it is essential that it should be turned from left to right, and not more than half a turn or so, to prevent the centre stem from unscrewing.

The centre stem which supports the chandelier is a metal tube or an iron gas pipe, concealed by outer tubes of silvered brass or Sheffield plate. The glass stem pieces are separated by metal washers.

Glass pieces

Many chandeliers are found to have chipped lustres and broken candle nozzles, greasepans, branches and bowls.

Damaged load-bearing sections, such as branches, canopies, pans, etc., should be replaced with an exact glass replica. Cracked glass should be repaired by a glass conservator. Glass branches are sometimes repaired with metal collars, which are not normally noticed from ground level. They can be left if found to be sound.

Smaller decorative parts, such as faceted spires and small crowns, may have been badly repaired with resin. It is possible for a glass conservator to take these apart and rejoin them so that the repair is more secure and less evident. Where the damage is too severe it may be necessary to replace the piece with an exact glass replica or sometimes a matching second-hand piece can be supplied by a chandelier restorer.

Lustres have tiny holes drilled in them which split if carelessly handled. If a lustre splits during handling, all pieces should be retained for reassembly by a glass conservator, as replacements are costly. Splitting most often occurs when iron wire or common pins have been used to thread the lustres together. Always use special brass pins and consult a chandelier restorer.

Linking pins or wires

Brass linking pins go between buttons, lustres and pans; some types of chandelier use silvered wire.

Check for broken, weak or corroded linking pins or silvered wires and replace where necessary. Always use those specially manufactured for the purpose. Soft brass linking pins bend easily and yet have sufficient strength to support the lustres and pendants. The linking pins on long vertical chains of lustres should be strengthened by fusing the ends together so that they do not stretch and open, causing the chains to fail. This is a job for a specialist chandelier restorer.

Opal glass 'candle' tubes

If the chandelier has been adapted for electricity, it is worthwhile changing all the light bulbs at the same time rather than be constantly replacing one or two, which wastes time and risks damage with the step-ladder on each occasion.

Always support the greasepan and nozzles by cupping one hand underneath to counterbalance the pressure required to insert the bulb. Glass 'candle' tubes break easily if compressed and excessive pressure could even break the glass branch.

Light bulbs with screw fittings are now available, so when the chandelier is rewired, consider changing the fittings to take screw rather than bayonet bulbs. This is a job for a chandelier specialist.

Cleaning

Once a year it may be necessary to dust each part of the chandelier. Use a ponyhair brush, working off a tower scaffold.

During the winter months when the house is closed, the amount of dust and dirt that settles on chandeliers is considerably reduced if they are protected by muslin bags. Do not fit a muslin bag if the chandelier is the only source of electric light in the room.

To make a muslin bag

Before cutting the butter muslin, first calculate the circumference of the chandelier by measuring the distance between the tips of two of the long arms and multiplying this figure by the number of long arms. Add an extra 460 mm to allow for gathering, shrinkage and a French seam on one side.

Next measure the height of the chandelier from the top of the glass parts to the lower finials. In order to allow for the bulge, add to this figure the diameter of the chandelier, allowing extra for shrinkage and hems top and bottom for the draw strings. The easiest way to measure the diameter is by taking the distance from the central stem to the tip of a long arm and then doubling it.

Cut out a rectangle so that the length of the material, folded over, becomes the width of the bag. Close the side with a French seam. Hem the top and bottom edges to form a casing through which to run the draw strings. Take care not to leave any raw edges or loose threads which might catch on the glass pieces or wires.

Before covering the chandelier, wrap each light fitting and greasepan loosely in acid-free tissue paper to prevent the muslin from catching on the pins and wires. Particular care must be taken if the chandelier is fitted with spires.

With two people working from step-ladders or a tower scaffold, slide the bag on from either side of the chandelier, drawing it up to the bottom of the chain, to which it should be attached by the draw string. Then gather up the bottom of the bag with the other draw string.

Textile sleeves and tassels

Dust can be removed from the textile sleeves and tassels, working off a tower scaffold, using a Hoover Dustette, fitted with the extension hose and crevice head covered in fine net. Keep the net in place with an elastic band (see Textiles, p. 262).

Dismantling

It may be necessary partly to dismantle the chandelier every three to five years in order to wash it. Keep a note of when this was done and record any damaged or missing parts (see below).

Before dismantling a chandelier, several photographs should be taken so that there is a clear record of where each piece belongs. Colour prints record details of cut glass and previous repairs more clearly than black and white.

The exact position of the pendants and chains need to be recorded only once, since their arrangement should be consistent for each segment of the chandelier. Bear in mind that since a chandelier will have been dismantled and cleaned many times since its installation, components may not necessarily be in their original positions.

First examine the chandelier for defects and damage (see Inspection, p. 125), then switch off the electricity supply. With at least two people, one working from a tower scaffold, prepare to place the glass sections in boxes or trays to be taken to a table near by, where they will be cleaned (see below).

For safety and ease of identification, the pendants and chains of lustres should be removed one segment at a time. They should be passed down from the working platform on plastic trays and then packed in plastic bags and labelled.

Next, the electric light bulbs and white opal glass 'candle' tubes are removed. In order not to put undue strain on the glass branches during this operation, each branch should be supported in turn by placing a hand under the greasepan (see Inspection, p. 125).

The remainder of the chandelier is cleaned *in situ* from the tower scaffold.

Washing

Place two screw-top jam jars on the working platform, one half-filled with a solution of 50:50 industrial methylated spirits and distilled water, and the second containing distilled water only. Moisten a swab of cotton wool with the mixture, squeezing it out well so that it does not drip. Gently wipe over each section of glass, frequently changing the swab. Do not dip a dirty swab into the solution. Try to avoid wetting the metal parts. Rinse each section immediately with a clean swab just moistened with distilled water. Gently dry each part with a lint-free duster, taking care not to put any pressure on the glass branches.

The dismantled pendants, chains and lustres should be tackled in the same way, working on the table top which should first be padded with a dust-sheet folded into several layers.

The metal fittings should be cleaned only by a chandelier specialist.

Recording damage

During cleaning, damage can be seen more clearly. Record any damaged or missing glass.

Re-assembling

Wearing thin cotton gloves to avoid leaving fingerprints on the glass, replace in reverse order to the way the pieces were taken down. If the room is cold and damp, set a fan-heater at cool on the platform of the tower scaffold to circulate air gently through the chandelier so as to ensure that the metal parts are completely dry.

Take great care over the removal and dismantling of the tower scaffold. This is when accidents happen, in the relief of a tricky job completed. The tower scaffold should be pushed well away before it is dismantled.

24. Rococo pier-glass at Petworth, with three ho-ho birds holding garlands of flowers in their beaks, probably carved by James Whittle in about 1757 but based on an engraved design by Lock and Copland

MIRRORS

It is rare to find an 18th-century mirror in perfect condition. Many old mirror frames have their original glass but the amalgam or silvering has corroded badly.

When tin amalgam corrodes, metallic mercury is released and may spread into intact areas or mercury may gather in droplets on the reverse of the mirror. It is important to prevent the deterioration of the amalgam or at least to slow it down, as the amalgam cannot be reconstituted. The main cause of deterioration is damp, which activates the soluble salts in dust and other air pollutants.

The National Trust accepts the appearance of corroded mirror silvering as a natural ageing process, but steps are being taken to monitor the continuing rate of deterioration and to improve the environmental conditions.

Mirrors, made up of metal (tin and mercury), wood and glass, should remain reasonably stable if kept within the target band of 50–65% relative humidity (see The Right Environment, p. 19).

General care and maintenance

When a mirror hangs on an outside wall or above a fireplace, where condensation may be a problem, it is advisable, provided that the back of the mirror is sealed, to have an air space between the backboard and the wall. However, where pier glasses and overmantel mirrors were designed to be fixed flat against the wall and a gap would be noticeable, aesthetic considerations should take precedence.

The fixings, hangings and condition of the wall should be checked regularly by a conservator, who would at the same time inspect mirror paintings for any signs of paint loss and *verre eglomisé* for areas where the metal foil is peeling away from the glass (see plates 25 and 26).

Do not attempt to move a large or elaborately carved mirror without the advice of a conservator (see Furniture, p. 107).

Never open the back of a mirror, as any released mercury is highly toxic.

Avoid hanging mirrors over radiators, as these cause heat and dust to rise up behind the mirror.

When a room is to be redecorated in oil-based paint, mirrors should be removed to prevent organic acids from the drying paint accelerating corrosion of the silvering. However, where the mirror is large and elaborately carved, it may be preferable to protect it *in situ* rather than risk moving it.

Replacing missing areas of amalgam

When a mirror has to be taken down, the conservator can renew or reseal the backing. However, opening the back of a mirror may also disturb areas of

25. Chinese Qianling mirror painting in an English giltwood frame, hanging against a contemporary hand-painted Chinese wallpaper at Saltram

26. 'A glass with my Ladies Arms' is listed in the 1601 inventory in Bess of Hardwick's withdrawing room, where this rare *verre eglomisé* panel still remains

silvering that previously appeared intact. While missing areas can be replaced with metallized plastic film to match the appearance of the original silvering, areas where deteriorated amalgam has been removed can appear hard-edged compared with the speckled effect of natural corrosion. (Aluminium foil should never be used behind mirror glass as it can set up corrosion in the amalgam.)

Cracked or missing glass

On a mirror with an elaborately carved frame, cracks, in small areas of glass, may be left until the mirror has to be taken down for other reasons.

Breaks in sheet glass can be repaired by glass conservators using an adhesive with the same refractive index as the glass. The adhesive must be strong enough to support the glass, pliable to allow some flexibility and have good ageing properties.

If original mirror glass shatters beyond repair, a conservator can arrange for a specialist firm to match modern glass to the colour of a fragment of the original glass. Do not replace broken glass with 'antique' glass sold in the high street.

Routine cleaning

Dust the glass with a ponyhair brush (see Appendix 3, p. 318), working away from the edges towards the centre. Hold a piece of white card against the inside of the frame to protect the gilding from abrasion. Dust large areas with a banister brush. Do not use a duster, as it could catch on carving, glass slips, decorative pins, etc. Large panels of glass in plain frames can be polished with a soft, dry chamois leather.

If the glass of an elaborately carved mirror becomes smeary, let a glass conservator clean it. If any dampness or liquid touches the frame it may damage the gilding and if either penetrates behind the glass, it would accelerate the corrosion of the amalgam.

To dust the frame, and on keeping a 'bit box', see Pictures, p. 216.

STAINED GLASS

See Walls, Windows and Ceilings, p. 287.

I would to God my name were not so terrible to
the enemy as it is: I were better eaten to death with
rust than to be scoured to nothing with perpetual
motion.

Shakespeare, 2 *Henry IV*, 1600

Since brass, nor stone, nor earth, nor boundless sea,
But sad mortality o'ersways their power

. . . rocks impregnable are not so stout,
Nor gates of steel so strong, but Time decays.

Shakespeare, *Sonnet 65*

CHAPTER EIGHT

METALWORK

General
137

Gold
139

Silver-gilt
139

Sheffield Plate and Electroplate
139

Silver
139

Bronze
142

Pewter
143

Ormolu
144

Brass and Copper
144

Steel Grates, Fireplaces, Fire-irons
145

Kitchen Ranges (Cast Iron)
149

Arms and Armour
149

Outdoor Metalwork
150

Metal Garden Sculpture
and Ornaments
152

27. Ambassadorial silver in the dining-room at Ickworth

·✤ METALWORK ✤·

GENERAL

It is a mistake to think that metals are hard and infinitely durable. Metal surfaces are easily scratched and worn away. Metalwork should be kept in dry conditions because most metals are naturally unstable in the atmosphere and tend to oxidize and corrode. This corrosion is greatly accelerated by the presence of moisture. It can be extremely rapid and can cause complete destruction of the object. Discuss any signs of corrosion or disfigurement such as white or green crystals or powders with a conservator (see The Right Environment, p. 25).

Extreme caution should be taken when handling a very neglected object, however mundane it may appear to be. No work should be done without consulting an expert.

Never try to polish up a neglected piece with patent cleaners. Untold damage could be done to the surface and the patination could be entirely destroyed.

Patina

Patina is the surface layer of a metal object. It can be a natural result of the ageing process of the metal and therefore part of its history, or it may have been applied by means of chemicals. The surface is often enhanced by the application of tinted varnishes or waxes. The patina is nearly always desirable. *Never* attempt to remove a patina without first consulting a metalwork conservator because the appearance of objects has sometimes been altered through the centuries to suit the tastes of the time. Occasionally preservatives have been applied, such as wax or oil, which have produced patinas. Sometimes objects have been painted as the easiest way of overcoming a conservation problem, perhaps to even out a blotchy appearance, e.g. the Le Sueur bust of Charles I at Stourhead, which was originally gilded and later painted. Lead statuary was frequently painted white to simulate marble or coloured to look like stone, and this has the added virtue of protecting the lead from the atmosphere. (See also Metal garden sculpture and ornaments, p. 152.)

Handling

Once metalwork has been polished or lacquered *never* touch it with bare hands because acidity in the skin will tarnish the metal. *Always* wear cotton gloves and keep them clean by washing them fairly frequently.

Lacquering

Metalwork that has been lacquered need not be touched again for five or ten years, except for the minimum of light dusting. Surfaces that are easily abraded or destroyed through constant polishing should be treated first, such as collections of silver-gilt and Sheffield plate. The National Trust also envisages lacquering silver, brass and copper in due course.

Metalwork should be lacquered only by experts, because the preparation of the item is complicated and must be left to a metal conservator.

It will help the conservator to decide on priorities if, when listing items to be lacquered, the thickness and colour of the tarnish is recorded. This gives an indication of the degree of tarnishing and of the length of time the object has been tarnished.

When helping a conservator to prepare objects for lacquering always wear cotton gloves, because the natural oils and grease in the skin inhibit the lacquer from adhering to the surface of the metal.

When items have been lacquered, a record should be kept listing the inventory number and date of treatment, to ensure that the piece, once lacquered, is not then polished by mistake. The date is important because it gives some idea of when the item will need to be lacquered again.

Day-to-day care

Dusting of metal objects should be kept to a minimum because dust can be abrasive. *Never* rub when dusting, just flick the dust lightly off the surface with a hogshair brush (see Appendix 3, p. 318). Do not use a feather duster because it cannot be washed; also the feathers break and then scratch the surface of the object. Where possible the dusting of metal should be limited to two or three times a year.

Never polish as part of day-to-day care. Any polishing, even with a dry duster, is abrasive and will eventually blunt and disfigure even the most apparently solid object. Constant polishing of, say, door handles and finger-plates will eventually mute and perhaps destroy the original decoration.

Where it is permissible to polish a metal object, cover the edge of the work table with something soft such as foam plastic or an old cushion or pillow, so that the object is not dented or scratched while it is being polished. But all polishing should be kept to an absolute minimum.

After cleaning, a light coat of Renaissance Wax can be applied to copper and brass to slow down tarnishing and to steel and cast-iron as a protection against rusting. This applies only to copper, brass, steel and cast-iron (see Cleaning plain steel, p. 148).

GOLD

Never touch the surface of gold except to dust lightly with a ponyhair brush (see Appendix 3, p. 318).

SILVER-GILT

Silver-gilt is silver with a thin coating of gold. *Never* polish or you will remove the gold, revealing the silver underneath, which will then tarnish in the atmosphere. Arrangements should be made for a metalwork conservator to lacquer silver-gilt objects. Dust lightly with a ponyhair brush.

SHEFFIELD PLATE (*c.* 1740–1840) AND ELECTROPLATE (1840 ONWARDS)

Sheffield plate is a thin coating of silver on a copper base. *Never* rub the surface by polishing, as this removes the silver, revealing the copper underneath. Just flick the dust off with a ponyhair brush when absolutely necessary.

Never replate. When the piece was made sterling silver would have been used which has some copper in it, but modern electrolytic techniques would deposit pure silver on the surface and so alter the appearance of the piece.

Electroplating has been in use as a manufacturing technique since 1840. The coating of silver is even thinner than that on Sheffield plate and the base metal can be a silvery-coloured alloy which makes it difficult to see when the silvery layer has been polished away.

SILVER

Cleaning

Arrangements should be made to lacquer silver not in use; in that case do not use Goddard's Long Term Silver Polish as it could inhibit lacquering at a later stage.

Never use plate powder for cleaning, as it is too abrasive. Use Goddard's Silver Dip (for use see pp. 140–41).

Plain (untooled) silver

Lightly tarnished silver

Wash in warm water to which a little Synperonic N has been added. Dry thoroughly with mutton cloth, or old, soft, linen tea towels. Do not dry with

28. The Countess of Stamford's toilet-service, by Magdalen Feline, 1754, at Dunham Massey

new dressed linen tea cloths because they are too abrasive. When thoroughly dry, polish with Goddard's Long Term Silver Cloth.

Heavily tarnished silver

Use only Goddard's Silver Dip. Never dip the silver into the Silver Dip. Apply with cotton-wool swabs. Rinse off under running water very thoroughly. Dry with mutton cloth or an old, soft, linen tea towel, and then polish with Goddard's Long Term Silver Cloth. When dealing with a large object, clean a small area at a time, rinsing off the Silver Dip before going on to clean the next area.

If silver is dipped into the Silver Dip, the liquid becomes overcharged with silver which gets deposited back on the metal surface as matt silver.

Keep your main supply of Silver Dip absolutely clean. Pour a little into a bowl for use and never pour back any left over into the clean main supply.

Tooled silver

Silver Dip is ideal for cleaning chasing as it will dissolve the tarnish in the decoration without abrasion caused by too much brushing.

Avoid getting Silver Dip into hollow decoration, such as fruit or small figures, or into hollow fabrication, such as cast handles or ball feet, as it is almost impossible to rinse it fully and is also difficult to dry thoroughly, though a hair-dryer, set hot, may help.

Small objects

Use a hogshair brush; do not use a toothbrush or household paint-brush, because their bristles will scratch and abrade the surface. Be sure to use these brushes for silver *only*. Do not over-insist or you may abrade the tops of the tooling leaving the valleys undisturbed. Where necessary take a wooden cuticle-stick with cotton wool wrapped round the end. Dip it in Silver Dip, work gently into crevices to remove tarnish, and rinse well and dry. Small bamboo satay sticks are flexible and long lasting. Wrap them round with cotton wool and use them in place of wooden cuticle-sticks.

Large objects

Use a plate brush (see Appendix 4, p. 318) to get into the grooves of the tooling; the correct type of bristle and the degree of stiffness are important. Consult a conservator when in doubt.

Drying

Silver that is thoroughly dried does not tarnish so easily. It is difficult to dry because of minute pores, cracks and crevices in the surface of the silver.

The silver should first be dried with a soft linen cloth and then, in order to drive off the remaining moisture, be placed in a drying cabinet, set at 50–60° C (120–140° F) for 15–30 minutes, depending on the size of the pieces and the intricacy of the decoration. Alternatively, use a heavy-duty hair-dryer. This is considerably cheaper to buy but allows only one piece of silver to be dried at a time. When using the hair-dryer, keep the nozzle at least 150 mm away from the silver, while rotating the piece, wearing cotton gloves. Let the hot air play over the surface until the last traces of moisture have evaporated.

Do not use any form of hot-air drying on silver which has handles or any other fittings of wood or ivory, for these components could be seriously damaged.

Using a drying cabinet, a collection of silver which used to be cleaned twice a year now lasts for two years without cleaning.

Storing silver

Pollutants in the atmosphere, especially hydrogen sulphide, tarnish silver, so silver which is to be stored should be wrapped in plenty of acid-free tissue paper or placed in a Tarnprufe bag. These are made of a material impregnated with a tarnish inhibitor.

Do not use baize, felt or chamois leather for wrapping silver as these give off hydrogen sulphide, which is the active blackening tarnishing agent in the atmosphere. Do not wrap silver in cling-wrap or use plastic bags, because condensation can form inside the covering.

Silver which has been lacquered can be stored without any special protection provided that there is enough space on the shelf to avoid the danger of scratching the surface of one object against another. It is worthwhile, however, to make each item an acid-free tissue paper hat so as to keep the dust off (see Ceramics, p. 67). Remember to wear cotton gloves when handling lacquered silver.

If silver is to be stored in boxes, use good strong acid-free boxes, making sure that there is adequate packing. Do not use crumpled newspaper, which is highly acidic. Wrap each piece in acid-free tissue paper or in a Tarnprufe bag (see above) and place the heavier items at the bottom of the box.

BRONZE

The treatment of bronze is specialized and difficult. *Never* try to clean bronze statues or statuettes. There are many types of patination, some of which could easily come off, revealing flaws or repairs (see Patina, p. 137). As part of the patina, there may be a build-up of varnishes and waxes, so *never* use any solvents, such as water, methylated spirits or white spirit, on bronze.

The surface of bronze should not be touched except once or twice a year when it can be dusted lightly. Dust is abrasive, so do not rub the surface when dusting.

Once a year remove carefully the dust trapped in the tooling of the bronze with a hogshair brush. This is important, because the dust lying in the grooves can act like a sponge and attract moisture, which could cause bronze disease.

Do not keep brushing away at the tops of the tooling. When necessary take a wooden cuticle-stick with clean *dry* cotton wool wrapped round the end and carefully remove the dust from crevices.

Never attempt to clean neglected bronze, because only after careful tests is it possible to know how the patina was formed.

Never wash bronze, because this could cause active corrosion. The appearance of bright green spots or patches is a sign of corrosion, and could be 'bronze disease'. Consult a conservator.

29. Gilt-bronze door furniture, designed by Robert Adam, in the Saloon at Saltram

PEWTER

It is often preferable to leave the dull grey patination on pewter. *Never* do more than dust it with a soft dry cloth or chamois leather.

Keep a look-out for pewter disease. This is a white powdery substance appearing on the surface of the pewter which sometimes leads to flaking and peeling of small areas of metal. Report any signs at once to a metal conservator.

If the environment of pewter is to be changed either by putting it into a showcase or by decorating the room, the object could become unstable through bringing it into contact with some form of acidity. Pewter should be kept out of rooms while they are being decorated and should never be in direct contact with untreated, unseasoned wood. While an oak dresser is the traditional place for displaying pewter, serious deterioration can be caused by organic acids from the oak. Pewter can be displayed on an oak surface provided there is plenty of air circulating around it, but *never* put pewter away in a drawer or cupboard made of oak.

ORMOLU

The gold-coloured mounts on furniture, clocks and candelabra are made of bronze or brass coated with a thin layer of gold. This is true ormolu, and the gold coat is as vulnerable as the gold layer on silver-gilt, or the silver layer on Sheffield plate.

Mounts that look like ormolu may also be of brass coated with coloured lacquer.

The base metal of some gilded pieces may not be bronze but the more brittle zinc (spelter), and this can easily fracture. The gilding on zinc is also less securely attached.

Never wash, rub or polish ormolu, whether true or imitation. Dust lightly with a ponyhair brush and only once or twice a year.

If ormolu candlesticks are used, protect them with candle grease catchers, small circles of plastic or glass placed on top of the candle holder. If candle grease gets on to ormolu, it can be softened with white spirit. On no account use anything hard or abrasive to remove the grease from the gilded surface.

BRASS AND COPPER

Although much of this ware is domestic and utilitarian, some of it has beautifully chased or engraved decoration which would be worn away by constant polishing. This applies particularly to door furniture. Lacquering should be envisaged for the more important pieces.

If the brass or copper is not used and has not yet been lacquered, apply a very light coat of Renaissance Wax on the clean, dry surface to slow down tarnishing (see Cleaning plain steel, p. 148).

Cleaning

Lightly tarnished

Rub with Goddard's Long Term Silver Cloth, or a special cloth for brass and copper (see Appendix 4). Brass and copper should each have their own cloths, and *never* use either of these cloths on silver.

Heavily tarnished

Use a mild cream metal polish, Peek or Midas Touch (see Appendix 4), which is available in tubes that have a long shelf life, even when opened, provided the tops are replaced.

Apply with pads of cotton wool. Burnish with a soft clean cloth. A plate brush is useful for getting the polish out of cracks and corners. Keep one brush for brass and another for copper.

30. The kitchen at Hardwick, with its copper *batterie de cuisine*

If copper pots are standing on a stone floor, isolate them from the stone with wooden slats or mats, as damp from the floor can corrode the metal.

As a matter of policy, brass fittings on furniture such as handles or knobs should not be polished. The brass should look cared for but not gleaming or shiny. To get this effect brass on furniture needs no special polishing (see Furniture, p. 111).

STEEL GRATES, FIREPLACES, FIRE-IRONS

It may be difficult to distinguish the raised decorations and materials used when they are obscured by dirt and rust. A metal conservator would make careful cleaning tests.

Gilding and engraving on steel

An object in steel should be checked carefully to see whether there is any gilding or engraving. When obscured by dirt or rust, gilding is often discernible only by an expert, who can test likely areas before work is begun. For example, in Adam-type fireplaces some of the embellishments may be in gilt-bronze (often the lozenge-shaped decoration). Engraving would be rubbed out completely if emery paper were used to remove rust.

Blueing

The colouring of the metal is literally blue – in shades of dark blue through to peacock blue. This is difficult to distinguish under a layer of dirt. Where there is any doubt, do not touch until the next visit of a metal conservator, except to wipe over with white spirit on pads made out of soft white kitchen paper towels to remove the surface dirt. In order to help stabilize the surface and prevent any further deterioration, a light coating of Renaissance Wax can then be applied (see Cleaning plain steel, below). As this will have to be removed in order to carry out the necessary conservation work, do not do so if a visit is imminent.

Cleaning plain steel

Whether action can be taken without the help of a metal conservator depends on the degree of rust.

Steel with no rust

Clean with a mild cream metal polish, Peek or Midas Touch. Apply with small swabs of cotton wool or pads made out of very soft white kitchen paper towel. Keep polishing in the same direction, using a lateral and not a circular motion. When polishing bars, go backwards and forwards along the bar, rather than round it. Care should be taken not to get a build-up of white powder in cracks and corners. A plate brush is useful for this. Keep one brush for steel only.

Steel affected by rust

Rust shows up in brown patches. It can be cleaned off with a mild cream metal polish, Peek or Midas Touch, fine steel wool, grade ooo or oooo. Any coarser grade will make scratches on the surface, leaving untouched valleys in between and, as well as damaging the surface, it will take far more work before you get a smooth unblemished finish.

31. A polished steel grate and chimney-surround at Castle Coole and (below) a detail of the central inscription

Very rusted steel

Heavy rust which has eaten into the surface should be left alone until the amount of metal which is left can be checked by a metal conservator. Iron and steel can be completely eaten away in places.

Never use a patent rust remover.
Never use an electric or any other form of mechanical burnisher.
Never use a wire brush on polished steel grates.

Protection after cleaning

After cleaning, apply a thin coat of Renaissance Wax to give some protection. Using small circular movements, apply with a plate brush or a pad made out of very soft white kitchen paper towel. Deal with small areas at a time because it is essential to buff up the wax within ten minutes of applying it, as the wax is hard and so is difficult to polish if the solvent dries out before buffing. If the wax does harden, moisten a paper towel pad with a little white spirit to remove the wax and re-apply.

Dismantling

No attempt should be made to dismantle a fireplace, or other object, without first consulting a metal conservator in order that the necessary precautions may be taken.

Grates

If black lead is already being used, continue to use it. Black lead is available in tubes (Zebrite). An alternative, if the grate is not in use, is to paint it with exterior-quality matt black paint such as Manders Black Ebony, Finish M.757, or International Matt Black. Apply only a very thin coat; a thick coat of paint would change the appearance of the grate and obliterate decoration and evidence of natural wear, which is all part of the history of the grate. Thin the paint, if necessary, with a little white spirit.

Apply a little Renaissance Wax over the matt black paint to give a little life to the surface and produce an effect nearer to that achieved by applying black lead (Zebrite). Do not be tempted to use exterior gloss paint because it is much too shiny.

KITCHEN RANGES (CAST IRON)

When rusty, brush over the surface with a wire brush. Use a bristle brush to remove any loose dirt or dust. Wipe over the surface with white spirit on swabs made out of soft white kitchen paper towel. *Never* use water. If not in use paint with a thin coat of exterior-quality matt black paint (see Grates, above), but first try a small area on a part that does not show and leave for about a week. The paint may peel off if the surface is unsuitable, so it is unwise to paint the whole thing until it is certain that the paint will adhere. If it does peel off, ask a metal conservator for another suggestion.

Check inside the range, which should also be cleaned and painted.

Never use a wire brush on any other object or metal surface.

ARMS AND ARMOUR

Arms, armour and swords should be looked at by a specialist metal conservator before they are touched. It is difficult to recognize the various metals and materials, let alone distinguish the decoration. Arms, armour and fire-arms could be blued, silvered, russeted, or have brass inlays. There may also remain traces of fine engraving. Inexpert cleaning, even wiping over with a dry duster, can lift and remove minute particles of valuable decoration.

Cleaning is best left to a metal conservator, as it depends on the amount and type of decoration. Arms and armour must be dismantled by an expert, or damage on the parts out of sight will be overlooked. For example, the barrel of a blunderbuss may be made of either steel or brass. It must be dismantled to be cleaned properly, as the underside is inaccessible until the barrel is separated from the wooden stock. This also applies to the mechanical sections of the lock and other detachable embellishments. The construction of fire-arms varies according to period and type; a comprehensive knowledge of the history of a fire-arm is necessary to be able to ensure that no damage is done in handling it.

No fire-arm should be taken apart by an amateur, as it is important for the metal conservator to be able to see its general condition and how it is at present put together. He can then judge the degree of cleaning and conservation necessary.

Security can be a problem, as weapons are now popular and have increased in value during the last few years. Consult a metal conservator about how they should be exhibited and the correct type of supports. All fixing or hanging points for arms or armour should be covered with plastic tubing and any part of the armour or weapon that touches an outside wall should be insulated from it by means of a piece of cork or, even better, black Plastazote.

If armour is kept in a room where there are signs of condensation, expert advice should be sought.

OUTDOOR METALWORK

Decorative and utilitarian metalwork forms part of the history of a country house. It is sometimes combined with other materials such as stone or wood or used as decoration in the form of gold leaf. Examples vary from weather vanes, decorated lead hoppers and rainwater cisterns, finials and balustrades, to stable fittings, hand pumps and cattle troughs, and to fine examples of, say, 18th-century wrought-iron gates, lead statuary and bronze urns.

Outdoor metalwork is often neglected. Metalwork corrodes rapidly when exposed to moisture and air. Much outdoor metalwork has been lost or suffered irreparably. As always with conservation, regular inspection and maintenance is more effective and less expensive than neglect resulting in costly restoration.

Metalwork suffers most in heavily polluted industrial areas, or coastal districts with salt-laden air, and when it is positioned under trees or in semi-sheltered housing, such as garden temples, where moisture from rain or condensation can remain on the surface.

Metal gates and railings

Metal gates and railings are usually constructed of wrought iron or cast iron or a combination of the two.

Wrought iron

Wrought iron was ductile, durable and could be worked into very elaborate shapes.

Cast iron

Cast iron is fabricated by being cast into moulds. It will not bend but snaps or fractures when stressed. Cast iron generally superseded wrought iron in the late 19th and early 20th centuries.

Protection and maintenance

Outdoor ironwork corrodes rapidly and has traditionally been painted for decoration and protection. As long as the paint layer remains intact, rusting is prevented.

The painted surface should be checked regularly as once the paint starts to break down, moisture enters the damaged area and attacks the metal. The expansion of the rust loosens the paint while the metal continues to corrode beneath it.

32. Wrought-iron gates at the entrance to Chirk Castle, made by Robert and John Davies of Bersham in 1712–19

Once rust is established on painted iron, it is a waste of time to paint over the moist rusting metal, as the metal will continue to corrode beneath the new paint and the rust will in a short time break through. Preparation of the surface is vital in achieving long-term protection, so seek advice from a metalwork conservator on the most suitable products and techniques to use.

Even with well-maintained metalwork, layer upon layer of paint obscures decorative details and so, from time to time, outdoor metalwork may need to be stripped. It is essential that all historical information is saved and recorded first. Wrought and cast iron were not necessarily painted black and traces of a former colour may be found in the detail under accumulated layers of paint. This research should be left to the conservator. It is particularly important where, for example, there is a gilded and coloured coat of arms on a gate.

Metal garden furniture

Painted metal garden furniture should be inspected regularly and painted as often as necessary (see Metal gates and railings, above).

METAL GARDEN SCULPTURE AND ORNAMENTS

Bronze

Bronze garden urns and statues were originally varnished or waxed to create the rich brown to black finish found on indoor bronze statuettes. The surface nowadays rarely has this patina but is streaked and mottled green and black because of corrosion.

Maintenance

Even though bronze corrodes slowly, it is important to slow down the rate of corrosion by removing polluted grime, bird droppings, moss and other plant matter. In the first instance this should be carried out by a conservator, who can ensure that the bronze is structurally sound and check that there are no serious corrosion problems. Ideally bronze statuary should be regularly maintained by cleaning and waxing, but this is specialist work and should be carried out only by trained people.

Plinths and liners for urns

See Stone garden sculpture and ornaments, p. 249.

Copper

Copper statuary may sometimes be mistaken for bronze, but in any event it should be maintained in the same manner as bronze (see above).

Lead

Garden statuary and urns were frequently made of lead and many 18th-century examples are of high artistic quality. The lead was usually painted white to simulate marble, or it was sometimes stone or bronze coloured. The paint had the additional virtue of protecting the lead from atmospheric pollution, which causes corrosion. More research is needed on the extraordinary range of finishes, including polychrome, given to lead statues in the past, but from evidence to date they were never left to look like lead before the beginning of the 19th century.

After conservation, if lead statuary is to be painted, the type of finish should be considered carefully and applied by a conservator. Aesthetic considerations should always prevail, but they should be based, as with colour schemes inside historic houses, on a combination of knowledge and taste.

Lead sculptures normally have an iron armature or skeleton which supports the weight internally, and sculptures and urns often have iron pins or dowels.

33. A lead rainwater hopper at Lyme Park

The iron corrodes and loses its supportive strength over the years. Any signs of sagging or splitting should be investigated by a conservator and the corroded iron replaced with stainless steel. Repairs must be carried out by a specialist.

Unstable plinths are often a problem, since if the plinth is not level it puts an uneven strain on the sculpture erected upon it (see Stone garden sculpture and ornaments, p. 249).

Late-19th and early-20th-century examples of lead-work produced by slush casting are usually not of very high quality and, in view of the cost of lead repairs, a replacement may be preferable.

Old lead water cisterns frequently have pleasing decorative mouldings and their date of manufacture on them. When used as garden ornaments, they should be raised off the ground on a grid of flat stones or slate with the gaps between the supports sufficiently narrow to prevent the lead from sagging. It is better not to fill a cistern with earth and plants, since the strain will eventually fracture it and there will be a steady corrosive action from earth, decaying vegetation and fertilizers. If the cistern is to be planted, it should have a fibreglass liner and drainage holes with pipes going through the base of the liner and the lead so that water does not rest on the bottom of the cistern (see Stone garden sculpture and ornaments, p. 249).

Zinc

Though not often found in historic house gardens, sculpture made of zinc may be mistaken for lead.

The methods of manufacture in the late 19th century and subsequent rapid corrosion make their care a conservation nightmare.

Handling and storage

Do not attempt to move large sculpture. Fixings can be difficult to remove and the correct method of support is a job for specialists.

If metal sculpture has to go into storage, the relative humidity should be kept as low as possible and should never rise above 60%. A cheap and effective way of achieving this is by constructing a polythene tent and removing water from the air within with a dehumidifier (see The Right Environment, p. 28).

Inside the tent, it is best to leave the metal objects uncovered, as this allows them to be inspected easily. Light-weight dust-sheets could be used but in any case never *wrap* metalwork in polythene as there would be a risk of condensation forming on the surface of the metal.

And that you may know how to shelter your Lute, in the worst of Ill weathers, (which is moist) you shall do well, ever when you Lay it by in the daytime, to put It into a Bed, that is constantly used, between The Rug and Blanket; but never between the Sheets, because they may be moist with Sweat, etc. . . . a Bed will . . . keep your Glew so Hard as Glass, and All safe and sure; only to be excepted, That no Person be so inconsiderate, as to Tumble down upon the Bed whilst the Lute is There; For I have known several Good Lutes spoil'd with such a Trick.

Thomas Mace, *Musick's Monument*, 1676

CHAPTER NINE

MUSICAL INSTRUMENTS

Introduction
159

Avoiding Accidents
160

Enemies and Snags
169

34. The 17th-century organ in the church at Staunton Harold

·✤ MUSICAL INSTRUMENTS ✤·

The conservation of musical instruments depends on proper care being taken of the materials and adhesives used in their construction. Five factors make adherence to this obvious direction more difficult.

The variety of component materials

In most musical instruments a diversity of materials is to be found, many of them organic and therefore particularly susceptible to alterations in temperature and humidity as well as to attack by pests of various sorts. Different materials vary in their reaction to atmospheric change and this fact leads not only to obvious damage like loose Boulle work and to ivories becoming detached from their keylevers but also to problems of mechanical regulation. Instruments made largely of relatively stable materials often incorporate less stable parts of organic origin; the skin forming the head of a brass kettle-drum is an obvious instance but not an isolated one. An ivory flute will have joints of cork or thread and key-pads of leather. A modern iron-framed grand piano will still have action parts of wood and garniture of leather and felt.

The delicate nature of the component parts

Parts of many musical instruments are of a size or thickness which renders them vulnerable. Some are manifestly fragile, like the elaborate roses of early guitars and of some harpsichords. Some are robust enough for their job but too delicate to mishandle, like return springs of hog's bristle or whalebone. The strength or weakness of other parts is not so obvious. Harpsichord soundboards can be less than 2 mm thick in places and the tables of lutes, theorbos (a type of bass lute), guitars and similar instruments are often equally thin. Although their backs and ribs are usually of hardwood, they are almost as delicate and just as liable to damage.

Such thin material readily reacts to alterations in humidity. The problem is acute in the case of fronts and soundboards, which are commonly made of quarter-sawn softwood. Expansion and contraction is most marked in this dimension. General joinery practice allows such panels room for movement by loose-tonguing them into the rabbets of the surrounding frame. Such freedom of movement cannot be allowed to a soundboard since it would rattle and buzz when energized. It is therefore glued in position around its edge and can only react to high humidity by distorting and to low humidity by splitting.

Tension

Stringed instruments, with or without keyboards, are load-bearing structures. The modern grand piano supports an aggregate string tension of about twenty tons, more or less the weight of an empty railway carriage. Earlier examples of the piano and, obviously, other types of instrument with fewer strings, are not subjected to such considerable loading, but in all cases tension can both provoke and accentuate distortion.

Tolerances

The tolerances involved in the proper functioning of musical instruments are often very small. The thickness of tissue paper rather than that of a visiting card gives an idea of the distance between good and bad regulation. Moving parts must function freely but noiselessly. The difference between mechanical stiffness and audible action slop is measured in hundredths of a millimetre and provoked by relatively small variations in humidity. Similarly small movements can prevent the effective closure of organ pallets and impair the wind-tightness of oboes, bassoons and the like.

The domestic environment

The conservation of instruments in their domestic surroundings can subject them to conditions unavoidably inferior to those afforded by the controlled environment of a good museum or, for the smaller examples, a showcase. Physical and mechanical damage is more likely, dust and airborne pollution can present more of a problem, fluctuations in temperature and humidity are likely to be greater, attack by moth and worm is more probable. Sunlight has to be considered a threat, not only in its discolouring effects but also as a source of heat.

AVOIDING ACCIDENTS

Lids

Some harpsichords and pianos have loose-pin spine hinges to make lid-removal easier. Make sure the pins are in place before opening the lids of such instruments. Many lids are secured when shut either by visible hooks or by concealed fastenings which are operated by drop-handles or knobs. Make sure all are released before endeavouring to raise the lid. The fractured remains of the slim brass hooks which secured their lid flaps against warping can be seen at the right-hand end of countless 18th-century square pianos.

When a lid is distorted or warped, considerable strain is thrown on its fastenings. Take up this strain by applying gentle pressure to the top surface of the lid before opening or closing the fastening beneath.

Lock keeps and the eyes engaged by the lid hooks are often let into material of no great thickness and secured by screws whose length affords insufficient purchase to resist mishandling.

Many harpsichords and earlier pianos have separate foreboards to close off the keywell area. If such a foreboard is furnished with a lock, check that the front flap is free before endeavouring to raise it and restrain the foreboard in the process to prevent it falling. Do not leave foreboards lying round where they can be damaged.

Where the lid-prop is a separate item and not hinged to the cheekpiece of the instrument, make sure that it is within reach of one hand before raising the lid with the other. If the ends of the prop are bevelled, make sure the faces are correctly offered to lid and case. Where no special housings are present, support the bottom of the prop in the angle formed by the cheekpiece and the cheekpiece moulding and not on the edge of the soundboard. Make sure that the top of the prop is securely restrained by the lid moulding and that the moulding itself is not loose. In instruments in which the lid is designed to open beyond the vertical, make sure that the cord intended to restrain it remains adequate for the purpose and that it is securely attached.

In opening and closing the lids of harpsichords which incorporate a nag's-head swell, bear in mind the mechanical linkage involved between pedal and swell and avoid forcing it into or out of engagement. Even greater care should be taken in raising or lowering the secondary, louvred lid of instruments with a Venetian swell. Such devices are heavy and awkward to handle. If the swell mechanism is temporarily to be dispensed with, the frame of louvres is most safely raised by one person while another holds open the lid. The secure positioning of the lid-prop is of even greater importance when it supports the combined weight of lid and swell. Assistance is equally desirable in lowering the swell mechanism.

Some instruments have front lid flaps which open back beyond the comfortable reach of someone standing at the keyboard. Handle them from the cheekpiece side, folding back the flap with the left hand and supporting it towards the centre with the right.

In instruments with two hinged front flaps, avoid raising or lowering one flap by the other and throwing unnecessary strain on the hinge screws. Fold back the first flap and move to the cheekpiece of the instrument. Hold the first flap with the right hand and the second with the left. Keep the first lid flap horizontal while folding both back towards the tail of the instrument.

In many square pianos, the two hinged flaps which make up the front section of the lid have bevelled edges where they meet each other at the treble end of the keywell. In closing such a lid, make sure that the right-hand flap is shut before the left.

Lids left constantly open tend to sag. Shut them after use or display and in so doing avoid closing them on to lid-props, jack rails, damper rulers and lid closures in their shut position. Some music desks are of deck-chair complexity. Make sure that they are in completely closed order before lowering the lid.

Legs and stands

The legs and stands of most instruments are designed to afford vertical support and not to resist the strains imposed by pulling them along floors or carpets. Earlier instrument stands often comprise a pair of two-legged frames, coach-bolted into two stretchers. Since they are designed to be dismantled when necessary, the tenons of the stretchers are not as snug a fit in their mortices as those which form part of permanent, glued joints. Great care should be taken not to loosen them further.

Where castors are fitted, they should not be employed in the movement of an instrument from one place to another. Many castors were designed with an eye to elegance rather than efficiency and wear has rendered them still less serviceable. Exceptions are some modern grands whose legs are equipped with patent rollers or mounted on steel trolley frames. (Castors can also cause great damage to floors.)

Moving instruments

Some instrument stands are equipped with pedals for the operation of mechanisms within the instrument. Rods and linkages should be disconnected before instrument and stand are parted.

If there are locating battens on the underside of an instrument, their relation with the top rails of the stand should also be observed.

Some linkages are awkward to re-engage. The sostenuto mechanism of those Broadwood squares which have 'peacock' under-dampers is operated by a pull-down which extends well up into the instrument. In this and all other cases of possible difficulty it is a sensible precaution to check that linkages can be reconnected before the relationship between stand and instrument is disturbed.

Without the restraint of their attendant rods, the pedals themselves are free to flap about on their hinges. Whoever moves the stand should avoid catching the pedals on the floor, particularly when the stand is being set down in its new position. It should also be borne in mind that stands are almost as wide as the instruments they support. A number of dents in the architraves of doorways

35. A harpsichord by Abraham and Joseph Kirkman at Tatton Park, dated 1789

must have been caused by the front ends of harpsichord stands proving obstinately wider than the tail ends.

Professional harpsichord hirers work single-handed wonders with trolleys and instrument shoes but they do not commonly move valuable antiques. With one person to move the stand, three others are required to move safely all but the smallest harpsichords, one taking the weight of the tail, each of the others taking one of the front corners. Avoid damage to the side of the instrument from belt buckles; if one person alone is to carry the front of the instrument, the foreboard is particularly vulnerable in this regard.

If more help is available, and for the movement of heavier instruments like all but the earliest pianos it may be essential, five people make up a more efficient team than four, though the negotiation of doorways becomes more difficult. The efforts of a fourth person at the spine or the bentside unbalance the activities of the other three.

If a harpsichord is to be moved up or down stairs, it should be carried the same way round in both cases: tail first in ascent, keyboard first in descent. Bear in mind that though the weight falls more heavily on those carrying the front, the instrument will tend to slip from the grasp of whomever is carrying the tail. The negotiation of stairs too narrow for an instrument to remain flat is more difficult to accomplish safely and therefore not advised unless absolutely unavoidable.

Virginals and spinets can safely be moved by two people, again with a third person being responsible for the stand. Remember that bentside spinets have an odd centre of gravity and that the treble end of the keyboard will require support.

Earlier square pianos are light enough for two to handle, but instruments like the Longman and Broderips of the 1790s are awkward to lift from and replace on their French stands. Some examples have finger reliefs in the top of their back rails, but the location of the piano within the top moulding of the stand remains an awkward operation. The instrument is best aligned in the length, held clear of the stand by the locating dowels if these exist, before being moved forward into position from underneath.

Four people are needed to move the later square pianos. A vast increase in the thickness of their bottom boards and framing, as well as the inclusion of cast-iron members to resist the increased tension of their heavier stringing, makes them prodigiously heavy for their size.

Moving grand pianos, particularly over any great distance, is best left to teams of professionals. Wisdom is not an automatic adjunct of strength, however, and the value and vulnerability of the instrument should be stressed. If the legs are to be removed, care should be taken to ensure that each is reintroduced into its correct housing and that pedal lyres are removed with caution and replaced correctly.

Whenever an instrument is to be moved, one person should be in charge and should make clear to all concerned what is to be involved in the operation. A ruler is a more efficient tool for measuring the width of a doorway than is the instrument itself. The best time for discussion is before an instrument is uplifted, as the removal trade used to have it, rather than after the operation has begun.

In spite of the example afforded by one-man bands, instruments should be carried separately, no matter how small. Flutes, oboes, recorders and the like may have dried-out joints and tend to fall apart. When an instrument has a case, it should be used.

Handstops, pedals, etc.

Many keyboard instruments are furnished with handstops, pedals, knee-levers or other controls, the use of which should be denied to those not conversant with their function, otherwise damage may result.

An obvious example is afforded by the Venetian swell. In the later English harpsichords most commonly equipped with the device, it is usually controlled by a pedal on the right-hand side of the stand. Any endeavour to operate the pedal while the main lid is closed will be not only ineffective but eventually damaging, since movement of the louvres will be impossible and the mechanism subjected to undesirable stress.

36. A double-manual harpsichord by Shudi & Broadwood, 1770. The louvres of the Venetian swell are shown open

A slightly more common feature in English harpsichords is a pedal designed to facilitate changes in registration by achieving in one movement of the foot what would otherwise require the movement of one or more handstops. Such devices are usually operated by a pedal on the left-hand side of the stand. They vary in complexity but appear in their most elaborate form as the machine stop on double manual harpsichords with lute stops.

When such a machine is engaged, the force of a spring pulls on the dog-leg and 4-foot registers and pushes off the lute. Pressure on the pedal overcomes the force of the spring, pushing off the dog-leg and 4-foot and bringing on the lute register. The lower manual 8-foot remains hand-controlled. In its on position, it forms part of the full harpsichord chorus when the machine stop is engaged but its pedal not depressed, and affords a lower manual contrast to the lute stop on the upper manual when the machine pedal is operated.

Such machine stops are engaged and disengaged by moving a stop lever which projects through the spine of the instrument at the left-hand side of the keywell. A movement of 10–12 mm is involved, towards the tail of the instrument to engage the mechanism, towards the front to disengage it. Slight pressure on the pedal facilitates movement of the knob in both directions.

If an appreciation of the functioning of the mechanism is needed, it can be gained by removing the screws which secure its cover to the outside of the spine. The movements involved will be apparent, as will the considerable strength of the spring necessary to achieve them. The possibility of damage through misuse will be evident.

It should be remembered that the movement of engaging or disengaging the machine stop may leave registers neither fully on nor fully off. Whatever registration is subsequently desired must be set by hand.

The handstops of harpsichords control lateral movements within the instrument and for that reason should be moved sideways, rather than pushed or pulled. Some forward and backward movement of the knobs results from the cranking of the levers they control but this is incidental to their functioning. Some few mid-18th-century Flemish instruments equipped with bell-cranks or inclined planes exist as exceptions to this rule.

The movements involved are small. Some registers move scarcely 1 mm between their on and off positions and the movement of their attendant handstops is little more. Even a harp rack moves only about 2 mm.

A harp rack should not be left engaged when an instrument is not in use, otherwise the pressure of the strings will cause indentations in, or leave rust or oxide deposits on, the buffalo hide or other leather employed in the stop. This applies not only to harpsichords but to those earlier square pianos which have a similar device. In some of these instruments, the lever controlling the harp stop can be mistaken for one of two others which relate to the divided sostenuto mechanism. Normally, the harp stop is controlled by the lever which lies below the other two.

The sostenuto mechanism of such instruments should not be left engaged either. When the piano is not in use, the dampers should be left in contact with the strings, otherwise the whalebone springs which ensure their smart return will be weakened.

As a general rule, when any instrument is not in use, those moving parts which can be relieved of strain should be. This applies not only to things like the pedals of double-action harps but to the hair of the bows of instruments of the violin family.

In early grand pianos in which lateral movement of the keyboard can be achieved by the use of a pedal to produce *una corda* effects, a small dovetail wedge is sometimes let into the right-hand keyblock to limit the sideways travel of the action and produce a *due corde* result. In those few examples in which the wedge can be raised above the keyblock, it should not be so left when not in use but pushed back down into the safety of its recess.

Keyboard movement in a front-to-back direction was the means usually chosen on the Continent to couple and uncouple harpsichord manuals. The system was also in use, both here and abroad, to couple the manuals of tracker action organs before tumbler or ram couplers became the norm. In double-manual instruments it is normally, though not always, the upper manual which shifts – away from the player to couple, towards the player to uncouple. In an organ, small spurs were often mounted on the keys of both manuals, and their size and half-round profile render them less liable to damage. In the harpsichord, the system operates by the engagement or otherwise with the upper manual keylevers of wooden dogs mounted on the lower. Their shape and length render them more vulnerable than the organ variety.

The risk of damage is increased by the existence of some modern harpsichords with shift couplers which are furnished with spring-loaded dollies instead of rigid dogs. These enable the upper manual to be moved without damage to the mechanism, even though lower manual keys are depressed. A roller system prevents the upper manual jamming even when purchase is applied only to the bass or treble end.

In the classical instrument, it is essential that lower manual keys are not depressed while the upper manual is being moved, otherwise the coupler dogs may be broken off by the distal ends of the upper manual keys. It follows that both hands are free to move the upper manual, each grasping one of the keyblocks to do so.

Cleaning, polishing and dusting

It is to be hoped that smaller instruments of the woodwind group, as well as those of the violin family, will normally be kept in their cases and therefore not require the attention of a cleaner.

If smaller instruments are left on view and require cleaning, bear in mind the vulnerable nature of such things as the tables of lutes, in particular of their roses, and the bellies of violins, especially the areas around the 'f' holes.

Unless their formulation is known and has been approved, avoid proprietary cleaners of all sorts, whatever the claims made for them on their labels as 'varnish revivers'. A clean, soft cloth will suffice to remove dust from all areas of such instruments except those too intricate or delicate to tackle. For these, the softest of small brushes and the blowing action of a vacuum cleaner will prove effective.

This blowing and brushing technique should be used to clean harp-lutes, harp-guitars and the other similar instruments designed to fill the space left in the Victorian drawing-room by the removal of the harp proper to the concert hall (for which its growing potential, complexity and cost increasingly suited it).

The moving parts of instruments, like the forks, levers, plates and studs in the actions of post-Hochbrucker harps, are best not touched during routine cleaning, and the same applies to the actions of keyboard instruments. These areas should remain relatively clean and dust is preferable to damage.

37. A polygonal virginal by Marcus Siculus, 1540; detail showing the rose and jackrail

Stringed keyboard instruments have their own defences against dusters in the form of hitch- and bridge-pins. If dust builds up for any reason on the soundboard of such an instrument it should be blown out, away from the action, but no endeavour made to remove it in any other way. In the case of a painted soundboard, even blowing dust from the surface should not be attempted if there is any doubt about the stability of the paint.

Brushing the dust from soundboards is not to be recommended. Access is made difficult by the presence of strings, and dirt will tend to accumulate in those areas which are awkward to reach. The roses of English and Italian virginals, of many south European harpsichords and of the earlier guitars, are often vulnerable creations of leather, vellum or fine fretwork. They should not be disturbed by cleaning.

Cleaning should never be carried out on areas of casework which are damaged or unsound. Particularly avoid introducing wax polish into cracks which may subsequently be repaired. Polish renders unfinished surfaces impossible to glue satisfactorily and a split which might have been closed will have to be spliced instead.

Beware of loose veneers. Stringers and inlay, whether of wood or metal, like the Boulle decoration of some 19th-century pianos, are particularly liable to lift because of the difference between their rates of contraction and expansion and that of the carcase material beneath.

Never clean fretwork with a duster but use a soft brush and great care. The short-grain features of many of the designs which decorate music desks and nameboards are very easily damaged.

Never use metal polishes on brass or silver instruments or on the metal furniture of others. Apart from creating an undesirably new look by removing the patination, the abrasive effect of such polishes destroys the crispness of the original design, rubs out the repoussé work which decorates, for example, the lid hinges of many earlier English bentside spinets, removes gold from items that may look like brass but are in fact ormolu or brass-gilt, and leaves a stubbornly persistent deposit around the feature cleaned.

Take extreme care in removing dust from painted, gilded or papered surfaces. Such finishes can only be as stable as the material they decorate and the adhesives used in their application. Movement in the one and failure in the other can lead to flaking and peeling.

ENEMIES AND SNAGS

The atmosphere

The effects of high humidity on wood, leather, felt and other hygroscopic materials can be imagined: expansion due to water absorption, distortion and

38. The Music Room at Snowshill Manor

consequent malfunction. The formation of mould growths is encouraged. The strength of water-reversible adhesives is reduced.

High humidity also encourages the formation of deposits on metal items such as the fulcra on which moving parts turn. In extreme cases, iron balance pins can not only rust solidly into the mortices of the early keyboards in which they are encountered but can actually destroy the material of the surrounding keylevers. Rusty tuning pins can similarly affect a wrestplank. Humid conditions can rapidly lead to the formation of sufficient oxide on key-loadings to jam adjacent keys, especially when the same conditions provoke distortion of the levers themselves. The gold leaf applied to the lead roses of many north European harpsichords can be dulled and eventually penetrated if oxide is able to form underneath.

Conditions of low humidity result in the loss of cellular moisture in wooden parts, leading to distortion and splitting. Oddly, some baizes and felts tend initially to expand and become fluffier as they dry out. Leather shrinks and eventually perishes altogether. In dry conditions, organ pallets cease to be wind-tight and leaks appear in bellows and trunking. The use of electric blowers to supply instruments previously hand-pumped can accentuate the problem, since the air may be warmed in its passage through the blower and its relative humidity reduced.

The range of relative humidity within which musical instruments are best conserved is 50–60%, bearing in mind the slightly conflicting demands of their component parts. In endeavouring to preserve this range avoid sudden changes, since these are more damaging than gradual alterations. The introduction of efficient heating systems into churches previously without them brings work to the organ builders when it might perhaps better bring work to the humidification experts. The same problem is encountered in a house with the advent of each new heating season and particular care should be taken in winter. An increase of perhaps 16°C (30°F) in the temperature of winter air indoors above the outside temperature can produce a most dangerous drop in the relative humidity. An increase of 5°C (10°F) will keep the relative humidity within the recommended range in most weather conditions (see The Right Environment, p. 25).

Alterations in temperature are rather less serious *per se* but obviously affect the relative humidity and, again, sudden changes should be avoided. The most obvious effect is on the tuning of instruments. Considerable heat is generated by the additional lighting involved in film and television work. Remember this when there are camera crews in the house.

Instruments are not usually subjected to conditions of extreme cold. If they are, however, a phenomenon known as allotropy can occur, in which metal parts such as the lead-gilt roses of harpsichords and the tin alloy pipes of organs can actually crumble into powder.

The regular inspection of instruments is essential, of those kept in their cases or in store as well as those on display. Poorly ventilated surroundings encourage mould growth, particularly when the atmosphere is hot and humid.

Of the airborne pollutants, the chlorides are the most corrosive of metal items but their presence in quantity is likely only in industrial or marine environments. Of the harmful airborne gases, sulphur dioxide is particularly destructive of leather, felt and baize. It is more likely to be a problem in urban environments. If either of these is causing damage, instruments must be kept covered by glass or dust-sheets when not in use or on display.

Pests

Woodworm and moth are the two parasites most likely to attack musical instruments. A constant watch must be kept for evidence of the activity of either pest.

Woodworm have dietary preferences and are particularly likely to relish the pine and spruce-fir of which most soundboards are made, the beech commonly used for bridges and nuts and the walnut casework of English bentside spinets. Many other woods are liable to attack, however, though worm activity in some timbers like oak tends to be concentrated in the sapwood rather than in the heart. Animal glues also attract woodworm, and damage often runs along the line of a joint.

Left unchecked, woodworm can irreversibly damage an instrument. The structural weakness resulting from extensive galleries of activity can often be remedied, but tonal alteration is almost bound to result from any of the expedients used to stabilize a severely damaged soundboard, even when the actual replacement of deceased timber is avoided.

Small heaps or tracks of wood dust are commonly looked for as evidence of infestation but such telltales can well remain unobserved within an instrument. The presence of worm is often more certainly diagnosed by looking for fresh flight-holes. These usually appear during April and May, as the grubs which have spent the last one or more years eating their way to maturity emerge and take wing to find suitable locations for the laying of more eggs. Once hatched, these in their turn burrow into the wood to continue the destructive cycle.

Fresh flight-holes can best be seen in a raking light, which will reveal the paler colour and sharper arris of recent damage (see Pests, Moulds and Insects, p. 192).

The topical application of an insecticide like Cuprinol is not always to be recommended with musical instruments. It can reduce the elasticity and increase the density of the resonating parts of an instrument, with resulting tonal loss. Advice should be sought as to whether a more effective treatment would be the subjection of the instrument to exposure for forty-eight hours to an atmosphere of methyl bromide. Other fumigants can be effective but all of them involve poisonous gas, and treatment must be carried out by specialists.

The wool and other natural fibres which make up the baizes and felts found in many musical instruments are the favourite diet of the larvae of moths. Unfortunately, although the eggs from which the larvae develop can be removed by a vacuum cleaner, they are seldom laid in the most accessible places, so a conservator should be consulted.

Moulds, insects and other pests thrive on damp, dirt and disregard. Musical instruments, especially those not in regular use or stored away, should be kept in surroundings which are dry, clean and regularly inspected.

Tension and distortion

Stringed instruments should be kept at or below the pitch for which they were designed. If there is any reason to believe that an instrument is unable to withstand this tension, or any ground for thinking that the string gauges have been increased during earlier repairs, the load should be reduced evenly throughout the compass. The pitch of the instrument should be lowered by a third or fourth and advice sought about the structural instability which provoked the anxiety.

The effects of distortion are difficult to remedy in the workshop. Modern restoration practice properly rejects the use of reinforcement and the alternative, if it must be undertaken, can involve the complete disassembly of an instrument.

In guitars and lutes, distortion is commonly seen in the deepening of the action as the neck pulls forward. The longer the neck, the more acute the possible problem; chitarrones (large long-necked lutes) are particularly vulnerable. Tension can also distort the tables of instruments whose strings are hitched to the bridge, rather than being secured to a tail-piece or tail-buttons. The more lightly barred the belly, the more susceptible the instrument; the earlier guitar is therefore much at risk.

The effect of tension on the various stringed keyboard instruments is obviously directly related to the ability of their framing to withstand the load imposed. Increases in the compass and sustaining power of the piano, for example, were not always matched by adequate increases in structural strength. If proper consideration is given to their original string gauges and probable pitch, however, wooden-framed instruments are not necessarily unstable; nor are later pianos, particularly those examples with metal spreaders and hitchplates rather than complete cast frames, necessarily stable.

String tension is responsible for the distortion of numbers of square pianos. The cases of the earlier examples tend to lift from the horizontal at the front-right-hand or back-left-hand corner. The foreboards of such instruments become jammed when shut and removal of their nameboards for action regulation is difficult because they are pinched between the returns of the keywell.

The framing typical of the 18th-century harpsichord made in this country seems to have contributed to the dropping of the cheekpiece at its junction with the bentside, a distortion so frequently encountered that it is commonly called 'the English accent'. The top edge of the bentside is frequently pulled in and the junction between bentside and tail is often distorted. Action gaps between wrestplank and belly-rail tend to close and hitchpin rails to pull away from the case sides. Four-foot bridges are often pushed downwards and four-foot hitchpin rails often pulled up. Wrestplanks can bend both forwards and upwards, become insecurely anchored and in some cases split their housings in spine or cheekpiece. Italian instruments, especially those lightly constructed virginals and harpsichords with separate outer cases, can literally curl up under tension.

The bows of instruments of the violin and viol family can suffer in the same way. Pernambuco and snakewood sticks lose their elegant and functional shape unless relieved of the tension of the horsehair after use.

Instruments should be inspected at least once a year for signs of such distortion. Remember that if an instrument is not tuned regularly, conditions can combine to produce a rise rather than a fall in pitch and a resulting increase in the tension. The load on a harpsichord with three choirs of strings, for instance, increases by more than a quarter of a ton if its pitch is raised by a semitone. For this reason, advice must be sought before an instrument designed for a lower pitch is tuned to a higher, a request most likely to be made by those who wish to use it in concert with a modern flute or oboe, for example.

Tuners

Present-day piano-tuners are not infrequently skilled technicians, capable also of carrying out not only the regulation but the mechanical repair of the modern instruments which they commonly encounter. The same is true of organ-tuners, for whom tuning is likely to be only a part of the skilled work they do for the firms who employ them. Neither, though, may be sympathetic to or conversant with historical examples of the instruments with which they deal.

Care must therefore be taken in the choice of tuners. Open metal pipework is not best attended to by those accustomed only to tuning slides; slim, oblong-headed wrestpins must be protected from ill-fitting tuning hammers in the hands of those who instinctively 'set' the pins.

Recommendations offered about regulation and repair should be treated with caution, and advice obtained before they are implemented. Proposals involving any degree of modification or 'improvement' should be rejected. The authentic pitch, or an approved alternative, should be preserved, as should the tuning of those instruments for which the temperament can be deduced.

Conservators

The number of instrument-makers devoting their attention to building copies of historical originals has vastly increased over the last twenty years. Skills and scholarship vary widely, in the same way that the instruments available range from assembled kits to valuable examples of the work of excellent and informed craftsmen.

It is important to remember that even a good instrument-maker is not necessarily a good conservator. The techniques, disciplines and attitudes involved are subtly different, and a historical humility is required of the conservator which is not necessarily demanded of the builder.

A simultaneous though smaller growth can be seen in the numbers of those who specialize in instrument restoration and a similar variation can be seen in scholarship and skill. Proper documentation, in the form of reports, work schedules, photographic records and drawings, is an essential part of the process still too often regarded as an unnecessary chore.

Restoration may not be in all cases the best way of conserving a musical instrument. Improvements in remedial techniques continue to be made. In some instances it may be wiser to do no more than stabilize the condition of an instrument in the hope that repair can be undertaken in the future. A further, perhaps more ethical, consideration is that the use invited by an instrument in playing condition should not be allowed to accelerate its decline.

Advice must be obtained whenever the restoration of an instrument is contemplated.

Specialists and amateurs

Old instruments which survive in unaltered condition make up the least ambiguous part of the evidence about how the music of the past might once have sounded. Such originals, or copies of them, have played an essential part in the more historically informed interpretation of compositions from periods as remote as the Renaissance and as recent as the Classical. Owners of significant examples are used to requests from musicologists and musicians to take measurements or make drawings of them or to use the instruments themselves in performance. More recently, specialists have begun to revise our perception of the Romantic composers and the tonal and mechanical characteristics of relatively modern 19th-century instruments are receiving the sort of attention already devoted to their 16th-, 17th- and 18th-century predecessors.

Such interest is to be encouraged but the well-being of the instruments must remain of paramount importance. Damage can be caused by the enthusiastic but uninformed researcher, especially if any degree of disassembly is involved, and a performer eager to use an old instrument for concert or recording purposes may not be the person best qualified to advise on any necessary regulation or adjustment. It is never worth carrying out hasty or ill-considered repairs, even for the sake of a compact disc.

The playing of instruments not in a condition to be played is to be discouraged, since mechanical damage can result. Even the blowing of experimental passages on woodwind or brass instruments causes internal condensation which, if not disposed of, may damage the instrument. Serpents have suffered seriously in this way.

The matter of alterations in pitch for performance purposes has been mentioned. In this and in all cases in which requests are received to play or make detailed examinations of instruments, expert advice should be sought.

For musical boxes, see Miscellaneous, p. 295.

There is a fine stuffed chavender
A chavender, or chub.
That decks the rural pavender,
The pavender, or pub.
Wherein I eat my gravender,
My gravender, or grub.

W. St Leger
The Chavender, or Chub

CHAPTER TEN

NATURAL HISTORY COLLECTIONS

Mounted Mammals, Birds, Reptiles and Fish
179

Birds' Eggs, Shells and Corals
184

Insect Collections
186

Rocks, Minerals and Fossils
186

Plant Materials
187

39. Big game trophies in the Tenants' Hall at Tatton Park

With increasing loss of natural environments worldwide, historic houses may possess many natural history specimens which cannot be replaced legally or at all. The laws concerning collections of birds' eggs are now particularly severe. Every collection should be catalogued by a specialist who can identify the rare or extinct specimens.

MOUNTED MAMMALS, BIRDS, REPTILES AND FISH

Animals mounted for display consist of skin and sometimes bones, padded out with sawdust, cotton wadding, plaster of Paris, etc., over a rigid manikin of wood or iron wires. Mounts, therefore, are very susceptible to deterioration through changes of humidity. High humidity causes mould growth and rusts the wires inside the body; also in the legs of birds, which may collapse and fall off their perches. Low humidity may cause the skin to shrink and split. Splitting usually occurs where the skin is thinnest, such as around the eyes and mouth, or where it is under the greatest stress, such as along stitching.

Damage by light is irreversible. The first signs are a dulling of the colours, followed by fading and increasing fragility. Light levels should be kept below 50 lux and relative humidity ideally at a constant 55% (see The Right Environment, p. 21). Where specimens are displayed in a room with daylight, exclude damaging ultraviolet rays either by treating the window with UV-absorbent film or by treating the glass of the display cases.

Specimens should be placed in the darkest part of the room and never above radiators, fireplaces or where beams of sunlight can strike them. Wherever possible the specimens should be displayed in sealed cases, which not only keep out dust and pollutant gases but also deter insects. A tight seal must be maintained on these cases by renewing lifting or broken seals with gummed tape. (Self-adhesive tape, e.g. masking tape, should never be used as the adhesive degrades and the seal soon fails.)

Insect attack

Moth and carpet beetle are the chief pests and can ruin and even destroy a specimen. Fish are particularly difficult to prepare for display. Traces of fat are left within the skin and body which sometimes appear as drops of grease under the fish. When this happens, beware of the bacon beetle. If there is evidence of attack, an expert must be consulted (see Pests, Moulds and Insects, p. 191).

Holes, falling hair or feather, moth wings and discarded larval cases are all signs of an insect infestation. The effect of insect attack on the skin itself is worst on thin skins, especially of birds, fish and pads of feet, and can lead to collapse.

Specimens in glazed cases may seem to be protected but insects can penetrate through very narrow cracks. Once inside the insects thrive on neglect. All cases should be inspected carefully once a year. If the display case is sealed, do not disturb unless there is evidence of dust in the case indicating that insects may also have got in.

Protection and treatment

Old birds' nests on buildings should be removed from eaves and chimneys as they provide a haven and breeding ground for a variety of insect pests that attack objects in houses.

Do not introduce a new specimen into a collection without first checking very carefully for signs of insect attack.

Ideally all specimens should be inspected annually in good light when the insects are most active in May to July and then any treatment needed should be carried out for eight to twelve weeks during this period. However, this time of year is seldom possible in historic houses which are open to the public (see Cleaning and handling, below). If many specimens are affected expert advice must be sought. When the attack is confined to one or two specimens, the recommended insecticide is a dichlorvos fumigant, generally available as 'Vapona' or 'Mafu'. Place the affected specimen in a sealed polythene bag or tent using polythene sheeting on a simple wooden frame. Ensure that there is plenty of air around the specimen. The polythene should not touch the specimen. Pin dichlorvos-based strips high in the bag or tent using only the number recommended on the packet. The strips occasionally exude a sticky liquid so suspend them where any drips will not fall on the specimen. Seal the tent by folding the sheet over twice and stapling in place. Leave sealed for eight to twelve weeks. Dichlorvos strips have a natural life of about six months, so use fresh supplies.

Insecticides are toxic, so avoid breathing in the vapour or wear a mask with appropriate filter. Fix and remove the strips in a well ventilated space – ideally out of doors. The use of dichlorvos has been banned in some countries.

Cleaning and handling

Cleaning should be carried out only if the specimen is robust. Most mounts become fragile in time, so specimens should be handled as little as possible and with extra care, by those who are experienced in dealing with them. A bird bobbing on its slender legs may fall off its perch. If a mounted animal is to be packed and transported, it should first be covered with a closely fitting cloak of smooth material, e.g. acid-free tissue, that will not ruffle hair or feathers. The specimen may then be given one layer of Bubblewrap, again fitted to its shape, before being laid on a bed of cushioning material that provides overall support. Large animals require purpose-made supports and trolleys for safe transport. All the heavy parts should be secured from movement or vibration.

All cleaning should be kept to a minimum and should take place when the specimens are examined for insect attack. Free-standing specimens will need cleaning more frequently than those protected by glass. Note the condition and record any treatment carried out. When cleaning, isolate the specimen from the rest of the collection so that if insects are discovered they will not be brushed off near other specimens and so contaminate them. Dust should never be sucked off with a vacuum cleaner.

Cleaning mammals

Always test for weakness in hair by lightly brushing an area over a piece of paper. There are three likely causes: (a) insect attack may be isolated in patches or concentrated along the surface of the skin, creating a mat of hair which may come away leaving a bald patch; (b) poor initial curing of the skin creates weakness in the hair follicles which over time release their grip on the hairs; (c) some hair is so badly degraded by the effects of light or pollutants that it breaks

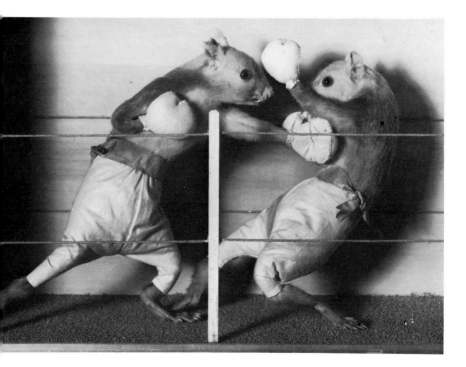

40. Boxing squirrels. One of a collection of tableaux at Castle Ward in which squirrels are 'set up' and are engaged in human activities

41. A picturesque caseful of curiosities collected by the Trevelyan family at Wallington, posing particular problems for the conservator

at touch. All three causes can lead to catastrophic loss of hair for which there is no treatment at present. Where there is a trace of hair loss but no sign of insect attack an expert should be consulted to establish the cause. If there is no sign of loose hair, blow (not suck) with a domestic cylinder vacuum cleaner on its lowest setting and then rearrange the fur by combing gently, using a plastic comb with wide-spaced teeth.

Ears and tails

Be very careful of ears and tails as they are fragile and can tear easily.

Eyes and teeth

Glass eyes and teeth may be dusted with a ponyhair brush (see Appendix 3, p. 318) and then, if necessary, wiped with a cotton bud stick just dampened with water. It should not be possible to squeeze water out of the swab, which must be changed before it gets dirty.

Noses

Dust with a hogshair brush (see Appendix 3, p. 318). If the nose is very dry, consult a taxidermist.

Antlers, horns and hooves

Rough surfaces can be dusted with a hogshair brush; smooth surfaces with a soft, clean duster. If necessary, antlers, horns and hooves may be wiped with small swabs of cotton wool very lightly dampened with methylated spirits, but first test a small area, especially on antler, to ensure that any added dyes are not removed by the swabs.

Lions

Lions can have their manes brushed with a soft brush, but be very careful of the ears which can tear easily.

Elephants and rhinoceroses

Brush with a 50 mm wide paint brush, while at the same time collecting the dust in a Hoover Dustette fitted with the crevice tool.

Cleaning birds

Feathers are generally tougher than hair though they can suffer 'grazing' and cutting by insect attack. Seek expert advice if a lot of damage is noted. Taxidermists use a bird's wing, with feathers, for brushing dust off specimen birds. After brushing, the feathers can be rearranged with a needle or a pair of very pointed tweezers. Some specimens, particularly birds, were preserved using arsenic soaps. Care must be taken not to inhale the dust during cleaning.

Claws and beaks

Claws and beaks may be dusted with a ponyhair brush and then, if necessary, wiped with small swabs very lightly dampened with water.

Cleaning reptiles and fish

Birds are sometimes called flying reptiles. The skin of reptiles and fish can be treated in the same way as claws and beaks. The skins were frequently varnished or even painted, so care must be taken not to soften the surface. Some mounted fish are actually plaster of Paris copies of the original. These are surprisingly heavy and fragile.

Cleaning other materials

Taxidermists took considerable pride in dressing the cases for mounted animals, using appropriate plants and stage settings. Most of these are now fragile and should be touched only lightly, if at all.

BIRDS' EGGS, SHELLS AND CORALS

These are all composed of calcium carbonate with a small amount of organic binder and frequently an organic pigment. They are therefore as susceptible as skin to high light levels which can cause fading and reduction in strength. The mineral component is also attacked chemically by acids from the air and most frequently from the wood or cardboard of storage cabinets. This chemical reaction takes the form of white growths on the surface, looking rather like mould, which is known as Byne's disease, after the Mr Byne who investigated the problem in the late 19th century. It can occur only in damp conditions so it is important to monitor the relative humidity and if possible keep it below 55% (see The Right Environment, p. 25).

Storage

It is dangerous to store these materials in cabinets made of oak or chestnut or in poor-quality packaging materials. Use acid-free tissue paper and boxes, or good-quality polythene bags (see Appendix 4).

CLEANING

Birds' eggs

Dust only with a ponyhair brush. Never use water or any other liquid as the colour may come off.

42. Mother-of-pearl suffering from Byne's disease

Shells and coral

Most can be brushed with a hogshair brush and then wiped over with a damp cloth or swab of cotton wool. However, others may be fragile, either because they are of delicate construction or because the surface is flaking. These should be left for expert attention. Great care must be taken when cleaning spiral shells to prevent water getting inside, or the desiccated remains of the creature, which are often still inside these shells, will start decomposing and smell vile. Bivalves such as mussels, clams, etc., are easy to wash as the dead mollusc has been removed. Dry well. A hair-dryer set at cool could be useful here.

INSECT COLLECTIONS

Most butterflies and moths live a short time and so their wings and bodies are delicate and unstable to light. Never touch the specimens and store in the dark. Collections of insects should be illuminated as little and seldom as possible.

Handling and cleaning

When moving a tray of insects, keep it level and free from vibration. Do not attempt to remove rusted pins, even though they are a cause of deterioration, as attempts to do so usually result in the disintegration of the pinned specimen.

Specks of dust in the drawer can be lifted out carefully on the tip of a ponyhair brush very slightly moistened with water. Do not wet the brush. Glass lids can be cleaned, well away from the insects, with a chamois leather. If a lot of dust is getting in, consult an entomologist on how best to seal the cabinet.

Insect attack

Insect collections are so fragile that it is best to seek the advice of an entomologist. Cleaning up the drawer or cabinet is a job for an expert. If the attack is slight, place the drawer and its contents, taking care not to shake it, in a polythene bag with a strip of 'Vapona' or 'Mafu' at the dosage rate stated on the packet (see Insect Attack, p. 180). Close the bag tightly and leave sealed for eight to twelve weeks. This treatment should be carried out between May and July when insect pests are most active. Remember this dichlorvos fumigant is toxic to humans, so open the bag in a well-ventilated room (see above). Rare specimens should always be treated by an expert.

ROCKS, MINERALS AND FOSSILS

Geological specimens vary greatly. Some are soft, others brittle; some light-sensitive and others attacked by acids from packaging materials. Unless expert advice has been sought, it is therefore better to treat all specimens as though they suffer from all these problems. Keep light levels low and use acid-free tissue paper and boxes (see Appendix 4 and also The Right Environment, Display cases, p. 31).

Iron pyrites is a component of many fossils and some mineral specimens. The most serious deterioration that can affect geological specimens is 'pyrite disease', a form of oxidation of iron pyrites. Pustules of grey dust appear on the surface, leading to the complete collapse of the specimen.

Pyrite disease produces sulphuric acid, so remove any affected material for the sake of neighbouring specimens. Once started it can be stopped only by prompt conservation treatment by an expert. Pyrite disease can be minimized by storage in dry conditions in an RH of less than 50%. Specialist advice must be sought.

PLANT MATERIALS

Pressed flower pictures, dried flower arrangements and other botanical specimens are even more sensitive to light and fluctuations in humidity than water-colours. Insects can also attack them.

To ruinate proud buildings with thy hours,
And smear with dust their glittering golden towers;

To fill with worm-holes stately monuments,
To feed Oblivion with decay of things

To spoil antiquities of hammered steel,
And turn the giddy round of fortune's wheel.

Shakespeare, *Rape of Lucrece*,
lines 944–7, 951–2

Lay up not for yourselves treasures upon earth,
Where moth and rust doth corrupt,
And where thieves break through and steal: . . .

Matthew vi, 19

Thou makest his beauty to consume away, like as it
were a moth fretting a garment: every man therefore is
but vanity.

Psalm 39

CHAPTER ELEVEN

PESTS, MOULDS AND INSECTS

Fungi
191

Insects
191

43. A death watch beetle grub attacking a book

·✤ PESTS, MOULDS AND INSECTS ✤·

Rats and mice, moulds, fungi, mildew and insects are a major threat to historical material. Prevention is better than cure, since the chemically based insecticides and fungicides are often hazardous to antiques and people.

FUNGI

Fungi are types of plants which grow on live or dead materials as moulds, mushrooms, mildew, rots, yeasts and even athlete's foot.

They grow in warm damp conditions from minute spores which are in the air. The presence of fungi in the material often results in the development of fluffy masses of minute threads, which may be visible on the surface of an object, or can grow root-like through it.

Prevention and cure

Fungi will not grow in dry conditions where the relative humidity in the air is below 65% (see The Right Environment, p. 25), and where there is plenty of ventilation. High levels of damp are generally damaging, so always establish the cause of the growth and do not rely on fungicides to solve the problem. Lower the level of moisture in the air and increase ventilation.

Avoid common sources of fungal growth, such as storing or displaying objects against cold outside walls (which cause high humidities) or on damp floors. Cellars, kitchens and bathrooms are naturally damp areas. Mopping floors, washing down walls, drying of emulsion paints, cooking, laundering, etc., all cause high humidities. Never store objects in damp, stagnant conditions, wrapped in polythene bags or sealed in boxes.

Any fungi found growing on part of the building should be surveyed professionally, as the fungi may have weakened the structure. Many fungicides can stain or damage certain materials and most are poisonous, so always seek professional advice before using them.

INSECTS

Insects are the group of animals that include beetles, butterflies, moths and flies, of which fortunately only a small number attack historic material. These are usually of two types: those that eat material of vegetable origin such as cotton, wood and paper; and those that attack animal-based material such as wool, leather, fur and feathers.

Generally insects have a similar life style that follows the seasons. Eggs are laid on or near a suitable food in the autumn and these hatch out into grubs or larvae in the spring. Depending on the type, the larvae feed and grow for either months or years until fully grown, when they pupate in a chrysalis, eventually to emerge as fully grown insects in the summer. The adults often feed outside during the summer before returning indoors in the autumn to lay their eggs and restart the cycle.

Woodworm

There are a number of insects that attack and damage wood, but the most common and widespread in Britain is the common furniture beetle.

The larvae of this beetle are a severe pest of most seasoned soft and hardwoods, though many tropical hardwoods are immune to attack. They also attack wicker and basketwork and early plywoods which are bonded with animal glues.

The eggs are laid in corners, cracks and crevices, old woodworm holes and on unfinished timber, particularly the rough grain end. In the spring the minute larvae hatch and bore into the wood, where they normally burrow for at least three years and often more, before pupating just underneath the surface of the wood, emerging in early summer as the adult beetle. The flight hole cut by the emerging beetle is the so-called woodworm hole. Freshly cut round holes about 2 mm wide, with perhaps some wood dust, which has a gritty feel to it, are sure signs of an active infestation.

Treatment

The standard method of eradicating woodworm is to paint the surface of the wood with an insecticidal liquid such as Cuprinol Low Odour Woodworm Killer. Never apply woodworm fluid by any method near objects or materials which could be stained, such as textiles, wallpaper, or the frames, stretcher bars or backing of pictures. Gilded wood should be treated only by a gilding conservator.

Treat polished wood from the back, as polished surfaces will not absorb the fluid. Take care to wipe off all traces of the liquid should any get on to the polished surface. Inject old woodworm holes carefully with a syringe or special applicator, so that the fluid penetrates the wood. Where there are a large number of holes it is only necessary to inject every 50 mm or so in order to saturate the wood under the surface (see Furniture, p. 114). Old woodworm holes often harbour eggs.

Where there are a large number of objects to be treated, or where the affected areas are difficult to treat, as with upholstered furniture, fumigation may be appropriate. The objects are placed in a portable plastic fumigation chamber, such as the Rentokil 'Bubble', into which insecticidal gas is introduced which kills all stages of the insect: eggs, larvae and adults. It has, however, no residual properties to prevent the objects from being re-infested. The different gases used for fumigation are all highly poisonous so expert advice should always be sought.

Moths and beetles

The larvae of a number of moths and beetles will live on natural materials such as wool, fur and feathers, 'grazing' bald patches and eating irregular holes in the fabric. Clothes, carpets and furnishings are particularly threatened.

Prevention

The chances of an infestation are greatly reduced by removing and burning all the old birds' nests from lofts, attics and disused chimneys; vacuuming thoroughly any areas where dirt and fluff may accumulate, such as along the edge of skirting-boards, behind furniture and along the cracks between floorboards; also by inspecting carefully any fresh or dried flower arrangements for beetles before bringing them indoors.

Infestations may first be noticed by spotting the insects. Carpet beetles are often found on windowsills in early summer, trying to fly outside, while moths flutter near windows and lights.

As the feeding larvae are naturally secretive, preferring to live in dark, damp undisturbed areas, they can cause irreparable harm and reach epidemic numbers before being noticed. The best weapon and defence is constant vigilance, good housekeeping and knowing your enemy.

House moths and clothes moths

House moths are usually recognized as small (about 10 mm long), speckled moths with dark spots on their wings. They tend to jump or fly short distances and when alighted hold their wings out flat.

Clothes moths are smaller (about 5 mm long), often a shiny gold colour with a 'tufted' head. When disturbed they have a scuttling run that is quite distinctive.

Both types prefer damp conditions and mild temperatures but can live in quite dry areas. The source of infestation is often from birds' nests in lofts and attics from which they spread, for example, to edges of carpets, woollen underlays, upholstery, fluff under the skirting-boards, where they can live and breed.

The larvae are messy feeders, living in a mess of white silky tubes and webbing, mixed up with small round balls of faeces of the same colour as the foodstuff. The larvae, if found, are usually small white or cream grubs, about 10 mm long. They produce ragged holes, falling hair, and bald patches, especially on soiled woollen fabrics.

Carpet beetles

The larvae of the carpet beetle is the well-known 'woolly bear', which is a voracious feeder not only of woollen textiles, such as carpets, clothes and upholstery, but also of animal-based materials such as horn, tortoiseshell, stuffed birds and animals and entomological collections of butterflies and moths, etc. Their damage is usually recognizable as the holes and 'grazed' areas which are irregular but clean cut, lacking the silk webbing and mess of moth larvae damage. Often pale brown cast skins of the larvae are also found. The 'woolly bears' are small (about 5 mm long), squat golden-brown hairy larvae with a tuft of hairs at the rear end. The adult carpet beetles look like small speckled ladybirds, or like small black beetles with a tiny white spot on each wing. The beetles live on the pollen and nectar of certain flowers, such as spirea, during the summer, coming indoors to lay their eggs in the autumn. Infestations, as with moths, often start with beetles flying in through open windows and laying eggs directly on suitable material such as carpets, stuffed animals, undisturbed debris such as dead flies or carpet fluff.

Booklice and silverfish

Booklice are minute fast-moving insects often found on books and papers in damp surroundings. They live on microscopic moulds growing on the paper.

Silverfish are small silvery insects that live on mouldy starch and are a common pest of larders and libraries.

Both insects damage by removing the surface of their foodstuff and both require very damp conditions to survive. Treatment is normally to improve the conditions. Airing and drying the books also has the added benefit of killing the mould growth (see Books, p. 49).

The roseate hues of early dawn,
The brightness of the day,
The crimson of the sunset sky,
How fast they fade away.

Mrs C. F. Alexander, from
Hymns Ancient and Modern,
1861 edition

CHAPTER TWELVE

PHOTOGRAPHS

Black-and-white Photographs and
Photograph Albums
199

Colour Photographs
201

44. William Henry Fox Talbot, one of the pioneers of modern photography, from a daguerreotype of about 1850 at Laycock Abbey

·✤ PHOTOGRAPHS ✤·

It is only in recent years that the historic value of photography has come to be realized. Unique examples must exist in many English houses, and there may well be members of the family or people living locally who can identify the subjects of old photographs.

BLACK-AND-WHITE PHOTOGRAPHS AND PHOTOGRAPH ALBUMS

A photograph is essentially a chemically sensitized paper which has reacted to exposure to light and produced an image after chemical processing. The image layer is frequently unstable and particularly sensitive to deterioration by light and pollution. The paper layer is subject to the same problems as all paper items, but especially to fluctuations in relative humidity.

Cartes-de-visite, card mounts, coloured backboards in frames and card-album pages were made from poor-quality groundwood pulp, and so are highly acidic and discolour and deteriorate rapidly. Thus, although the paper layer itself may be of good quality, migration of acidic by-products from supports and their manner of attachment will cause deterioration.

Storage and display

Relative humidity and temperature should be kept as constant as possible, as variations will cause expansion and contraction of the photographic emulsions and lead to cracking and flaking. Temperature should not exceed 15°C (59°F) and relative humidity should be in the range 45–55%. Mould growth will be encouraged in a relative humidity of over 65% and there is unfortunately no recommended fungicide for photographs.

Photographs should be stored in the dark. On display, light should be restricted to 50 lux maximum with an ultraviolet filter. Tungsten lights may need heat filters.

Never touch the surface of the image. Collections that are handled, for example, for study purposes should be stored in transparent polyester envelopes with acid-free card supports for fragile or large items. Any adhesive seam should be positioned on the reverse side of the image. Sellotape should be avoided.

Never store photographs near or in wood furniture, or in newly painted or varnished areas. Wood gives off organic acids which react adversely with the image layer. Ideal storage would be an enamel-finish steel cabinet with air vents, fitted with dust filters, in a clean, dry area. Mounted photographs can be stored in acid-free boxes and kept on open shelves. Albums should be wrapped in strong acid-free paper and tied with flat cloth tape until they can be boxed.

Atmospheric pollutants which degrade photographs include:

(a) ozone, given off, for example, by photocopying machines
(b) hydrogen sulphide, nitrogen oxides in the air
(c) organic acids given off by wood
(d) ammonia from household cleaners
(e) sulphur from deteriorating rubber, e.g. rubber adhesives, rubber bands
(f) salt carried by coastal winds.

Photographic copies can be made through the polyester envelopes recommended. Commissions for new photographs and orders for copies should include the necessary processing recommendations for maximum permanence. (Consult a paper conservator.) Resin-coated photographic papers are not recommended for archival use; photographs should not be dry-mounted. Acid-free card mounts should be specified.

Specific problems

Gelatine and albumin photographs

These are especially subject to cracking and flaking – usually caused by high relative humidity – and mould and insect attack, such as silverfish.

Nitrate film

This was in use from 1899 to 1939, and is a severe fire risk, as chemical decomposition can produce spontaneous combustion. Film should be copied and the original destroyed or stored at a temperature between 2 and 5°C (37–41°F). Storage in fireproof steel cabinets (preferably away from other collections) is the main priority. Cellulose acetate safety film became generally available only in about 1930.

Daguerreotypes, Ambrotypes

Never touch the surface. Store in the original cases wherever possible and keep closed. Do not attempt to clean the surround – a velvet or gilt frame, for example – as the dislodged dust particles will damage the image surface.

45. A screen with Victorian family photographs in the library at Clandon

Lantern slides and glass negatives

These should be isolated from each other by the recommended transparent polyester envelopes (see Appendix 4), and stored in their original boxes in cupboards. Do not attempt to stick broken photographs together (glass or paper). Keep all relevant pieces in a labelled envelope until the problem can be discussed with a conservator.

COLOUR PHOTOGRAPHS

These were commercially in use and widely available by the 1950s, although early colour processes, such as Autochrome, were selectively available from the late 1930s.

Colour photographs are subject to the same problems as black-and-whites, but especially to fading, both from exposure to light and from the impermanence of the colours. The rate of fading is thought to be related to the film speed, lower film speeds giving a more permanent colour image.

In order to maximize the permanence of these images, exposure of original photographs should be avoided. Duplicates should be used for study and exhibition.

Storage

Ideally the temperature should be between 2 and 5°C (37–41°F), but a constant temperature between 8–12°C (46–54°F) is acceptable, with the relative humidity constant between 30 and 45%. Otherwise store as for black-and-white photographs.

The way to ensure summer in England is to have it framed and glazed in a comfortable room.

Horace Walpole,
letter to Dr William Cole, 28 May 1774

When Sir Joshua Reynolds died
All Nature was degraded;
The King dropped a tear into the Queen's ear
And all his pictures faded.

William Blake, *On Art and Artists*

For Time shall with his ready Pencil stand;
Retouch your Figures, with his ripening hand;
Mellow your Colours, and imbrown the Teint;
Add every Grace, which Time alone can grant;
To future Ages, shall your Fame convey;
And give more Beauties, than he takes away.

Dryden, *To Sir Godfrey Kneller*, 1694

CHAPTER THIRTEEN

PICTURES

PAINTINGS

Preventing Accidental Damage
207

Action in the Event of Damage
210

Carrying Pictures
211

Hanging and Taking Down
Pictures
211

Storing: Long-term
and Temporary
214

Frames and Framing
216

Transport
217

Routine Inspection
218

Environment
219

MINIATURES

Categories of Portrait Miniatures
221

Display
222

Storage and Transport
223

Cleaning
223

Inspection
223

WATER-COLOURS,
DRAWINGS AND PRINTS
224

Paper support
225

Artists' materials
226

Causes of Deterioration
229

Storage
231

Hanging
233

Cleaning Frames
234

Accidents
234

Conservation
234

PARCHMENT
235

46. Nash's original design for the Picture Gallery at Attingham and (below) as it is today

· ✤ PAINTINGS ✤·

Pictures play an essential role in the embellishment of any country house and many country-house collections contain paintings and frames of outstanding importance. The continued enjoyment of a picture depends on its survival in good condition.

The surface of a painting should not be touched by anyone but a picture conservator. In fact once a picture is hanging safely on the wall, it is best left entirely alone; even dusting the frame exposes the painting to risks of accidental damage.

The care of pictures through good housekeeping falls into three areas: avoidance of accidental damage; observing and reporting suspected deterioration; and maintaining an appropriate and stable environment.

PREVENTING ACCIDENTAL DAMAGE

Much of the repair work of paintings is made necessary by accidental damage received in the course of handling, storage and display. All possible steps should therefore be taken to minimize risks.

Visitors and house staff

Pictures should wherever possible be safeguarded by placing furniture below them. Topographical views in particular tempt visitors to point out local features. Room stewards should discourage visitors from pointing at details in paintings, as the distance may be misjudged or the hand accidentally jolted. Apart from the risk of inadvertent damage, fingers deposit grease and grime on the painted surface.

Paintings should not be hung where they are liable to be knocked by visitors pushing through narrow passages or bottlenecks; nor in vulnerable positions on staircases. Any painting that is in danger of being knocked or scraped and which cannot be hung elsewhere should be glazed.

Be aware of the vulnerability of pictures when moving furniture and other objects in a room. Always have at least two people to carry long objects, especially on staircases where paintings suffer from ladders being carried up and down. Never allow one person to move tall step-ladders single-handed, as they are easily unbalanced.

Tower scaffolding should be erected and dismantled well away from the paintings; avoid loose tools on the platform which could drop down on to a painting.

Never hold a tool above a picture or attempt to position something above a painting. First remove the painting right out of the way. This also applies when taking down or hanging one painting above another. Always take down the lower register before handling the upper register.

While in principle no work should take place above a painting, in some circumstances it is impractical to take down all the pictures before dusting cornices with a vacuum cleaner. Clean, lightweight dust-sheets can be carefully draped over the frame, taking care that the surface of the painting is not touched.

When planned ahead, it is generally possible to arrange for a picture conservator to be working in the house while special cleaning, which gives rise to these problems, is taking place.

Try to avoid creating dust in a room, especially when dry-sweeping a stone floor. Avoid leaving excessive damp after washing a floor, as this may raise the relative humidity (see The Right Environment, p. 25).

Aerosols and other sprays must not be allowed in the vicinity of pictures. Do not use insecticides or oil-based pesticides, such as Cuprinol or Rentokil, on picture frames or any part of the paintings, such as panels or stretcher bars, as the non-volatile base can cause serious damage.

Building and decorating

Always remove paintings out of the way of builders and their scaffolding. Paintings should not be left in an area where decorations or repairs are to be carried out.

Never hang a painting on a freshly plastered wall until the wall has quite dried out, which may be a matter of months; nor in a newly painted room until the smell has dispersed. Smell is an indication that volatile chemicals in the paint are still evaporating.

The redecoration of a room presents a good opportunity to remove and treat paintings in fixed architectural frames. Also where special scaffolding is needed, such as on staircases, the conservation of the paintings can be planned ahead to coincide with building work.

Paintings set in panelling or fixed architectural frames had space allowed for air movement and were not set directly on to brick or rendered walls. Never plaster or paint behind a painting set in the wall. Modern plastic paints should not be used on the wall surrounding a painting inset into the wall, or round a wall-painting, because any dampness in the wall could then only come out behind the painting or through the wall-painting.

Photography and filming

See that all equipment is kept well clear of paintings and other objects, to avoid accidental damage. Filming can be profitable, but only if it does not result in damage to valuable objects. For example, chandeliers have been damaged by photographers moving their equipment round a room without proper supervision.

Oil paintings on canvas are less vulnerable to exposure to tungsten-halogen lights (as used in photo-floods) than are textiles, drawings and water-colours. However, even short periods of floodlighting can raise the temperature and lower the relative humidity (see The Right Environment, p. 25).

Photo-flood lights should always be kept at least 2 m away from all picture surfaces. There should be adequate ventilation such as open windows, cooling fans and reflectors, to deflect the heat, and the lights must be switched off immediately after the photograph has been taken.

When photographing pictures, photographers should not be left alone with the painting and no picture should be handled or unframed by the photographer. A glazed water-colour, print, drawing, etc., must never be unframed except by experts. Sealing works of art on paper into a frame is a specialized job which only a few framers do correctly.

47. An illustration of the 18th-century practice of hanging pictures from chair rail to cornice at Saltram

Photographers should not be allowed to touch the surface of the painting in any way, and should on no account be allowed to wipe the surface, either dry or with any liquid.

ACTION IN THE EVENT OF DAMAGE

In the case of a painting being damaged, advice should be sought without delay from a picture conservator.

Accidents

If damage such as a dent, scrape or tear is found, do not take the painting down, and avoid the almost irresistible temptation to touch the surface. Give details of the nature, location and extent of the damage to a picture conservator.

If the painting has fallen off the wall or has been badly jolted, record the incident, even if there is no apparent damage, so that the picture and frame can be checked carefully on the next visit of a picture conservator. Before moving the painting, check whether any chips of paint have fallen off newly damaged areas in case these could be retrieved from the frame, furniture or floor by the picture conservator. Do not touch the damaged surface of the painting.

Floods, splashes

If the picture has been splashed with a liquid or streaked by water from a burst pipe, do not wipe the surface. Leave the painting hanging unless it is necessary to remove it from further risk. Do not be alarmed if the varnish becomes opaque and white as it dries – a paintings conservator should be able to reverse this damage.

If the painting has been in a flood, take it down and lay it flat, *face upwards*, supporting its frame on blocks so that the air can circulate underneath. Be sure that the blocks do not touch the back of the painting. It should be left to dry out in a well-ventilated room with no extra heating and in a safe place where no one will step on it.

Birds' mess

If birds habitually fly into a room, stretch soft-fruit cage netting over the window opening. At a distance, it will be hardly visible.

If a bird gets in by accident, no attempt should be made to remove the white splashes it may leave on the surface of the painting, as there is a danger of rubbing the mess in or smearing it over the surface. The picture conservator should be able to remove it without disturbing the varnish.

CARRYING PICTURES

Before attempting to move a picture, be sure that there are enough helpers and time to do so safely. Most pictures should be carried by two people. One person should be responsible for the front of the painting and the other for the back throughout the operation, so that it can safely be manoeuvred round corners and past door knobs. Decide exactly where you intend moving the painting and inspect the route for hazards. Always carry a painting vertically by its shortest sides. This lowers its centre of gravity and makes it more stable and manageable. In carrying large paintings particular attention should be given to heights of doors and stair-flights.

Do not take hold of a framed painting by anything but the frame, and never lift holding only the top section of the frame. It is very tempting to lift a framed picture by the stretcher bars of the painting, but this should not be done because hands may press into the back of the canvas, causing dents. Inexperienced furniture removers have to be carefully instructed and supervised.

When carrying unframed paintings fingers should not come into contact with the painted surface.

HANGING AND TAKING DOWN PICTURES

How and where a picture is hung has a great bearing on its preservation. Pictures should not be hung above radiators or on sections of wall carrying hot pipes or internal flues which can heat up the wall quite considerably. Hanging pictures above a fireplace which is in use cannot be recommended. In no case should panel paintings be hung over any source of heat. If the dining-room is used, hot-plates or greasy, steaming dishes should not be placed below a painting. (See also The Right Environment, p. 25.)

Air should circulate to the back of a picture – normally the frame leans forwards at a slight angle so that only the bottom edge touches the wall. Outside walls are subject to condensation so stick corks to the bottom corners of the frame to isolate the picture from the wall completely and to allow maximum circulation of air.

In most houses there is a traditional method of hanging which should be followed. In a room without picture rails and where picture chains or wires do not need to be visible, hang the painting from two screws plugged into the wall with washers over the screw-heads, to prevent the picture chain from slipping off. Fix two hooks on the back of the frame and suspend it on short lengths of picture chain. The positioning of the hooks on the side members will control the forward tilt of the painting.

Check periodically that the fixings and fittings on walls and frames are sound and that chains, wires or cords are in good condition. Note any that need to be replaced. Wires and cords fray and rot at the fixings.

48. Different methods of picture hanging: (above) with cords, in the Stone Hall at Uppark;
(right) an unusual hanging of enamels on brass rails in the drawing-room at Kingston Lacy

Large, heavy frames should be supported underneath to prevent the mitres from opening under the strain. Upper-register paintings can be canted forward by being supported at the base and by lowering the hooks on the frame towards the centre of the side members. In every case where the weight of the frame is resting on a support, a short length of picture wire should be twisted through the link of the picture chain to prevent the hook from disengaging.

When hanging a painting, check that there are no obstructions in contact with the back of the painting such as alarm systems, picture-light wires or plugs. When picture wire is used, check that no loose ends are touching the back of the canvas which could later cause a protrusion in the front of the picture.

Before taking down a painting, remove all ornaments below the picture as well as any furniture that would get in the way. If the painting is hung on a picture chain, slip a treasurer's filing tag or a paperclip into the link of both chains from which the picture is hanging. This saves all the time and bother of re-establishing the correct height and level when rehanging the painting.

When lifting the picture clear of the wall, make sure that nothing can fall down and hit the front or back of the picture. This is particularly important where there is a heavy hook over a picture rail. A bang on the back of the canvas will cause whorled craquelure on the painted surface and the damage is irreparable. Keep the painting vertical when lowering it gently to the floor. A plain carved frame should be tipped slightly backwards so that it rests on the straight edge behind the carved moulding.

If the picture is in a decorated carved frame or in a fragile plaster frame, lower it on to a padded surface made up of, say, two bolsters placed on the floor at right angles to the wall; or use offcuts of rubber-backed carpet, which a local carpet dealer should be able to supply free, and which have the additional advantage of not slipping.

STORING: LONG-TERM AND TEMPORARY

Conditions

Suitable long-term storage room in a house open to visitors should be planned at the same time as space is allocated for shops, tearooms and information centres.

Do not store paintings or anything else near boilers, water pipes or in damp areas. Avoid stone floors, which can get cold and damp, and never use a newly painted or plastered room for storage until it has completely dried out and the smell evaporated.

Basements are generally cold and damp or, when the boiler is sited there, hot and damp. Attics should be used only if the roof is insulated, because otherwise the temperature can drop below freezing in winter or heat up unacceptably in summer.

The greatest care should be taken over the conditions in a store-room because the objects in store are inspected less often than when displayed in a room. The relative humidity should be checked at regular intervals and light should be eliminated by keeping shutters closed or by draping black cloth over the windows. An inexpensive but effective way of controlling the relative humidity in a store is to construct a polythene tent round the paintings and install a dehumidifier controlled with a humidistat.

Methods of storing paintings

Framed pictures are safest hung, so whenever possible hang them like postage stamps on the store-room walls. Avoid external walls. Stick corks on the bottom corners of the back of the frame so that the picture is isolated from any condensation that may form on the wall. Check all fixings, wires and chains so that there is no danger of the picture falling off the wall.

Simple wooden racks can be built if there are more paintings than can be hung on the available wall-space in the store-room. Protect the frames by making triangular 'paper hats' out of Bubblewrap or Fast Foam to slip over the corners of the frames. Use masking tape (*not* Sellotape) to attach the corner protection to the back of the frame, taking care that the sticky tape does not touch the gilding or any part of the painting.

Temporary stacking

Avoid stacking immediately under windows, near radiators or on a stone floor.

Never put framed and unframed paintings in the same stack.

Ensure that nothing touches the canvas of the painting from the front or the back.

Cover the stack loosely with a lightweight dust-sheet, ensuring that it does not come in contact with the paint surface. A polythene sheet can be placed over the dust-sheet for extra short-term protection particularly if builders are in the house, but it should not prevent air circulation.

Stacking framed paintings

Remove all projections such as picture lights, brackets, wires, chain, etc. If frame hooks are not removed, care must be taken that they do not touch the gilded surface of another frame. Never remove any historical fixtures, such as leather thongs or hand-forged hooks, or any labels whatsoever.

Stack in descending order of size and not more than three deep, because the angle of the frame gets progressively less upright and the weight of the stack would rest too heavily on the first picture. Should it be necessary, through lack of space, temporarily to stack more than three deep, place a sheet of hardboard behind the third frame and then stack another two or three frames against the hardboard sheet.

Pads of tissue paper between the frames will protect the gilding from damage during stacking. However, in subsequent handling the pads invariably fall down and touch the picture surface.

Paintings in plain frames can be stacked with the painting facing inwards, so that dust will not collect on the painted surface and the stretcher bars give the picture some protection against accidental damage.

Paintings in elaborately carved and decorated frames should not be stacked. Pad the floor with bolsters or equivalent, and lean the frame against the wall face outwards. If necessary a piece of hardboard should be placed against the frame before covering with a dust-sheet.

Stacking unframed paintings

Check that the wall is clear of projections, such as light switches or mouldings. Stack face inwards in order of diminishing size and ensure that only the edge of the picture surface, that would normally rest under the rebate of the frame, is touching the stretcher bar of the back of the painting against which it is stacked. Paintings in one stack should be more or less of the same size or there is a danger that the corner of the smaller painting will swivel and touch the back of the canvas of the picture in front of it.

FRAMES AND FRAMING

The framing of a painting plays an important role in preserving the painting. Apart from its aesthetic function, a frame protects the edges of the painting and makes handling and storage safer. The same care is needed in selecting frame-makers with a historical knowledge of frames and an understanding of conservation, as is taken in other fields of conservation.

Until the importance and condition of a frame have been established it is advisable not to touch it. Original frames of great importance are too often ruined by modern frame-makers and amateurs alike treating the gilding inappropriately. In long-established country-house collections, knowledge of frames may provide evidence to help the art historian in dating a picture and in suggesting its provenance.

Dusting frames

Dusting the picture frame puts the painting at risk. Most country-house picture frames are grimy and cannot be safely cleaned except by a gilder trained in conservation. Dusting the frame will not greatly improve its appearance and it is often better to put up with a little dust than put the painting at risk. A picture hanging on the wall is best left entirely alone.

Do not attempt to dust a frame if the gilding is flaking; report any sign of woodworm to a conservator. (No part of a painting or frame should be treated for woodworm by the house staff because the non-volatile base of pesticides could cause serious damage.) A 'bit box' should be kept for any pieces of carving, plaster or other bits that may become detached. Identify the bit and give it to the frame conservator to refix, when he should at the same time be able to consolidate and touch out any flaking frames. *Never* touch in gilding with any form of gold paint because it gives a totally different effect and will discolour anyway.

Do not dust with a cloth or feather duster, either of which would abrade the surface. No liquid whatsoever should touch the surface of the frame. A damp cloth would remove water gilding and in the past many frames have been damaged in this way.

If it is decided that a frame can be safely dusted, this is best done when the picture is down off the wall by standing at the back of the frame and dusting the top back edge with a Hoover Dustette. The bottom member of the front of the frame can also be brushed gently with a ponyhair brush (see Appendix 3, p. 318), collecting the dust in a Hoover Dustette.

The surface of the painting should not be touched while dusting the frame and if there is any danger of dust flying on to the painting, it is better to leave the dust settled on the frame.

Numbering picture frames

Country-house collections were often numbered and identified on the frame. In houses where this has not been the practice in the past, other ways of giving information to visitors should be considered. One possibility is to have a 'bat' in each room on which is sketched the layout of each wall, with the pictures listed underneath. This is particularly appropriate where ropes keep visitors from approaching the pictures to read the numbers. Where this is not the case, tablets can be hung under the pictures, suspended on chains from the back of the frame. A good example of this method can be seen at Ickworth; it avoids all danger of damaging the carved and gilded face of the frame.

Framing and unframing

It will not normally be necessary for paintings to be framed and unframed in the house, except when conservation is to take place *in situ*.

The picture conservator will use brass framing plates and balsa wood spacing pieces.

Panels and paintings on metal or unusual materials, such as slate, are delicate and should be framed and unframed only by a picture conservator because there are too many problems that may arise.

TRANSPORT

Any painting that is going to be transported should be carefully inspected to make sure it is not flaking (see Routine inspection, below). If there is flaking the picture must be prepared for transport by a picture conservator.

Few trade carriers are experts at transporting paintings. Quite apart from causing damage to a painting, the cost of conservation is very high and good conservators object strongly to spending time repairing avoidable damage through careless handling. The extra cost of specialist picture transporters is worthwhile. Never let a painting leave the house unless the driver is accompanied. Otherwise, in case of breakdown, the van would be left unattended.

Always check that the carrier has packed the painting and loaded the van in the following way. Framed paintings should have their corners protected with pads made from Bubblewrap or an expanded polyethylene foam such as Fast Foam. They should then be sealed in a polythene parcel. Unframed paintings should be wrapped in Melinex, and then cornered with Bubblewrap or Fast Foam. The painting should be loaded upright, supported on soft padding, and strapped to the van's sides by means of flat webbing. Crated pictures must also travel upright and be similarly secured.

See that paintings, whether crated or not, are handled gently and not bumped around. Uncrated paintings should be handled by the frames only and not by the back of the picture stretchers. Only unframed paintings should be handled by the stretcher bars.

ROUTINE INSPECTION

Signs of suspected deterioration can be determined without touching the surface of the picture. Only a picture conservator should touch the surface of a painting.

Flaking

It takes a trained eye to distinguish signs of incipient flaking from natural ageing and the normal craquelure found on all old paintings, but chips of paint that have almost become detached can be noticed easily by using a torch to provide a raking light on the surface.

Panels

Movement in panel paintings renders them particularly susceptible to flaking.

Look out for independent movement of the members which make up a panel. Old splits have usually been restored and are dark, with old discoloured retouchings and grime in the crack. A fresh break would appear light.

Some convex warping is to be expected but watch for signs of change in the curvature. This can be seen by an increase in the gap on the inner sides of the frame between the paint surface and frame rebate.

In cases of extreme humidity the curve can become concave, which is highly dangerous as the paint surface is then contracted. Notify a conservator immediately if a concave warp is noticed, but do not remove the panel from the room in which it hangs as the change in environment must be most carefully controlled by the picture conservator to avoid cracking and loss of paint.

Canvases

The tension of the canvas may vary with changes in the weather and relative humidity, but this should cause no undue concern. Correct stretching should be left to the picture conservator. However, buckling at corners and edges should be noted and reported.

Occasionally a wedge from the stretcher will slip between the canvas and the bottom stretcher bar and will cause a distortion; accumulations of dust and other matter can have the same effect. *Never* attempt to remove these foreign bodies; leave it to the picture conservator. The reasons for this are that the edges of the canvas of an unlined painting can be weak and can tear away from the stretcher bar. Also foreign matter is easy to shift but difficult to remove. Shifting the obstruction without removing it would distort and bruise the canvas in more than one place, so that twice the amount of damage would be caused.

ENVIRONMENT

One of the difficulties in caring for the contents of a historic house is that the damage caused by negligence is often not immediately apparent. The life of a painting will be greatly prolonged by the attention given to maintaining a stable environment.

The supports of most paintings are canvas, wood or copper. All are sensitive to changes of relative humidity or temperature. Excessive expansion and contraction of the support can lead to lifting and flaking of the paint, which is too rigid to follow these movements.

Slow seasonal changes can be tolerated relatively safely, but if a room has to be heated for a winter function, it should be done gradually to avoid potentially destructive sudden change.

Paintings on wooden panels are particularly susceptible to adverse environmental conditions. Rooms in which important panel paintings hang should have the relative humidity checked regularly and extra readings taken in exceptional circumstances, such as extreme changes in the weather conditions or the heating-up of a house for a function. The relative humidity should not fall below 50%.

Daylight

Never let sunlight fall on a painting. The cumulative effect of sunlight will greatly accelerate the decay of the painting. As well as causing heating, ultraviolet rays present in daylight degrade the materials of a painting.

Light falling on the painted surface should not exceed 200 lux. Use the blinds and keep shutters closed whenever possible, to reduce the length of time the picture is exposed to light.

49. Portraits of the 17th century in the ballroom at Knole, with Edwardian brass picture lights

Picture lights

The types of picture light at present available are not recommended from a conservation point of view. They can cause patches of overheating of the picture surface.

Also, existing picture lights do not illuminate the whole surface evenly but reflect pools of light in the varnish. It is sometimes possible to cant forward the upper register of paintings in a room, which reduces reflection and makes it easier for the pictures to be seen without resorting to picture lights.

Never fit picture lights to paintings on wood, metal, paper or vellum. Avoid placing a standard or table lamp immediately beneath a picture because light is also a source of heat.

·✢ MINIATURES ✢·

The term miniature is derived from the Latin name for red lead, *minium*, which was abundantly used by the medieval illuminators. The term 'portrait miniature' defined a type of painting which is intended to be viewed from a very close range on account of the minuteness of its technique rather than because of its small size. Miniatures can differ immensely in size, from those painted for finger rings, which may be no more than 10 mm in height, to large full-length or group portraits which may be as much as 600 mm in their larger dimension.

CATEGORIES OF PORTRAIT MINIATURES

Miniatures in oil

These were normally painted on a metal ground, such as copper or silver, in much finer techniques than those usually employed in oil painting. They are normally small, between 30 and 70 mm in height, and date from the 16th to the early 18th centuries.

Miniatures in enamel

Of all miniatures these are the most stable, being painted in metallic oxides over a white enamel ground laid on a metal base, and then fired at high temperatures. They are invariably slightly convex, and have a glossy surface. Under normal conditions they are very stable, but rapid fluctuations of temperature can cause separation of the enamel from its metal base and the enamel, being brittle, cannot withstand severe physical shocks. A further problem which sometimes arises with enamels on copper or brass plates is that acidity can cause green corrosion to form on the metal, and this can gradually throw off the enamel coating.

Miniatures painted in water-colour on vellum

These can usually be recognized by their very matt paint surfaces and by the fact that this technique was restricted to the early years of portrait miniatures, that is from *c.* 1530 to *c.* 1720.

The attachment of water-colour paint to vellum is better than that of water-colour to ivory, and the nature of the paint renders it less susceptible to mould growth. Vellum is more flexible than ivory, and is thus better able to adapt itself to changes of temperature and humidity, but in too dry an atmosphere the vellum may warp and separate from its card support.

Miniatures painted in water-colour on ivory

In the early 18th century ivory was substituted for vellum as the most common support for miniature painting. It is often difficult to distinguish early-18th-century examples from those painted on vellum, as at first the techniques of applying and mixing the paint were virtually the same as those used for painting on vellum. Towards the end of the 18th century, however, much more gum was added to the pigments, making them more transparent and glossy, and this trend continued in the 19th century, to the extent that many water-colour miniatures of that period were so heavily gummed that they appear to have been varnished.

In the 1830s a machine was patented which could cut thin slivers of ivory from the circumference of the tusk and these were then flattened to produce sheets of ivory of very large dimensions; full-length and group portraits of 600 mm or more in their greater dimension were not uncommon at that period.

Ivory is extremely sensitive to changes in humidity, and a very dry atmosphere can cause it to warp or crack in the direction of its grain and become very brittle. Gum arabic is hygroscopic and in conditions of high humidity it can become sticky and this will encourage rapid mould growth. The adhesion between water-colour and ivory is not good and in very dry conditions it is common for the paint to flake away from the ivory.

DISPLAY

Light, temperature and relative humidity

The light falling on the miniature should not exceed a maximum of 50 lux with a relative humidity of 55%, while the temperature should not exceed 15°C (59°F).

Central heating, although it may produce a constant temperature, is dangerous because it tends to make the atmosphere too dry.

Cabinets and display cases

Collections of miniatures are best housed in cabinets with drawers or in display cases with covers (see Display cases, p. 31). The pigments of water-colour miniatures are frequently extremely sensitive to light and should where possible be kept covered except when being looked at. Subdued artificial light is preferable to daylight. Make sure that all cabinets, drawers and cases are kept locked.

Hanging

Miniatures should never be hung near fireplaces or radiators, where there may be draughts, or where sunlight will travel across them during the course of the day. Avoid exterior walls which are subject to condensation. There should always be a small gap between the frame and the wall to allow a free passage of air around the miniature.

Where possible, it is safest to hang a group of miniatures in a shadow box, or hanging display case, as the fixing on the frame of the miniature is weaker than any security screw.

STORAGE AND TRANSPORT

Protect miniatures by wrapping them loosely in crumpled acid-free tissue paper. *Never* use cotton wool, cloth or other hygroscopic material. Loosely wrapped tissue paper not only protects the miniatures but allows air to circulate around them.

Bubblewrap is a useful material for packing for transport.

CLEANING

No attempt should be made to clean the frames or lockets of miniature paintings with proprietary metal cleaners. The effect of capillary action can draw such mixtures into the frame and the solvents and reagents used in such cleaners could cause corrosion of metal supports and damage to painted surfaces. For the same reason household glass cleaners should not be used to clean the cover glasses of miniatures. If it is necessary to clean the outside of a cover glass, it should be carefully wiped with a soft, dry chamois leather. If necessary the glass may be *very* gently breathed upon during the process.

INSPECTION

It is essential that collections of miniatures should be examined at frequent intervals to ensure that they are free of the ailments to which they are vulnerable. Water-colour miniatures are most at risk, and it is fortunate that in this case it is possible to recognize potential dangers long before corrective treatment becomes necessary.

On no account should any attempt be made to open the miniature frame, or to carry out any sort of treatment and, in fact, most of the lockets and frames designed to contain miniatures are impossible to open unless one has professional knowledge and experience.

Miniatures in water-colour

Support

Note any warping or distortion in vellum and ivory miniatures because distortion of the vellum support can lead to flake losses of the pigment layer; such movements eventually split or crack the ivory.

Mould

Look for signs of mould growth, especially on miniatures in water-colour on ivory. Mould is usually evident, in the early stage, as white hairy deposits on the glass or on the paint surface, or as yellowish, raised spots. Such growths eventually infect the paint layer.

Condensation

A further phenomenon, which may be evident in either vellum or ivory miniatures, is the formation of minute droplets of moisture on the inside surface of the cover glass. Check for these by tilting the miniature so that the light is at an acute angle to its surface, and if condensation is observed inform a conservator without delay.

Sulphiding

Another disfiguring phenomenon to which miniatures in water-colour are prone is the blackening of lead whites caused by the action of atmospheric hydrogen sulphide.

Miniatures in enamel or oil

Support

It is essential that regular examinations are made to ensure that corrosion of the metal surface is not causing separation of the enamel or paint layer. Green corrosion can usually be seen as a green deposit round the edge of the painting.

·✤ WATER-COLOURS, DRAWINGS AND PRINTS ✤·

There are many different types of works of art on paper found in historic houses: water-colours, drawings, prints, photographs, maps, plans and documents. Some will be framed, others stored in drawers or kept in albums, boxes and portfolios.

PAPER SUPPORT

Paper was in use in China by the 2nd century A D, and spread through the Arab world to Europe, where it was progressively adopted during the 13th to 15th centuries.

Oriental papers were manufactured from various types of plant fibre, using sizes of vegetable origin, and are remarkably permanent if kept in an appropriate environment. European papers before about 1800 were made from recycled plant fibres in the form of cotton and linen rags. Many of these papers are also extremely permanent.

So rapidly did the demand for paper increase during the early 19th century that different plant fibres were introduced to supplement the inadequate supply of rags, and from the middle of the century more and more papers were made using wood fibres.

Paper deteriorates as a result of the breakdown of its fibres, and this can occur for a number of reasons. Acidity and light are the main causes of deterioration. The acid may be introduced at the manufacturing stage, particularly through the use of alum with the size. Acid can also be introduced as a

50. A water-colour of the North Gallery at Petworth by Mrs Percy Wyndham, about 1860, showing the upper register of pictures canted out from the walls

result of absorbing sulphur dioxide from air polluted by the burning of fossil fuels. Wood fibre papers have a very limited life, and pose a major conservation problem.

ARTISTS' MATERIALS

Even with the advent of the commercially successful artists' colourmen in the late 17th century, artists continued to mix their own materials from dry pigments and a variety of binding media. This is true of almost all works of art in ink, water-colour, chalk and pastel before *c.* 1830.

Water-colours, gouache

Painting in water-colours became something of an English speciality and developed into a separate genre. In the 18th and 19th centuries water-colours were produced in great numbers by painters and amateurs of varying accomplishment.

In dry conditions, gum arabic will crack and flake off, often taking the pigment and paper surface with it. In wet conditions, it will attract and encourage mould growths. Honey, which is hygroscopic and encourages mould, was often added to water-colour pigments to keep them moist. Lead white or pigments mixed with lead white will react with hydrogen sulphide in the air and blacken. This is a chemical change which in most cases can be reversed by the paper conservator.

Water-colours will fade quickly and irreversibly if blinds are not kept down and artificial light sources kept below 50 lux. *Never* use a picture light on framed water-colours or hang them directly above table lamps. Display-case lighting should be checked by an expert. Treat the windows of the room with ultraviolet filter varnish or film. When a room is not in use, light should be excluded from water-colours by placing the frame face down on a table, after protecting the surface with a dust-sheet. Or suspend a piece of thick, dark cloth over the front of the frame, which is left hanging on the wall.

Paintings in gouache are essentially water-colour pigments mixed with white body-colour and have a dull, chalk-like surface which is prone to flaking. *Never* touch the surface because grease and moisture leave irreversible stains.

Drawings

Ink drawings

There are four types of ink most commonly used by artists: carbon-black, iron-gall, bistre and sepia. Carbon-black inks were prepared by the ancient

Egyptians and Chinese. Iron-gall inks were produced by a chemical reaction from mixing gall extracts with ferrous sulphate. Galls are formed on oak trees by gall wasps, and contain concentrations of tannic and gallic acids. Iron-gall inks may be extremely acidic and some iron-gall ink drawings now have a lace-like appearance where the chemicals in the ink have attacked and destroyed the paper below the pen strokes. Bistre is a brown ink prepared by extracting soluble tars from wood soot; and sepia, made from the ink sacs of cuttlefish, squid and octopus, was widely used for drawings and washes in the 19th century.

Inks are especially sensitive to light and will fade irreversibly in even a short period of time. Do not touch the surface of ink drawings, as moisture can reactivate the ink and so cause smearing.

Chalk, pastel and crayon

A few coloured earths were useful to the artist. Natural red chalk was important as a drawing medium in the 15th and 16th centuries. Black chalk made up of carbon and clay was gradually replaced by graphite pencils. Two varieties of natural white chalk, calcite and soapstone, were used to heighten modelling.

The interest in pastel painting in the 18th century led to the preparation of papers with textured grounds, and to the use of other supports, such as vellum, taffeta and linen, roughened with pumice or covered with a coat of glue on to which marble dust or pumice had been sifted.

Binding media included gum arabic, gum tragacanth, sugar candy, milk, whey, beer, glue, stale size, honey, starch and plaster of Paris. As most artists' pigments, including white, could be used to produce pastel sticks, a wide range of colours became possible.

Pastel drawings can be the dimensions of full-length oil portrait paintings, made up of many sheets of paper attached to poor-quality canvas or board. They are particularly prone to mould growths, especially when framed and pressed up against the glass, as was customary. Pastels contain very little binding medium, so even small vibrations loosen the adhesion. Pastels should therefore *never* be moved or transported unnecessarily. Pastel and chalk will also smudge and stain irreversibly if the surface is touched. For these reasons, a pastel or chalk drawing should be removed from its frame only by a paper conservator.

Crayons are distinguished from natural or fabricated chalks by the presence of fatty materials in their composition. Experiments with a variety of crayon formulas at the end of the 18th century resulted in the invention of lithography, which encouraged the use of crayon by artists for drawings in the 19th century.

Prints

Perhaps because prints were produced in greater numbers, they have in general been less well looked after than other works of art on paper. Many houses have fairly extensive collections of prints, often not on show and badly stored.

Prints have from the earliest times been coloured by hand. Attempts were made in the 17th and 18th centuries to devise methods for printing in colours but these were complicated and the mass production of coloured prints only became widespread in the 19th century.

There is a bewildering range of print-making techniques which can be divided into three categories – relief, intaglio and planographic printing.

Relief printing

Relief printing was known to the Chinese well before AD 1000. The image is produced on paper from the inked surface of a block. Lines and areas which are to print black are left raised, while the white areas are cut away. Woodcuts used in European books from the 15th century onwards are the most common form of relief printing.

Intaglio printing

Intaglio printing was discovered by metal engravers, who took impressions on dampened paper by rubbing ink into the incised decoration on armour. Engraving on copper plates developed rapidly throughout Europe in the 16th century. Great skill was required to engrave the design in reverse on the metal. In the 17th century, etching made print-making considerably easier and quicker. The design is scratched with a drawing needle into a wax coating on the plate and relies on the use of acid to bite the design into the metal. Etching produced freer images and was much favoured by artists in the 18th and 19th centuries. Engravings are characterized by more formal and rigid lines suitable for reproducing paintings. Other intaglio processes include the velvety-black mezzotint and the granular images called aquatints.

All intaglio prints are recognizable from the impression made in the paper by the edge of the metal plate, which is called the plate mark.

Planographic printing

Planographic printing uses a flat printing surface and depends on the antipathy of grease and water. Lithography – the original planographic process – was introduced in the last years of the 18th century. The design was drawn in greasy crayon on the treated surface of a slab of finely grained limestone; when the stone was wetted and then inked up, the printing ink adhered to the design but was rejected by the rest of the stone. Lithographic prints have a distinctly flat surface quality.

CAUSES OF DETERIORATION

Problems common to all works of art on paper may be divided into three categories, as follows.

Acidity

This may be introduced into the paper from either primary or secondary sources.

Primary sources

The addition of chemicals, such as alum, during the manufacture of the paper; the medium of the work, e.g. iron-gall ink and certain pigments.

Secondary sources

The migration into the paper of acidic by-products from poor-quality mounts and supports, degraded adhesive layers and the backing used in frames such as wood, strawboard and hardboard. Also atmospheric pollutants such as sulphur dioxide.

Biological attack

Insect pests

Insects which attack paper are usually feeding on impurities such as sizing agents or the binding media of pigments. Silverfish will follow and eat the ink outlines of prints giving a lace-like appearance to the image and also damaging the paper surface. The common woodworm will eat through paper to find more wood. Thrips (hay bugs) easily get inside frames; once there, their body fluids provide food for mould growths.

Mould

This includes the easily recognizable irregular brown spots known as 'foxing'. Mould growth is encouraged by high relative humidity (over 65%), direct contact of the paper with the glass of the frame and poor ventilation caused by the frame being hung flat against the wall.

51. An example of damage due to variations in relative humidity. The engraving, laid down on canvas, is showing tears and losses due to movement between the paper and the canvas

Light, temperature and relative humidity

Works of art on paper should ideally be kept below a maximum light level of 50 lux and at as low a temperature as possible – certainly no higher than 15°C (60°F), with relative humidity at a constant level between 55 and 65%. Variations in relative humidity will lead to loss of adhesion of the paint, gum and chalk layers, and the eventual disintegration of the image since paper responds quickly to changes in humidity. Even at low light levels, paper will continue to deteriorate as light oxidises the bonds of the paper fibres and reacts with structural impurities in the paper. Some types of paper, such as those with a high percentage of lignin, are especially sensitive. Such deterioration is progressive and can be slowed down only through careful conservation and improved display or storage conditions. Water-colours, ink drawings and tinted papers are especially sensitive to light.

STORAGE

The room in which works are stored should be clean, dry and well ventilated. Metallic salts in household dust act as a catalyst to chemical change and therefore speed up the rate of deterioration. Stagnant air can contain high levels of pollutants and will also accelerate decay. Water-staining is unsightly, and the resulting wrinkling and curling of the paper support can cause loss of pigment, smearing or fractures if a secondary backing is involved. The water will also draw any impurities from the canvas, glue, wood, etc. into the paper and cause further problems.

Unframed works

Unframed works are particularly vulnerable to surface abrasion, scratches and loss of paint. An unframed pastel or chalk drawing is most at risk and should be laid face up on clean white blotting paper until a paper conservator can handle the problem.

Unmounted prints, drawings and water-colours should be separated from those which have mounts or backboards, and any which show signs of 'foxing', water-staining or insect attack should be kept separately from those that appear to be in good condition. *Never* store mounted and unmounted works in the same pile and do not mix deteriorating and undamaged works.

An artists' portfolio can be used temporarily for gathering together the unframed works and this will help the conservator to assess the extent of the problem.

Interleave the unframed works with acid-free tissue paper and store the portfolio *horizontally*. Do not store the portfolio upright or the contents will slide down, and crease and buckle along the bottom edge.

52. A pastel portrait, probably in its original frame, of Sir Richard Hoare, 1st Bart, by Francis Cotes RA at Stourhead

'Hospital' portfolios should be marked and kept only for infected paper and should not later be re-used for undamaged work.

Artists' portfolios are not suitable as permanent storage because dust and insects can get in and too much movement can lead to abrasion and surface scratches. Where appropriate, Solander boxes of suitable sizes can be ordered in bulk for more permanent storage. The works should be interleaved with acid-free tissue paper and the boxes stored horizontally. Important collections can be stored on mounts of acid-free card in Solander boxes measured to the exact size of the mount plus a 10 mm gap to facilitate handling.

Framed works

Some of the most important frames in the house may be framing works on paper, such as the pastel frames of about 1760 at Stourhead. The glass may well be original.

Framed works should not be stored for any length of time at floor level, where insects and dust can collect and where damage can be caused by cleaning equipment. Simple wooden racks should be made with divisions every foot or so against which the frames can be leant. When storing small frames, first line the shelf with Bubblewrap and then set the frames upright on the shelf, leaning against each other and against the divisions along the shelves. Place small pieces of Bubblewrap in between the top edges so as to protect the gilding and the glass. Allow enough clearance on the shelf to lift the frames out as they will not slide on the Bubblewrap.

Before storing a frame, remove the wire, chain, hooks or rings which could scratch or damage other frames.

Framed paper should never be unframed except by a paper conservator. Great care should be taken to preserve any labels or other information which may be on the frame or backboard.

HANGING

Hang the frames whenever possible on an inside wall, where there is no danger of shafts of sunlight passing over the face of the picture. Do not hang immediately above a source of heat, such as a radiator or table lamp. Do not hang near outside doors where light and temperature cannot be controlled.

The darkest wall of the room is usually between the windows and so it is sometimes better to hang water-colours on this outside wall rather than try to reduce the light level of the whole room. Stick corks on the back of the bottom corners of the frame in order to insulate it from the wall and allow air to circulate behind the frame.

The simplest way to hang light frames is to suspend them on rings from two X-picture hooks in the wall. When using picture wire, Aubo Bronze picture wire is stronger and longer-lasting than ordinary brass-coated picture wire, the steel core of which rusts. Never use string. If cord is traditional in a house, use cotton glacie cord. Do not use nylon cord, which looks too modern, stretches and does not dye evenly. (See also Hanging, p. 211.)

CLEANING FRAMES

Any dust which has collected on the top and bottom edges of the frame can be dusted off lightly. Remove dust from gilded surfaces with a ponyhair brush.

Never polish the glass of a pastel or chalk drawing as static electricity will attract the looser pigment particles on to the inside of the glass, leaving a fuzzy, unfocused image, which cannot be restored.

Never use patent window cleaners or any other liquid, including water, to clean the glass. Buff it up with a soft, clean, dry chamois leather, using a little spit on cotton wool to remove marks such as fly dots. Often the dirt will be found to be on the inside of the glass. Do not unframe the work but leave it to a paper conservator, who will re-set the work correctly in its frame. Avoid rubbing the frame and try protecting the gilded edge by holding a postcard against it when dusting the glass.

ACCIDENTS

If the frame should fall off the wall and the glass break, place the frame face downwards on a flat surface and notify a conservator.

Take care that the bits of glass do not slide around, cutting and abrading the surface of the paper. Do not remove fragments of glass if it is difficult to do so. Correct framing is crucial to the preservation of the work and unfortunately it is as yet practised by only a few specialist framers.

In an emergency, should water get inside a frame, remove the work and lay it face upwards on clean white blotting paper. Do not attempt to remove the print or drawing from its backing or mount and do not heat the room excessively, but let the work dry out slowly. Do not wipe a wet frame or you could remove the gilding.

CONSERVATION

The conservation of paper must take into account all the materials with which the paper comes into contact. The mount and the way the work is framed are important in the preservation of paper. Once a print or drawing has been sealed into its frame, it is impossible to check whether correct methods and materials have been used until signs of deterioration appear. It is therefore essential that a paper conservator should supervise the mount-cutter and framer. It should be remembered that the framer handles the work itself and bad workshop habits or simply lack of available clean surfaces could lead to irreparable damage.

There is little point in re-mounting and re-setting a work correctly in its frame without first checking its condition. Deterioration involving mould growth, and acidic build-up from contact with poor-quality materials, would only contaminate the new environment.

·✛ PARCHMENT ✛·

Parchment is made from the skins of animals soaked in lime water, scraped clean and dried under tension. It may be made from the skins of different animals, but calf (correctly called vellum), goat and sheep are the most common. Sheep parchment is often what is meant when the word parchment is used on its own. It has been used as a material for writing on since long before the birth of Christ, but has also been used as a covering material for books, both over stiff boards and on its own (known as limp parchment bindings). It has been used from the Middle Ages up to the present day as a material for painting on, giving a surface particularly suited to finely detailed work, especially for flower and heraldic paintings.

It is normally a strong, durable material if stored under suitable conditions, but will degrade rapidly if exposed to too much light, will grow moulds in damp conditions and become brittle if too dry. It reacts rapidly to changes in humidity, softening and expanding at high levels and shrinking and hardening at low levels. This movement is especially damaging to layers of pigment or gesso on the surface of the vellum, and can result in losses. It is therefore important to ensure constant relative humidity at all times. Unless on display or in use, items on vellum, whether bound or not, should be kept under light restraint or pressure to prevent excessive cockling. Specially designed boxes, folders and mounting systems will be required to do this.

Environment

Ideal humidity levels are towards the higher end of those recommended for paper, around 60% relative humidity, but not over 65%. It is better to have constant relative humidity at a slightly lower level, than fluctuating conditions which only occasionally reach the ideal. Temperatures should be kept as low as the desired humidity levels will permit, and light levels should not exceed 50 lux.

Transport

It is important to ensure that items on vellum are well buffered against changes in humidity when in transit. They should be packed with lots of absorbent material such as acid-free tissue paper. The package should be enclosed in Bubblewrap and sealed along all the edges with masking tape. The wrapped items should not be left in bad conditions for longer than is absolutely necessary. Important items should be packed by a conservator.

Framing

Framed parchment must not be allowed to come into contact with the glass, as both it and the pigment layers may adhere to it in damp conditions. Deep mounts or fillets will be required to prevent this, and should give at least a 25 mm gap for large maps and plans. A gap of 12 mm will be sufficient for small items. The parchment should not be fixed too firmly to its mount or be drummed over a frame, as it may be damaged if it is placed in dry conditions and shrinks. It is, though, necessary to secure it on all four edges to control its natural tendency to cockle.

Various mounting systems can be used according to the size of the piece of parchment, but they will normally need to be carried out by a trained conservator.

Conservation

The repair of parchment differs considerably from that of paper and is highly specialized work. It must never be immersed in water or subjected to treatments involving heat, as both will result in severe damage. Cleaning with moisture is dangerous and dry cleaning with an eraser can also be dangerous if there are friable or loose inks and pigments on the surface. Any work should be undertaken only by a suitably qualified conservator.

Can storied urn or animated bust
Back to its mansion call the fleeting breath?

Thomas Gray,
*Elegy Written in a
Country Churchyard,* 1751

CHAPTER FOURTEEN

STONE, INCLUDING MARBLE AND ALABASTER

Causes of Damage and Decay
241

Routine Maintenance
242

Inspection
245

Handling and Fixing
246

Decorators and Builders
247

Packing Small Statuary for Transport
247

Storage
249

Stone Garden Sculpture and Ornaments
249

53. A marble statue of a companion of Diana by Claude-Augustin Cayot (1677–1722), on the Borghese balustrade at Cliveden. The statue is now shown indoors

STONE, INCLUDING MARBLE AND ALABASTER

Most historic houses have some structural decoration on the exterior and urns, sculpture or balustrades in the garden. In some there are important marble fireplaces and often busts or statues. A few have collections of sculpture.

CAUSES OF DAMAGE AND DECAY

All materials deteriorate, but the common saying 'as hard as rock' leads us to expect stone and marble to be durable. In fact they can easily be damaged by both physical and chemical action, and objects made of stone may be vulnerable because of the way in which they have been put together.

Marble, for example, is made up of a mass of crystals and a blow will bruise the surface, causing irreversible disruption of the crystals surrounding the point of impact. Because it is porous, the smoke from a fire can turn it permanently brown or black, and it can also be stained by absorbing colour such as rust and verdigris, stains from mould growths, wine from glasses left on pedestals, or paints and dyes from unsuitable packing materials.

Statues, fireplaces and decorative friezes were made up of various sections joined together by a wide variety of methods and materials; antique marble sculpture, collected on the Grand Tour, often has 18th-century additions and restorations to complete the composition. Iron set in some protective coating such as lead or shellac was the metal most commonly used to join pieces. This can vary from large dowels running up the legs and supporting the whole weight of the sculpture, to many small iron pins where corroded surfaces have been patched. Recent repairs where iron cramps have been set in mortars, cements and plasters are likely to cause damage.

Moisture starts off a harmful process of chemical change which attacks adhesive and metal used in the construction. Internal iron supports will expand as the iron changes to iron oxides (rusts) and this will eventually split the object apart. Changes in temperature and the level of relative humidity in a house may easily cause condensation on the surface of alabaster with potentially disastrous results, since alabaster is slightly soluble in water. The siting of objects can also cause damage. For example, a marble bust should not be placed by an open window in a damp draught, since the moisture would bring out iron-staining and cause permanent discoloration of the surface.

Rain not only dissolves away the surface of stone and marble, but also, when the atmosphere is polluted by sulphur dioxide, corrodes it chemically. A white crust forms on the surface which 'spalls' away, leaving a roughened area which is quickly blackened by grime and dirt, and the surface continues to corrode away. Not only will carved detail be lost, but water will penetrate in winter; the pockets of water then freeze and expand, causing fracturing and splitting.

The pollution of the atmosphere in Britain is not confined to the towns, but is spread across the countryside as well – indeed we export much of it to Scandinavia, since the prevailing winds blow in from the Atlantic. Experiments have shown that the sulphur dioxide content of the air indoors is about one third of that outside, so even objects indoors are not exempt from this type of attack.

ROUTINE MAINTENANCE

Cleaning should be left to a sculpture conservator, with the exception of routine maintenance which mainly consists in brushing out finely carved mouldings with a hogshair brush (see Appendix 3, p. 318) once a year to remove surface dirt. Avoid black bristles, which could leave marks on white marble. The brush must be used dry and should be kept scrupulously clean. To prevent the dust from floating all over the room, brush out with one hand while holding a Hoover Dustette in the other so that the dust is sucked up. Use the extension hose and crevice head bound round with foam rubber and secured with a rubber band so as to protect the sculpture from accidental knocks.

Never dust marble with cloths which smear greasy grime over the surface. Never use feather dusters, which can break and scratch the surface.

Never use any liquid or cleaning packs on sculpture, since alabaster is easily mistaken for marble. Marble is porous and any liquid applied to the surface may drive dirt or stains further in. Acids attack marble and remove the surface layers. Alabaster is not porous, but it dissolves in water, so unskilled cleaning could result in the complete loss of surface detail. In addition there is a danger of water activating harmful salts or the iron which is present in some stone – for example, as iron pyrites – which, in conjunction with water, can cause irreversible staining.

Stains such as ink or lipstick, and the marks made by cigarettes being stubbed out on marble bases or wine glasses being left on stone or marble surfaces, should be left to a sculpture conservator to treat. Tests are carried out before the conservator embarks on any cleaning, and the overall effect should be discussed with him, taking into account old restorations and repairs and irreversible damage such as iron-staining, all of which will become more apparent after cleaning.

During cleaning the conservator should also note historical information like tool marks, traces of pigmentation or even signatures, which may be hidden under dirt layers. A photographic and written record should be kept of the presence of iron, and, as a priority, where there is movement, the joints will be separated and refixed. Any filler used will be softer than the sound marble. Conservation methods do not require any mechanical keying or cutting of the surface.

54. Spalling of a Portland stone façade at Castle Coole, caused by the rusting of internal iron cramps

55. Marble chimneypiece, attributed to Sir Henry Cheere, West Wycombe Park

Chimneypieces

Chimneypieces can be of marble, alabaster or other stone – sometimes with plasterwork overmantles (see Walls, Ceilings and Windows, p. 284). They should never be washed (see Causes of damage and decay, p. 241, and Routine maintenance, p. 242). Washing in any case would not remove or reduce the layer of tarry dirt on fireplaces. This can be safely removed only by a sculpture conservator, who should undertake a programme of *in situ* cleaning when necessary. When the fireplace is no longer in use the conservator can apply a protective coating after treatment, to help restore the polished finish and inhibit re-soiling from household dirt.

Dusting

Fireplaces can be dusted using a white bristle hogshair brush, at the same time collecting up the dust with a Hoover Dustette.

INSPECTION

While cleaning has, therefore, to be restricted, the task of the sculpture conservator is greatly assisted if during routine dusting a look-out is kept for structural instability and discoloration or flaking of the surface.

Structural instability

The conservator should be informed immediately if anything is loose or unstable – a wobbly pedestal, for example – or where jointing material has dropped out of sections of a fireplace. It will sometimes be found that the surbase or socle, which is the smaller stand that is usually placed on top of a pedestal to serve as the base for a bust or statue, is dowelled neither to the pedestal nor to the bust.

Discoloration of the surface

A brownish discoloration is a fairly certain sign of a rusting iron cramp or dowel and it shows that the process of expansion by rusting has reached the danger point where cracks will soon appear.

Flaking or sugaring of the surface

A painted object should always be inspected for any slight lifting or blistering of the paint surface. Plaster and terracotta sometimes have protective surface coatings or layers which may also begin to flake in the wrong conditions.

Marble and stone surfaces were usually smoothly finished or polished. If a surface appears rough or granular, this should be reported, as it may be the beginning of a harmful salt formation caused by air pollution and an incorrect environment. In the case of marble, 'sugaring' usually begins on the underside of any carved area, and this can be detected by rubbing the little finger gently along these undercut areas to check for loose crystals.

HANDLING AND FIXING

Sculpture combines weight with fragility and it is easily scratched or bruised. Even a bust is made up of at least two pieces, more often than not dowelled with iron. Because of its weight marble can easily be broken in moving. The surface absorbs dirt and grease and it is advisable to wear clean white cotton gloves when handling it.

A sculpture conservator or mason should always advise beforehand and be present when large statues have to be moved, but bad handling can cause damage to smaller objects too. Take a bust lying on its back on a wooden floor: undue pressure would have been put on the socle joint while the bust was being lowered using the edge of the socle as a pivot, and while the bust remained horizontal. White marble would also pick up varnish or wax where it was in contact with the floor.

Sculptured reliefs

The lower edge of sculptured reliefs should be supported on stainless steel brackets, padded with chamois leather.

Marble, terracotta and plaster are not at all flexible. A wooden frame will undergo considerable dimensional change, particularly in a heated room, which could put pressure on the relief and crack it. Allowance must be made for this movement and the fitting of all framed reliefs should be checked by a conservator.

Reliefs should not be fixed above a radiator. Convected warm air passing over the surface of the sculpture will distort a wooden frame as well as depositing dirt on the surface of the relief.

Mortar

Wet mortar should not be used indoors for fixing or repairing, for example, fireplaces. The stone or marble is dry and would absorb the moisture, with the danger of activating dormant salts and affecting old iron dowels. The conservator or recommended mason would use modern, inert adhesives to embed the dowels.

Pedestals and socles

The most vulnerable pedestals are the tall, narrow-based, hollow wooden type. They are usually placed up against a wall for support, but the busts which stand on them are often too deep to allow this. Even when they are flush with a wall, sideways movement is still possible. Stability is best achieved by filling at least the base of the pedestal with clean, dry sand or, if possible, by fitting a collar round the pedestal and fixing it to the wall. If the floor under the pedestal is uneven, a suitable bed should be provided in order to eliminate movement. The use of wedges is not recommended because they are too easily moved by accident or by vibration.

The bust should be dowelled to its socle and the socle to the pedestal. The sculpture conservator will use stainless steel, as iron, bronze, steel and copper all have a tendency to corrode that would eventually cause staining and disruption.

DECORATORS AND BUILDERS

Move the sculpture out of the room or protect the statue from accidental damage by constructing a strong wooden box around it. Nothing – brooms, ladders, hands, elbows – should ever be leaned against sculpture.

PACKING SMALL STATUARY FOR TRANSPORT

To protect the surface from grease and dirt, first wrap the sculpture loosely in acid-free tissue paper; then cushion it against knocks and abrasion with a double covering of Bubblewrap, held in place with masking tape. Finally the package should be placed in a firm wooden or plastic box or crate, which has first been lined with a layer of polystyrene pellets (at least 50 mm thick). Surround the package with pellets, which is one of the safest ways of supporting sculpture in a crate. Foam plastic at least 50 mm thick can be used as a substitute for pellets. Wooden crates should be screwed together and not nailed.

Never wrap sculpture in coloured materials or baize. If there were the slightest moisture, the colour would migrate on to the sculpture.

To transport large sculpture requires careful and specialized preparation and so must be undertaken by a conservator.

56. A marble bust and pedestal perched precariously on a cracked plinth

STORAGE

Stone, marble, terracotta and so forth should be stored with the same care and attention as other more apparently fragile materials. Provided the storage is dry, outhouses and garages may be suitable, but only if the space is uncluttered and set aside for sculpture. Damp cellars must not be used and the temperature of the store should not drop below 5°C (41°F) or rise above 15°C (60°F); the relative humidity should be between 50 and 60%.

As a precaution against rising damp, keep the sculpture clear of the ground by placing it on a wooden pallet or, if this is not possible, on clean polythene sheeting. *Never* stand white marble on a carpet or on a polished floor, either of which could stain the marble. Cover the sculpture loosely with a dust-sheet. Do not cover with polythene, which could cause condensation.

Enough space should be allowed so that each piece can be inspected and so that there is no danger of one object knocking against another.

Any fragments or pieces that may have been accidentally knocked off, however small, should be saved and kept in a cardboard box, protected by crumpled acid-free tissue paper. Do not use newspaper, which is very acidic. Do not keep fragments in paper or polythene bags. Place a note in the box identifying the broken piece.

STONE GARDEN SCULPTURE AND ORNAMENTS

A photographic record of garden sculpture and ornaments is highly desirable so that signs of deterioration can be monitored. Black-and-white photographs are more suitable for detecting cracks and repairs, while colour photographs show surface changes, such as the spread of iron-staining or the growth of algae. Regular on-site inspections should be made to check the speed of degradation against good photographs. Be sure to date the photographs.

In the meantime any programme of repair and conservation must be planned by a sculpture conservator. There is no point in dealing with a plinth which is out of alignment if the foundation on which it stands is inadequate. In most cases the base needs to stand on a concrete raft which exceeds the width of the plinth. (The plinth is the lowest projecting member of the base of a column or pedestal.) The plinth and the concrete raft are then separated by a lead damp-proof membrane to prevent moisture containing harmful salts present in the earth from being drawn up by capillary action from the ground.

This damp-proof membrane must be above the level of the ground, otherwise earth will bridge the distance between the raft and the plinth and render the membrane useless. For this reason the concrete raft should be set slightly above ground level without becoming visually obtrusive. A specification for this work, which involves dismantling the base, must be drawn up and the work supervised by a sculpture conservator.

In some cases it is possible to dig a narrow trough on all four sides of the raft and then fill it with pebbles. This improves drainage, helps prevent the damp-proof membrane from being bridged by earth, plants and debris, and makes it easier to avoid knocking the plinth when cutting the grass. This practical but slightly municipal solution may not be desirable in some settings on aesthetic grounds.

Overhanging greenery should be trimmed back because a dripping, damp atmosphere encourages the growth of algae. Creepers, such as honeysuckle and ivy, should not be allowed to climb up the base because they feed on moisture and break down the surface of stone and marble.

Vandalism is an increasing problem, so a sculpture conservator should advise on security measures to prevent the statue or urn being toppled or stolen.

Repairs

In the past repairs have included unsuitable materials such as iron dowels and cement fillings. For this reason only a sculpture conservator should stipulate the materials to be used, and should carry out or at least supervise any repair work on statuary and its base.

Winter covers

Winter covers for garden sculpture should be placed in position during a spell of dry weather before the end of October (see Causes of damage and decay, p. 241).

Ventilation should be incorporated into the design to allow the residual moisture in the sculpture to dry out and to prevent damp being trapped inside the cover. The design should also include fixing posts to prevent wind knocking the cover against the sculpture.

Never use straw and canvas tied to the sculpture with ropes. This method does protect sculpture from freezing but it retains moisture, which promotes the growth of destructive soluble salts. There is also the danger of staining from straw, canvas or tarpaulin and the use of ropes, year after year, abrades fragile surfaces and leaves patches of rubbed stone.

Urns and vases

Stone and marble urns and vases are a pleasing feature of many gardens, and some of these have very high-quality decorations (see also Metalwork, p. 152). Urns and vases designed to be planted have a hole somewhere near the base for draining off water. In the past these urns were usually provided with metal liners for holding the earth and protecting the urn from the corrosive action of

57. Italian Renaissance well-heads at Cliveden as normally shown and (below) under protective covers for the winter

damp earth, decaying vegetation and fertilizers. Liners can now be made of lead, fibreglass or zinc. The lining should connect with the drainage hole in the urn and this hole should be lined with a lead tube. It is sometimes possible for a sculpture conservator to provide a drainage hole in the urn but its importance and the aesthetic effect need to be considered carefully. It may be desirable to arrange for the liner to be removed in winter, together with the earth and plants, for storage in a greenhouse.

Coade stone

Fired artificial stone began to be manufactured in the middle of the 18th century and the most notable work came from the Coade factory at Lambeth. Coade stone owed its success to its relative cheapness, durability and the high quality of the workmanship.

Although the manufacturing processes were kept a secret at the time, modern analysis has shown that Coade stone is a type of ceramic. While originally impervious to the worst of weathers, Coade stone is now in need of care and attention. A sculpture conservator should make sure that the decorations, which were applied in Wedgwood style, are well adhered and cannot be picked off. Firecracks should be well pointed.

A sculpture conservator should also check the foundations and base on which the Coade stone stands and design a suitable winter cover. Should a Coade stone urn be filled with plants, liners should be fitted (see Urns and vases, above).

Cement statuary

Statuary cast in cement or hydraulic lime mortars (Roman cement) and placed in a garden or on a building is often hard to distinguish from statuary carved in stone or marble.

At first cement is durable in all weathers, but flaws in manufacture can become a source of problems in later life. Cracks should be carefully pointed making sure that the pointing is weaker than the original cement. A sculpture conservator should be asked to consider whether further expensive treatment is worthwhile. If of sufficient value, protect with winter covers (see above).

Making casts

Few methods are not damaging to the surface of the original, and before a cast is taken the statue or carving should be inspected and prepared by the sculpture conservator, and not by the cast-maker.

See also Metal Garden Sculpture and Ornaments, p. 152.

. . . there was sweete tapestry hangings with small figures and very much silk, they look'd as fresh as if new tho' bought severall yeares . . .

Celia Fiennes at Chatsworth, 1697

I chose my wife, as she did her wedding gown, not for a fine glossy surface, but such qualities as would wear well.

Goldsmith, *The Vicar of Wakefield*, 1766

We'd take all the carpets up and take them up on Cage Hill in a pony cart and beat them. There'd be twenty odd fellows up there beating, brushing, sweeping the carpets. The housemaids beat the carpets? No. We used to beat the housemaids.

Harry Jackson . . . at Lyme Park,
from Kedrun Laurie, *Cricketer Preferred*

CHAPTER FIFTEEN

TEXTILES

Protection
257

Cleaning
261

Repairs
266

Pests and Mould
267

Handling
268

Storing
269

Display
270

Costume
270

58. The state bed and accompanying seat furniture made for James II, at Knole

Light

Textiles are as susceptible to damage from light as water-colours. The colours fade and the materials rot. Once fading is noticed, it is too late; the damage has been done and cannot be reversed. Further damage can be reduced by treating the windows with ultraviolet-absorbent film or varnish and by using shutters and sun blinds to reduce light levels.

Where textiles of exceptional importance are displayed, such as the state bed hangings at Knole, Erddig and Calke, daylight may need to be excluded so as to ensure that light levels do not exceed 50 lux and the relative humidity can be controlled (see The Right Environment, p. 21).

Siting of objects

Textiles are made to be handled – as curtains are made to be drawn, upholstery sat on and carpets walked on – and it is a natural impulse to want to feel what the material is made of; but when many thousands of people visit a historic house every year, they can cause a lot of wear and damage even to new textiles. Most visitors will curb the instinct to touch if this is explained to them, but the siting of objects can help avoid unnecessary wear.

Some irreversible damage from light is unavoidable unless textiles are stored in total darkness, but it is sometimes possible to place vulnerable objects in a darker part of the room.

Make sure that furniture is not pushed up against textiles – a chair against a wall, a sofa table biting into the back of a sofa or furniture against tapestries.

In houses open to the public, watch visitors in crowded rooms and notice the textiles which are constantly rubbed, touched or brushed against by visitors' clothes. If, for example, people lean on the back of a chair to peer at a photograph, it may be possible to re-site the photograph or move the chair.

Make it the responsibility of the room steward to see that information bats are not put down on upholstered chairs or stools. In selecting a suitable place, remember that these bats can scratch polished wood and also marble.

Use of ropes and cords

Bed hangings can be roped off, but it is still necessary to have a steward in the room when a house is open to the public. In the past, visitors have reached over the rope and damaged hangings while the part of the bed out of reach has remained in good condition.

Where stanchions and ropes are used to protect a carpet, remember that visitors walk right up to the rope, so the stanchions must stand well back on the drugget to prevent feet wearing the carpet along the line of the rope. Do not stand a stanchion directly on the carpet or it will leave a mark.

When cords are used to stop visitors sitting on chairs tie them loosely so as not to cut into the upholstery.

Carpets and rugs

All carpeting is expensive to replace and some is irreplaceable. Most carpets and rugs are walked on occasionally and carpeting along the route which visitors follow in a house open to the public takes an enormous amount of wear.

Carpet paper

A thick type of brown paper placed between the floor and underlay can protect the carpet from rising damp, prevent dust rising from between the floorboards and stop the underlay from marking the wooden floor.

Underlay

A good underlay greatly prolongs the life of a carpet. It reduces wear by taking up the unevenness of the floor. The underlay should come to the edge of the carpet. Never overlap or turn back underlay as this makes the surface uneven. The seams of underlay must be sewn together, otherwise it moves and gaps appear, making the surface supporting the carpet uneven and causing wear. Do not use adhesive tape to join the underlay, as the adhesive can migrate, marking the carpet and floor. Floors can be badly marked if double-sided adhesive tape is used to fix underfelt to stone, marble or wood floors.

The International Wool Secretariat recommends the use of hairfelt underlay of contract quality. Some other types deteriorate so badly that the underlay sticks to the wooden floor. Do not use foam rubber or composition-backed underlays, which deteriorate unevenly, or those with a dimpled surface, which could cause uneven wear. On stone floors and other places where underfelt could absorb damp, carpet paper should be laid under the felt.

Druggets

It is known from old records that coverings or druggets were supplied with carpets to give protection from dirt, light and wear, and were used to protect a good carpet except when it was uncovered for state occasions. Nowadays no antique carpet should be walked on by visitors to a historic house, but where

59. Wooden castor cups placed beneath legs of furniture protect valuable carpets (shown here before sanding and painting)

this is unavoidable, it can be protected with a drugget, particularly in doorways and where visitors are channelled round a corner. As some druggets can do more harm than good, research and experiments have been carried out with the help of the International Wool Secretariat (see Appendix 2, p. 312).

Turning and moving carpets

Carpets and rugs wear more evenly if turned round every year. Stair-carpets should be moved a few inches periodically by a professional carpet-layer, renewing the underlay on the treads where necessary.

If a carpet is too large for a room, do not turn it under, as great damage can be caused along the fold. Roll the spare carpet on to a roller right side outside so as to prevent any creases forming (see also To roll a carpet, p. 269).

Castors on furniture

Protect carpets by placing small cups under the legs of heavy furniture, especially when it is fitted with metal castors. The cups can be made of three-ply wood and coloured to blend in with the carpet (see Appendix 2, p. 314).

60. A conversation group, by J. H. Mortimer (1741–79), showing chairs and a settee with case covers in use and (below) an armchair at Petworth, with case cover copying those in the Mortimer picture

Table carpets

The sharp edges and corners of tables should be well padded out with several layers of blankets or cotton bump before a table carpet is placed in position. Sharp corners cut into the fibres and cause damage. When a house is closed for the winter, table carpets should be taken off and laid flat on the floor or rolled up right side outside (see To roll a carpet, p. 269). If this is not done the carpet will take up the shape of the table and the strain could cause splits.

Case covers and dust-sheets

Use of dust-sheets to cover upholstered furniture when a house is closed reduces the damage from light and dust (see Appendix 3, p. 320). Faded colours and brittle materials can never be restored to their original condition.

Even when the house is open, consider fitting all but one of a set of chairs with case covers. Great care must be taken when putting covers on and taking them off. Measuring for case covers should be left to a textile conservator as, if they are too tight, damage can be done to the textile underneath and the case cover will do more harm than good.

Curtains

Curtains can sometimes be given added protection from light by hanging an extra sun-curtain draped behind the drawn-back curtain and held out of sight in the tie-back.

During the months when the house is closed, release curtains from tie-backs and draw them slightly to relax the folds. The bottom of heavy curtains should be folded into three and lifted neatly over the back of a chair or on to the windowsill so as to take some weight off the rest of the curtain to allow the creases to relax.

Festoon or draw curtains should be let down during the winter to release the folds. This is also the time to check fixings, rings and cords.

CLEANING

Never attempt to wash or dry-clean textiles of any historic importance without first consulting a textile conservator.

The safest way to remove dust and dirt from textiles is by vacuuming. As textiles should be handled as little as possible leave tapestries and curtains for a year or so and limit day-to-day cleaning to the carpets that are walked on.

It is essential to look at the whole of a textile before vacuuming. If it is very fragile, leave it strictly alone until the next visit of a textile conservator. *Never* vacuum embroideries which have beads or sequins as the suction will remove any which are loose. The vacuum cleaner has also taken its toll of 17th- and 18th-century fringes. The pile of some velvets is also vulnerable.

Equipment should be suitable for the job, not only for the safety of the textile but also to save time. The general-purpose head should always be used unless otherwise specified. *Never* use brush attachments when cleaning textiles, as brushes of any description can rough up loose threads.

Vacuum equipment and its uses

Most large houses will need three different vacuum cleaners (see Appendix 3, p. 317):

Small: Hoover Dustette

Ideal for most textiles, including tapestries, upholstery and fragile carpets. It is supplied with the general-purpose head. The flexible extension hose and crevice head, which come with the set of attachments (sold separately), are essential when working with textiles. When fitted with the flexible extension hose the Dustette can be tied to the waist or hung from a shoulder, enabling both hands to be free.

Medium: Domestic cylinder vacuum cleaner

This vacuum cleaner should have variable suction and a flexible hose. For stronger textiles, such as antique carpets and rugs which are in good condition, use the suction at low or medium depending on the strength of the carpet and how dirty it is. The long flexible hose makes this vacuum ideal for stair-carpets.

Industrial vacuum cleaner

Never use an industrial vacuum cleaner on any textile except modern carpeting and druggets.

Nylon screening

This screening is used with the Hoover Dustette and the domestic cylinder vacuum cleaner to prevent the textile from being sucked into the nozzle of the vacuum cleaner; it holds down any loose threads and protects fringes.

On flat horizontal surfaces the vacuum cleaner head should glide over the nylon screening and must not be pressed down as this could cause damage without increasing the amount of dirt removed. Remember that it is the suction which removes the dirt. The nylon mesh is soft and pliable but heavy enough not to be sucked up by the vacuum cleaner. The sharp edges of the

61. Vacuuming fragile textiles with a Hoover Dustette fitted with an extension hose and a general-purpose head, using protective nylon screening

screening must be bound with tape, and it should be washed frequently.

On vertical or shaped surfaces it is easier to use the general-purpose head, covered in soft nylon net held in position by a strong elastic band.

Carpets and rugs

Dust and grit cause great damage, so carpets that are walked on should be vacuumed daily, even though this will inevitably remove fibres. Float the head across the carpet slowly. It is the suction which removes the dirt. Any pressure or scrubbing to and fro will only damage the fibres and make the work harder.

Fragile carpets must not be walked on and should be vacuumed only once or twice a year using the Hoover Dustette with protective nylon screening. The knotted type of carpet fringe is particularly vulnerable. Protect the fringe with nylon screening and use the Hoover Dustette.

Never attempt any washing or dry-cleaning of carpets or rugs without first consulting a textile conservator. Some commercial cleaning methods accelerate re-soiling.

Upholstery

Care should be taken when, for example, dusting chairs or stools that the duster does not come into contact with any part of the textile. Special care should be taken of fringes. Drop-in chair seats should be removed before dusting, and especially when polish is applied to the wood.

Upholstery in good condition can be cleaned by using the Hoover Dustette fitted with the extension hose and the general-purpose or crevice head. Where conditions in a house are very dusty, upholstery may need to be vacuumed more than once a year so that it does not become impregnated with dust.

Fragile upholstery should always be protected by nylon screening while vacuuming. The crevice head, covered with fine net held in place with an elastic band, is useful for vacuuming the spaces down the back and sides of seats, places where moths can attack the stuffing as well as the seat cover.

The repair of upholstery requires considerable historical knowledge. Seat shapes, for instance, vary according to the period and country of origin. Always seek advice from a textile or furniture conservator who specializes in historical upholstery before any evidence of original upholstery is disturbed. If re-upholstery is considered advisable, traditional methods should be followed, and often the original materials can be re-used.

Hangings

As textiles should be handled as little as possible, vacuum fragile curtains and tapestries only once every few years. In this way it is possible to deal with one or two rooms of a large house every winter.

Curtains, bed hangings

Always lift the end of floor-length curtains on to a chair or windowsill before polishing or washing the floor.

Pelmets and valances should not be taken down but vacuumed with the Hoover Dustette. On vertical and shaped surfaces use the Hoover Dustette with the crevice head covered in soft nylon net, which can be held in position by a strong elastic band. Where elaborately draped pelmets, heavy fringing or intricate textile-covered carvings are involved, a textile conservator should be asked to advise on methods of vacuuming.

Bed hangings or curtains which are strong enough can be taken down and vacuumed flat on a large table using the Hoover Dustette and protecting the

62. The state bed at Clandon, with case curtains half pulled, and a light frame to protect the elaborate armchair *en suite*

textile with nylon screening. The textile can then be folded into three length-wise, with the folds well padded with acid-free tissue paper, and wrapped in a dust-sheet for the winter while the rest of the room is thoroughly spring-cleaned.

Tapestries

Handle as little as possible and report all new splits and deterioration to a textile conservator.

It is better to leave some dust than to over-insist and agitate a weak place. *Never* use a stronger suction than the Hoover Dustette. Use the general-purpose head covered in nylon net if the tapestry is in good condition. Float it over the entire surface without touching the tapestry. If the tapestry is very fragile consult a conservator.

Tapestry chairs and other flat surfaces can be protected with nylon screening, and vacuumed with the Hoover Dustette, using the general-purpose head.

Banners and flags

These are often extremely fragile; they should be left hanging and not touched in any way unless otherwise advised by a textile conservator.

Embroideries

Handle as little as possible. Do not touch intricate embroideries such as stump work or gold work without seeking expert advice. Fine cotton gloves should be worn when handling metalwork embroidery.

Most embroideries can be vacuumed with the Hoover Dustette, first protecting the surface with nylon screening. *Never* vacuum embroideries which have beads or sequins, as the suction will remove any which are loose.

REPAIRS

When dealing with important or fragile textiles, do not attempt repairs of any kind without first consulting a qualified textile conservator.

Always sew and *never* use commercial adhesives on textiles. They can harden and discolour and are often impossible to remove.

Upholstery and hangings can be enormously improved by sewing down loose braid, cord or gimp.

Netting

Net can keep in place damaged and deteriorating textiles, but netting should be considered as a holding operation only until the textile can be properly conserved or renewed.

Net can trap dust and dirt and is also abrasive, so only the finest and softest should be used. It should be dyed to the background colour of the textile.

The placing of the net and the sewing down can cause more damage to silk and braid than if they had been left alone.

On curtains, net can balloon out and look unsightly. It must be taken up to the curtain heading; if this is not done the curtain is liable to tear lower down where it has been perforated by the sewing-on of the net.

Always consult a textile conservator before starting to net.

Linings

Most hanging textiles such as curtains, bed hangings and tapestries have linings or bound edges which may shrink in time. The way the textile hangs is then distorted and damage can occur along the creases. If the hangings are in good condition release the lining or edging – this should remove the cockling and allow the textile to hang straight once again. Do not touch anything fragile, as in some cases it is only the lining which is keeping the textile together.

Fixings

All fixings should be examined when vacuuming the hangings; missing rings and hooks should be replaced. Where a textile hangs straight on a wall, Velcro or a batten in a sleeve should be used for hanging so that there is no strain at any one point. Consult a conservator before altering the hanging as damage could be done in taking the textile down.

PESTS AND MOULD

The common clothes moth, brown house moth and carpet beetle do the greatest damage to textiles. The best protection against these is thorough dusting and vacuum cleaning. If they are found, a textile conservator will advise on the correct treatment.

Moths

The larva stage, which does the damage, can last for several months. Moths like to lay their eggs in enclosed spaces beneath heavy furniture, the inside of a drawer which may be slightly damp or the felt of card tables. The larvae feed on wool and other animal fibres.

Carpet beetle

Dirt and darkness attract the carpet beetle. At least once a year all woollen materials, including carpets and rugs, should be inspected carefully over their entire surface for signs of infestation even if this involves moving heavy furniture. The 'woolly bear', as the insect is called in its early stages, is far more active than a moth grub, so look out for holes scattered over a wide area. Care should be taken to vacuum thoroughly along the borders of carpets and under furniture.

Mould

The treatment of mould should be left to an expert. Check the temperature and humidity of the room and consult a conservator.

See also Pests, Moulds and Insects, p. 191.

HANDLING

Fringes

Never touch the fringe when carrying furniture. Chairs and stools with fringes should always be carried by the legs by two people (see Furniture, p. 106).

Carpets

A carpet can walk and ruck up against furniture which puts a strain on the fibres and may result in it getting torn. A carpet can be irreparably damaged by pulling at one end or corner when it is fully laid out. Its own weight can break

63. A rare 17th-century X-frame stool at Knole. Handling over the centuries has destroyed much of the original silver fringe

the warp or weft. *Always* roll a carpet and lift it into the new position even when moving the carpet only a few inches.

Textiles should be stored in the dark in a room which is both well ventilated and has a constant relative humidity. The relative humidity should be about 55% and the temperature 5–15°C (41–59°F).

Store-rooms can be a breeding ground for pests so they must be kept clean. All stores should be examined once a year for signs of pests and mould.

Dust-free cupboard and drawer units are expensive. However, textiles can safely be stored in cupboards, open shelves or in large acid-free boxes. Line shelves and boxes with acid-free tissue paper. Open shelves should be curtained or dust-sheeted. Do not overfill boxes or cram shelves because textiles crush very easily.

List the textiles in store and when additions are made note the date so that the textile conservator can check the objects on the next visit.

Flat textiles

Small pieces can be laid flat, with each layer protected by acid-free tissue paper. Large textiles such as tapestries, carpets or banners should be rolled round a PVC tube or drain-pipe, or cardboard tube 65–200 mm in diameter. The larger the dimensions of the object the greater the diameter of the tube must be. Rollers can sometimes be got from a local carpet shop. Cover all rollers with acid-free tissue paper before use.

Roll textiles firmly *right side out* in the direction of the warp threads, interleaving with acid-free tissue paper. *Never* roll a textile right side in or it will get crushed. Take care that there are no folds or creases. Wrap each roll in a dust-sheet to exclude dust and light and, if it needs to be tied, use wide, white cotton tape. *Never* use rope or string, which can cut into the textile.

To roll a carpet

Never crush the carpet by folding it right side in or bundling it up. Roll carpets fringe to fringe right side outside so that the pile is stretched rather than squeezed, interleaving with acid-free tissue paper. This is easy with small rugs which can be turned over before rolling. It is rather more difficult when coping with a large carpet which should be rolled round a core of PVC or a cardboard roller of 200–250 mm diameter.

Clear the carpet of furniture. The more fragile the carpet the more people will be needed, but do not start with fewer than three, and remove shoes before walking on the carpet. Stand on the carpet in a row facing one end of the carpet. Lift the edge and walk backwards for about three metres so that the carpet is lying underside uppermost. Place the roller in position and roll up the end over the doubled area of the carpet so that the right side is outside. Stand on the carpet again facing the roller. Pick up the roller, and walk backwards for another three metres and roll this area of carpet; repeat until the whole carpet is on the roller.

Shaped textiles

Items that cannot be rolled should be laid out as flat as possible. Creases must be prevented from forming, so each fold should be padded out by a roll or loose pad made up of acid-free tissue paper. Always re-fold in a different place, as holes will often appear along old crease lines.

DISPLAY

Lace

Lace may have to be washed and pinned out before being mounted. Consult a textile conservator.

Embroideries

Embroideries are sometimes framed and hung. The selection of acid-free mounts, the sealing of the glass and backing and the fitting of fillets to prevent the textile touching the glass should likewise be left to a conservator to arrange.

COSTUME

Cleaning and repairs

No cleaning or repairs should be done except under the direction of a textile conservator.

Display

Costume is best displayed on dummies in glass showcases where light and dust can be controlled. The room in which costume is displayed must be kept dry and aired throughout the year.

In winter, costume on open display should either be packed away in boxes or left on the dummy and covered with lightweight dust-sheets to exclude light and dust.

Dummies must be adapted to fit the particular costume. Do not use pins unless absolutely necessary. *Never* use steel pins, which rust; use fine pins of brass or stainless steel.

Storage

Hanging

Allow plenty of space between garments. A cotton cover can protect the costume from damage from buttons and hooks on adjoining garments. *Never* use polythene, as the static electricity which it produces attracts dust; polythene also inhibits ventilation.

Pad coat-hangers with polyester wadding and then cover with calico. Do not use cotton wool to pad the hangers as it absorbs moisture.

If a dress has a waistline, sew tapes to the inside and loop these over the coat-hanger. The weight of the skirt will then be supported by the tape instead of by the shoulders of the garment. Puff out the sleeves with crumpled acid-free tissue paper.

Folding

Costumes can be folded and stored in large acid-free boxes. The garment should be laid out as flat as possible. Boxes with lids the same depth as the side of the box exclude dust and light best. Line the boxes with acid-free tissue paper and do not overfill as this squashes the lower layers and reduces the circulation of air. Soften each fold with a roll of acid-free tissue paper. Always re-fold a garment in a different place to prevent creases from forming. Often holes appear along an old crease.

Small garments such as blouses, underclothes, shoes, hats, gloves, etc., should be stored in boxes with plenty of acid-free tissue paper.

. . . a great deal of Paper is nowadays printed to be pasted upon Walls to serve instead of Hangings: and truly if all Parts of the Sheet be well and close pasted on, it is very pritty, clean and will last with tolerable Care a great while: but there are some other done by Rolls in long sheets of a thick Paper made for the Purpose whose sheets are pasted together to be so long as the Height of a Room – and they are managed like Woollen Hangings, and there is a great Variety, with curious Cuts [wood-cuts] which are Cheap, and if kept from Wet, very lasting.

John Houghton, F R S,
A Collection of Letters for the Improvement of Husbandry and Trade, 1689–1703

I saw a Chinese wallpaper when I was at Maigret's house with Mme de Forget. Maigret told us that we have nothing to equal their skill in producing fast colours, and he said that when he tried to make a sample of part of the pink background it turned a dreadful colour in a very short time . . .

Extract from Eugène Delacroix's journal, 1847

CHAPTER SIXTEEN

WALLS, CEILINGS AND WINDOWS

Wallpaper
275

Chinese Wallpapers and English Papers in the Chinese Taste
276

Flock Wallpaper
278

Leather and 'Wax' Cloth
278

Wall-paintings
280

Decorative Plasterwork and Carved Wood
284

Panelling
285

Cleaning Paintwork
285

Windows
287

Equipment
288

64. Chinese wallpaper in the State Bedroom at Nostell Priory, supplied and hung by Thomas Chippendale in 1771

WALLPAPER

Although surviving 16th- and 17th-century wallpapers are rare and fragmentary, it is clear from contemporary records that wallpapers were both widely used and highly regarded.

The idiosyncratic production methods of the early manufacturers make it impossible to outline exact procedures for conservation. Expert advice should always be sought, as every case requires individual treatment. Problems may arise from the paper support, the ground and pigment layers, from adhesion between these components or between the paper and the wall surface. Similar difficulties exist with 18th- and 19th-century wall coverings and even modern papers.

If wallpapers are seen to be detached from the wall surface, the area should be investigated for the cause – this could be damp conditions, movement of the building, deterioration of the backing or even problems arising from previous layers. The wallpaper should not be re-attached without consulting an expert.

The paper-hanging makers

The success and ultimate prosperity of the English paper-hanging maker was due to several factors: the amount of technical knowledge already available to him, his ability to adapt to new forms of production to meet new fashions and his ability to produce convincing imitations of a variety of decorative hangings such as textiles, leather works and Chinese papers.

Although the 'superior' papers were usually put up by the maker, there is evidence to suggest that, from the early 1700s, do-it-yourself was acceptable. The detailed diagrams given in Diderot's *Encyclopédie* show that paper-hanging could be a very elaborate and complicated art indeed, and that the best work required the services of several expert operators, all of whom played a specially appointed part in the undertaking.

The early methods of hanging papers were varied, one of the commonest being described with deceptive simplicity by Robert Dunbar writing in 1734:

Please to observe the following Method of putting up the said Hangings in any Room viz:

First, Cut one Edge of each Piece or Breadth, even to the Work, then nail it with large Tacks to the Wall and paste the Edge of the next Breadth over the heads of the Tacks and so from one to another, till the Room be perfectly hung, observing to make ye Flowers join.

NB. Damp the Paper before you put it up, and begin next the window, and make stiff Paste of the best Flour and Water.

Gradually the papers themselves and the degree of finish expected of the hanging become finer. With the advent of roller-printed papers with accurate repeats, exact matching from piece to piece became possible, but it remained customary until relatively recent times to paste up sheets with an overlap. The edges of all papers required hand trimming and paper-hangers only adopted butted joints when accurate pre-trimming became widely available.

Until the late 19th century, the pastes were usually starch, the glues animal or fish based, and they were strong and water soluble. Modern pastes are derivatives of starch or polymethyl cellulose, and contain a fungicidal agent.

CHINESE WALLPAPERS AND ENGLISH PAPERS IN THE CHINESE TASTE

It is generally accepted that Chinese papers first appeared in Europe about 1650. They were called India papers as they were transported in the ships of the Dutch, French and English East India Companies during their trading ventures with Canton. The impact of Chinese decorative art was felt in France from the 1650s, but English awareness came much later. John Evelyn, inspecting the Queen's collection of rare *objets d'art* in 1693, gives a matter-of-fact description of these 'divers China and India articles' which suggests that he was familiar with the vogue at this date.

Most of the Chinese papers were sold in sets of about twenty-five rolls, each twelve feet long. The absence of any kind of repeat, and the studied dissimilarity of detail between one length and another, gave them a unique quality which was greatly prized by those who possessed a room decorated and furnished in the oriental style. Each Chinese room should be regarded as an individual achievement. The sheets were normally hung from cornice to dado. Some meticulous paper-hangers carefully cut the painted decoration and embellished the panels with specially made matching borders.

The favourite motifs of the Chinese papers up to 1750 were flowering trees, shrubs and flowers with additions of birds, butterflies and small insects. The highest branches of the trees reached the extreme top edge of the sheet, and this section is frequently missing owing to the problems of fitting the sheet or the panel on to the existing wall space. Later examples specialized in landscape and figure motifs, the latter sometimes depicting Chinese life and occupations.

Chinese papers were essentially a luxury article (three to five guineas a roll in the 18th century) and special care was taken with their display. It is generally accepted that the Chinese style passed out of fashion during the latter half of the 18th century largely because of over-exaggerated designs.

The quality and design of the chinoiserie papers made by English artists varied greatly, from very fair reproductions of the flowering tree and shrub variety to the quaintest imitations of the landscape and figure types in which men and women in 18th-century garb are depicted wandering through improbable Far Eastern scenery, or taking their ease on seats of unmistakably English design. A surprisingly early English imitator was the stationer James Minnikin, of St Martins le Grand, who advertised 'Japan' paper-hangings made on the premises for sale in 1680.

Structure

The rolls of panels were often formed of single sheets of paper, of approximately 510 × 760 mm, joined by a slight overlap of approximately 3 mm. This was backed with a long-fibred oriental paper of similar dimensions but with the seam falling in the centre of the decorated sheet, or sometimes even applied at right angles to the decorated sheet. The panels were often treated with alum before painting to prevent spreading of the pigments, which were bound with an animal-glue medium. The alum may be responsible for the slight yellowing often visible in such papers and may also cause problems when the paper has been applied directly on to a plaster surface or an exterior wall. The panels were generally applied to a European or English lining paper, or, if professionally hung, to a canvas lining which was then stretched over wooden battens. The latter method is the most prevalent; it does allow the ventilation necessary to discourage mould growth, but presents problems of discoloration from contact with the wood or poor-quality canvas.

General care

Too much light causes irreversible fading and deterioration. Blinds should be kept down at all times and artificial light must be kept as low as possible (50 lux maximum).

Pieces of furniture should not be pushed up against wallpapers, particularly those stretched on battens.

Metal fixtures such as blind cleats or light switches should be isolated from the paper layer by an acid-free cartridge paper cut-out. (Metallic salts react with the pigments in adverse conditions of relative humidity and cause irreversible colour changes.)

The papers should not be allowed to come into contact with moisture or solvent fumes such as those from metal-cleaning agents, wood preservatives or fungicide agents. Tears, sags or loose areas should be reported to a conservator and *not* re-attached.

Do not dust the surface as such papers are very fragile, and subject to flaking and general deterioration. A paper conservator should be consulted before any treatment is undertaken.

FLOCK WALLPAPER

Although flocking on textiles was available much earlier, the first known examples of flocked paper suggest that this had become the usual medium by the end of the 17th century. The first types were coarse flock grounds built up in layers to resemble velvet; designs of figures and flowers were introduced with improved manufacturing techniques during the 18th century.

The technique involves passing paper, on which the design has been printed or stencilled in slow-drying adhesive, through the flock or powdered wool. The beauty and expense of these papers ensured careful treatment, with the consequent preservation of many fine examples.

General care

Do not attempt to clean or dust. Some flocks were made using powdered coloured silk instead of wool, and others have additional constituents such as mica or metallic dusts to simulate gold and silver. These composites are particularly fragile and the adhesion of the various particles to the paper support may be weak.

LEATHER AND 'WAX' CLOTH

Leather hangings

From early times leather was in common use for wall covering. The earliest decorated leather hangings were introduced by the Arabs, who brought them from North Africa to Spain in the 11th century. In the reign of the Emperor Charles V Spanish craftsmen in turn brought the art of leather painting and gilding to the Netherlands, whence it spread to England in the 17th century. English craftsmen under Dutch and Flemish influence also made hangings, screens and table covers, and were subsequently associated with the production of 'paper-hangings'.

Treatment is under review; in the meantime take relative-humidity readings in any room in which leather is hanging and *never* let sunlight fall directly on to the leather. *Never* attempt to clean leather hangings.

'Wax' cloth hangings

These hangings were tough, durable and almost impervious to damp conditions. Their production coincided with the vogue for chinoiserie effects and designs, and dimensions usually compared with contemporary paper-hangings.

Linen or canvas was stretched on to a wooden frame and given a ground of chalk/varnish/soot. This was smoothed with pumice, the design painted or printed on and a layer or layers of varnish added. Although the final varnish layer will give protection, the instability of the original ground must be respected and protected from adverse conditions of relative humidity.

65. One panel of a series of early-18th-century wall hangings of embossed and gilded leather at Oxburgh Hall

WALL-PAINTINGS

Wall-paintings in the care of the National Trust vary from a simple masonry pattern representing brickwork in the King's Room at Oxburgh, to an elaborate figurative frieze of 1599 in the High Great Chamber at Hardwick; from full-scale allegorical schemes to decorate staircases and saloons, such as the Grand Staircase at Petworth, painted by Louis Laguerre in 1714/15, to the *trompe l'œil* decoration by Rex Whistler, painted at Mottisfont in the 1930s.

66. The Great Staircase at Knole of about 1603, decorated in grisaille after designs by Marten de Vos

In the 16th century when Vasari wrote 'of all the ways in which painters work, wall-painting is the finest and most masterly . . .' he was referring to *fresco*, a technical term for a sort of mural painting on plaster, where colour is applied to the newly laid *intonaco* while still wet. The paint is bound into the plaster as it sets by a complicated process of drying and carbonation.

North of the Alps pigments were frequently mixed with some binding material and applied to the plaster after it had dried. These 'secco' paintings are less stable than true fresco.

Mural decoration can be painted on canvas to be attached afterwards to a wall or ceiling, for example at Berrington Hall, or the Rex Whistler at Plas Newydd.

Wall-paintings were therefore executed in a variety of media, but were usually painted on to the very structure of the building, be it a partition wall made of plaster and timber, a masonry wall which had been plastered with several layers to achieve a smooth finish, or sometimes straight on to the masonry or brick walls with little or no priming.

As a wall-painting is effectively part of the architecture, its preservation depends in large measure on the condition of the building.

Causes and prevention of deterioration

Damp

In damp conditions, soluble salts in the wall or plaster tend to migrate through to the painted surface on which they crystallize, disfiguring and sometimes irrevocably damaging the paint. Damp may also cause the plaster to separate from the wall or from other plaster layers, giving rise to hollow bulges where the plaster is in danger of becoming completely detached. Damp can cause some pigments, most notably those containing lead or copper, to alter chemically and consequently change colour.

Condensation can also be a problem and may form on the painted surface, particularly where wall-paintings are on the interior face of an outside wall.

Preventing damage from damp

Where a wall-painting is on the interior face of an outside wall, it is particularly important to check rain gutters and downpipes, making sure that they are not blocked with leaves and are functioning properly. Rainwater should drain away from the base of walls and not be allowed to collect in pools adjacent to the building. If there is any sign of rising damp, an architect or structural surveyor should be consulted.

The walls should be kept well pointed with a suitable mortar and the roof regularly inspected for leaks.

Light and heat

Wall-paintings that have been protected from bright light have a brilliant intensity of colours which can be breathtaking. Light levels should not exceed 200 lux. Where sunlight may fall directly on the paintings, sun curtains or blinds should be fitted. Treat the windows with ultraviolet-absorbent varnish or film (see also The Right Environment, p. 23).

There may be a temptation to spotlight details of a wall-painting, but this should be resisted because the concentrated light and heat emitted by the spotlight would cause damage.

Ideally all water pipes should be diverted away from areas of wall-paintings or decorative plasterwork and radiators should be removed from their immediate vicinity. It is amazing how often water pipes in walls do leak and cause terrible damage. Any hot-water pipes running along walls with wall-paintings should be well lagged to prevent excessive warming of the wall. Heat and dryness will cause paint to become brittle and flake off.

Touching and vibration

Many wall-paintings extend down to floor level and consequently are easily scuffed, scratched or simply touched. Every effort should be made to prevent visitors from touching wall-paintings, preferably without recourse to the use of glass or Perspex covers. If covers have to be employed, it is important to ensure that they do not touch the surface of the painting and that air may circulate in front of the painting by leaving vents at the sides. Consult a wall-paintings conservator.

Heavy use of upstairs rooms causes vibrations to ceiling paintings and decorative plasterwork immediately beneath. This applies also to cantilevered upper landings of staircases. The vibration cracks and loosens the plaster and it has been known to cause paintings to fall on to the dining-room table when bedrooms above were put on the visitors' route.

General care

Do not attempt to dust a wall-painting. Inspect regularly for any cracks, bulges, flaking paint or signs of damp and if any changes occur, seek the advice of a wall-paintings conservator, who in any case should inspect the walls at least once every ten years.

67. The Long Gallery at Sudbury. Intricate plasterwork ceilings of this type have to be cleaned from a lightweight tower scaffold

DECORATIVE PLASTERWORK AND CARVED WOOD

Some 15th–17th-century houses still have original lime plaster. Traditional lime plaster is mortar made from sand and slaked lime, often with the addition of horsehair for increased strength and improved setting. It is quite different from modern interior plasters, which are gypsum based.

Spring cleaning

Decorative carved mouldings and cornices should be vacuumed once a year. Care should be taken that dust does not fall on the paintings and tapestries beneath, and wall- or ceiling-paintings should not be touched. Move all small or vulnerable objects out of the way before starting work.

68. Plasterwork overmantel in Bess of Hardwick's bed chamber

Use the Hoover Dustette strapped to the waist or hung from the shoulder, so that both hands are free. Fit it with the flexible hose and crevice head, protecting the plasterwork from accidental knocks by binding a piece of foam plastic round the crevice head; brush out finely carved mouldings with a hogshair brush (see Appendix 3, p. 318). For larger areas use a paper-hanger's brush. It is advisable to work off a tower scaffold (see Equipment, p. 289). By brushing out with one hand while holding the Dustette head in the other, the dust is sucked up and does not float all over the room.

Never use any liquid or cleaning packs on plasterwork. Painted plaster can be mistaken for terracotta, the paint may be flaking and the plaster may be affected by water.

During cleaning, the opportunity should be taken to examine woodwork for woodworm and all decorative work for loose areas, cracks or rust stains. Rust stains are evidence that the decoration has been put together with iron cramps or dowels, and when these rust they expand and cause the plasterwork to crack. Any problems should be reported to an architect or conservator.

PANELLING

Unpolished panelling

Dust over with a soft, dry duster or banister brush. Brush out carving with a hogshair brush used in conjunction with the Hoover Dustette (see Decorative plasterwork and carved wood, above).

Polished panelling

Treat in the same way as furniture (see Furniture, p. 108).

CLEANING PAINTWORK

Before attempting to clean any paintwork, inspect the surface carefully – it may be flaking; and be sure that you know the type of paint that has been used – some are adversely affected by water. If you do not know what kind of paint it is but the surface is sound, dust lightly with a banister brush (see Appendix 3). Even where it is permissible to wash paintwork, first consider the overall effect of leaving high water marks which may make the wall look dirtier than before.

Decorative paintwork (graining, marbling, etc.)

Decorative surfaces, such as graining or marbling etc. should not be touched but referred to an expert. See also Wall-paintings, p. 280.

Limewash

Limewash, often called whitewash, is diluted pure slaked lime, sometimes mixed with tallow. It acts as a disinfectant and was applied on virtually any kind of interior wall or ceiling after plague or illness, as well as during the regular maintenance of a building. Limewash now most commonly survives on the decorative plasterwork of ceilings and overmantels.

Unfortunately most limewashed surfaces have been covered with a modern paint, such as white emulsion, which has a completely different appearance and often lacks the permeability of limewash and so tends to flake and look shabby.

Limewashes require very little attention if the environment is stable. If the surface is sound, dust lightly with a banister brush. Never use a feather duster, which would scratch the surface. If there are any signs of dampness do not touch but seek the advice of a wall-paintings conservator.

Distemper paints

There are two types of distemper paint: a soft distemper, also known as size-bound distemper; and a hardened one, either casein-bound, such as Distemper Super, or oil-bound distemper, such as Walpamur.

Soft distemper

Soft distemper or size-bound distemper is held together with an animal glue, and is generally found on ceilings. It wipes off very easily. The only safe way to clean it is to dust the surface lightly with a banister brush. Water should never be used.

Casein-bound distemper

Dust lightly with a banister brush. If necessary wipe with a damp (not wet) cloth but never wash the surface.

Oil-bound distemper

Oil-bound distemper is generally harder-wearing than soft distemper.

Dust first with a banister brush. Sometimes this is all that is needed. Another very safe way to clean oil-bound distemper is to compress lumps of fresh white bread and roll them over the dry paint surface. If necessary wash gently with warm water to which a little Synperonic N has been added. Rinse off and dry. Use three cloths and two buckets.

Oil-based paints

Oil-based paints should be treated in the same way as oil-bound distemper.

In addition, obstinate marks such as those left round door handles and on skirting boards after polishing can sometimes be lifted by using a mixture of 300 ml white spirit and 300 ml water, to which 5 ml Fairy Liquid has been added. First test the surface as white spirit softens some paints. Apply the mixture with small swabs of cotton wool and use very sparingly. Rinse and dry well. White spirit can have a dramatic effect and caution should be used, as a cleaned area can stand out in sharp contrast to the surrounding painted surfaces.

Do not use any commercial cleaning detergents or abrasive powders, which can remove the surface of the paint or roughen it so that dirt will collect more easily.

Acrylic paints

Clean in the same way as oil-based paints.

WINDOWS

Stained glass and leaded windows

The term 'stained glass' usually refers to windows, coloured or otherwise, where a design has been painted in an opaque brown or black paint on the surface of pieces of glass and then fired into it. It is invariably assembled by means of 'H' section lead strips and waterproofed.

A variant, known as 'enamelled glass', is found frequently in heraldic work. Here various coloured enamels are fired on to the surface of the glass, partially eliminating the need for lead between one colour and the next. This type of glass is particularly delicate and liable to flake.

Stained glass

This should *never* be washed because the paint is often loose on old glass, particularly heraldic glass, and this can very easily be dislodged and lost by washing. *Never* treat stained glass with ultraviolet-absorbent varnish or film. Stained glass should only be cleaned by a specialist conservator.

Plain leaded glass

This can be wiped with a damp cloth, but do it very gently, as some of the glass will be old and extremely fragile. Do not use any commercial detergent or window-cleaning product. The importance of the plain leaded glass should be established before it is treated with UV-absorbent varnish or film.

All other types of windows

Every house should have a check-list of windows treated with UV-absorbent varnish or film with the date of the last application (see Appendix 1, p. 302).

Windows treated with UV-absorbent film or varnish

As there are many UV filters on the market, always check the manufacturer's cleaning instructions. Unless otherwise directed, wash with clean water using a *clean* soft cloth. Dry gently without rubbing, using a soft cloth. Any particle of dust or grit can scratch the surface and damage the filter so the cloths must be kept scrupulously clean.

Do *not* touch the windows for thirty days after treatment with UV-absorbent varnish.

Do *not* clean the window in hot sunlight or if there is any likelihood of frost.

Do *not* use any detergent, cleaning agent or alcohol. (Methylated spirits is the solvent used to remove this varnish.)

Do *not* use brushes, chamois leather or paper towels.

Do *not* put any sticky tape or notices on the treated glass.

Untreated windows

Wash with clean water to which a little methylated spirits has been added. Use a soft, clean cloth. Dry and then polish the glass with chamois leather. Avoid proprietary cleaners which are expensive and dry out leaving white powder in the corners and along the edges. Also, many of these products contain silicone, which inhibits the adhesion of UV-absorbent varnish and makes it impossible to treat the window.

EQUIPMENT

Step-ladders

Lightweight aluminium step-ladders suitable to the needs of the house are essential. It is a false economy not to replace existing wooden ladders, which are often heavy and unsteady. Cheap, badly designed equipment can be dangerous. Try out the step-ladder before buying it; some of the taller ones have back legs which bend and slip on polished floors (see Appendix 3, p. 320).

The vulnerability of objects and decoration in a room should always be considered. Except when short and light, step-ladders should be carried by two people; one person alone should not attempt to shift the position of a long step-ladder, as it is easily unbalanced. The cost of conservation and decoration is too great to take the risk of damaging plasterwork, paintings or furniture.

Tower scaffolding

Houses with carved cornices, plasterwork, chandeliers, tapestries, large curtains and elaborate pelmets or picture frames need a lightweight aluminium tower scaffold, which is also useful when moving large paintings. This is an expensive piece of equipment and should be chosen with care (see Appendix 3).

I sat down beside the fireplace and let my eyes wander over the miscellany of the room. There were many dusty objects lying around and heaped upon each other. It was like the lumber-room of Prince Prigio. Like him, I began to examine them. Each had its own significance as part of a place that breathed a story of its own. There are houses which have soul and spirit, inclined to joy or sorrow; there are places of dignity and grandeur. There are façades of brick and stone that hold images; there are little silent places where, in half-forgotten whispers in dusty corners, the stories of ages find voice.

Margaret Meade-Fetherstonhaugh,
Epilogue to *Uppark and its People*, 1964

CHAPTER SEVENTEEN

MISCELLANEOUS

Billiard Tables
293

Ephemera
293

Ethnographic Artefacts
294

Ivory
294

Model Ships
294

Musical Boxes and Automata
295

69. Model ships on display at Arlington Court

·✤ MISCELLANEOUS ✤·

BILLIARD TABLES

The nap on the bed-cloth of a billiard table runs from the balk end to the spot end. On the cushions the direction of the nap varies according to the make of the table. The cloth is stretched tightly over the table when first fitted, but its natural characteristics allow it to stretch and in time it becomes slack. When this stage is reached, re-stretching by a skilled fitter is required.

Cleaning

If the table is in use, regular brushing and ironing with special billiard-table equipment in the direction of the nap are essential to the maintenance of the table efficiency.

1. Brush to remove all the dirt, using only the tip of the brush at the ends of the table.
2. Go over the table again with a duster wrapped round the brush.
3. Iron, using a clean warm iron; an iron that is too hot dries out the wool fibres making them brittle and the cloth becomes more susceptible to wear. Iron the bed-cloth only. *Never* iron the cushions.
4. Brush the cushions with the run of the nap.

Billiard tables which are not used, especially when covered with their original cloth, should be cleaned as upholstery (see Textiles, p. 264). Treat the wood as polished furniture (see Furniture, p. 108).

EPHEMERA

Posters, postcards, programmes, menu-cards, souvenirs, advertisements and a wide range of 19th- and 20th-century paper items are involved in this category, the title of which admirably indicates their impermanence.

Owing to the transitory nature of the information they contain, these items were often made from poor-quality materials and were not usually treated with care. The high percentage of ground-wood fibres used in their manufacture is responsible for their rapid deterioration, which is accelerated by light, pollution and contact with other poor-quality items.

As they are often very brittle, ephemera should be handled as little as possible; do not attempt to unfold folded items – pick them up by the margins only. Unless on display, they should be stored in a Solander box, interleaved with acid-free tissue. The conservation of ephemera is highly specialized and a paper conservator should be consulted.

ETHNOGRAPHIC ARTEFACTS

Ethnographic artefacts, sometimes referred to as tribal art, are utilitarian or ritual objects made by peoples who have had little or no contact with the urban civilizations of the world. Such items were frequently brought back from abroad as curios, and were occasionally collected on a systematic basis.

Much of the interest in ethnographic objects relates to the way in which they were used, and their condition when collected. In particular, masks and other ceremonial objects may bear ritual deposits which should not be removed, and paints and pigments may frequently be very loosely attached to surfaces. Apart from light dusting, all cleaning of ethnographic objects should be left to a conservator specializing in such materials. In particular, no attempt should be made to polish metal components such as blades, and when objects are mounted or suspended for display, this must be done in such a way as to avoid any strain on fragile components. Care should be taken when handling arrows, which may still retain some poison.

As most of the objects in this category are wholly or mainly composed of organic materials, they should wherever possible be displayed at light levels not exceeding 50 lux, and at a relative humidity in the range 50–65%.

IVORY

Ivory has a strong directional grain and is especially sensitive to humidity changes. Keep out of direct sunlight and away from heaters and radiators.

Never allow ivory to come into contact with water, oil or any other liquid. Ivory should be examined by an expert before any cleaning is considered.

If ivory is to be stored, it should be wrapped in acid-free tissue paper. *Never* use coloured paper or cloth, as these materials contain dyes which may migrate into the ivory and stain it.

MODEL SHIPS

All model ships are extremely fragile. They must be handled as little as possible and should be displayed in glass cases.

They are made up from many types of organic materials such as bone, ivory, wood (especially pear wood) and textiles for the rigging and sails. All these materials are sensitive to variations in light levels, temperature and relative humidity. Above 50 lux colours will fade and the textile fibres deteriorate; direct sunlight or too strong electric light will increase the temperature inside a glass case. Temperature and relative-humidity levels are particularly important, as the delicate and finely cut parts of the model will dry out very quickly in adverse conditions, the deck planks will warp and overlap and marquetry will lift. If the relative humidity is too high and the case is damp, rigging will snap. Victorian rigging is painted to resemble tarring and is consequently more fragile than unpainted 18th-century rigging.

Ideal display conditions are a maximum light level of 50 lux and a relative humidity of 55% with a temperature of 15°C (59°F).

Display

If the ships are kept in dust-free glass cases in the recommended conditions they will need little maintenance. As they are so fragile, cleaning of any sort should be left to an expert, who should inspect them every four or five years. Models were often varnished over layers of dirt, and decks may have been treated with oil and so have become dust traps. This needs specialist attention. *Never* cut off loose or broken rigging.

Transport

As the glass of a showcase is especially vulnerable to traffic vibrations, advice should be sought before any form of packing or transport is considered.

If an uncased ship has to travel it should be placed on a board which is longer than its entire length from bowsprit to stern and wider than the mainsail yard. Side pieces can then be fixed. The bowsprit and rigging are particularly fragile and should be well protected. Under no circumstances should packing material be allowed to come in contact with the model.

MUSICAL BOXES AND AUTOMATA

Do not attempt to play a musical box unless it is known to be in safe working order. If in doubt consult an expert conservator of clocks who specializes in musical boxes.

Musical boxes and automata are usually driven with very strong springs and are highly stressed mechanisms. If operated regularly they will certainly wear out. However, occasional use, e.g. five or six times a year, will help to keep the lubrication fluid and is recommended.

If a box is played it is *essential* that the mechanism is left stopped only at the end of a tune. If the box is stopped or runs down in mid-tune the teeth of the comb are particularly vulnerable, especially if the box is moved.

In general the advice on positioning, storage care, maintenance and handling of musical boxes is exactly the same as that for clocks (see Clocks, p. 75).

Positioning

It is especially important that musical boxes are not kept in hot conditions, such as in direct sunlight or near heating units, because with cylinder musical boxes the shellac cement slowly melts and sinks to the bottom of the cylinder.

Care and maintenance

As with clockwork, *never* attempt to clean, oil or touch the mechanism. Musical boxes are particularly vulnerable and if tampered with will readily self-destruct.

Handling

When moving a box, after making sure that it has been stopped at the end of a tune, a folded wedge of paper should be placed in the fan blades of the governor to ensure that the movement does not start during transit.

Also, where possible, the mainspring should be well run down by playing the box, as this will reduce still further the risk of an accident.

A housemaid's duty is to keep the housemaid's cupboard in order, and to be dressed by four or half-past four in the afternoon . . .

From *The Servants Practical Guide*,
by the author of *Manners and Tone of Good Society*, 1880

APPENDICES

Appendix 1
METHODS OF PROTECTION AGAINST LIGHT
301

Appendix 2
SPECIAL EQUIPMENT AND PROTECTION

Light Meters
307

Hygrometers
308

Carpet Protection
312

Appendix 3
THE HOUSEMAIDS' CUPBOARD

Electrical Equipment
317

Brushes
318

Step-ladders and Tower Scaffolding
320

Miscellaneous
320

Appendix 4
SUPPLIERS OF EQUIPMENT AND MATERIALS
323

Appendix 5
SUPPLIERS' ADDRESSES
331

70. Double blinds in the Turner Room at Petworth

METHODS OF PROTECTION AGAINST LIGHT

As well as cutting down light levels to the recommended levels, by using sun-blinds and sun-curtains, it is essential to cut down the time objects are exposed to light by using shutters or dark blinds.

Shutters

Where shutters exist they should be put into working order and used.

Since the exclusion of light prolongs the life of the contents of the house, shutters should be kept closed for as long as possible. During the winter months when the house is closed, shutters should be opened only when a room is being cleaned. In the summer the shutters can be released from their security bars but kept closed, opening them only for cleaning the room, the staff closing them again on leaving. Just before the visitors arrive the shutters can be opened and the sun-blinds adjusted. In this way the contents of a house opening, say, five afternoons a week, need only be exposed to under thirty hours of light.

Sun-blinds

As light levels have to be reduced, it is recommended that plain cream or buff holland blinds are fitted. These transmit a sunny light, even on a grey day. White blinds are not only less effective in cutting down the amount of light, but make even a sunny day seem rather cold.

Blinds must be kept down if the sun is shining directly through a window, and should not be raised until the sun has moved round the house. Sunlight must never fall directly on to any object in a room.

If the sun is not shining through the window, the height of the blind should be adjusted according to the light level in the room. It is very difficult to judge this by eye, and it is strongly recommended that a light meter should be used as an aid in setting the level of sun-blinds. On gloomy days, it will probably be possible to have the blinds right up, to make the most of the available daylight.

On most days the light levels will vary quite considerably, depending on the weather and the time of day. A reasonable compromise, bearing in mind that there may not be time to adjust all the blinds each time a cloud passes in front of the sun, is to raise the blinds on windows that the sun is not shining through to the central transom, so that the bright light from the sky is prevented from entering the room, but the view outside can be seen.

In rooms with particularly sensitive contents, such as the Turner Room at Petworth, two sets of blinds can be fitted. The normal cream holland blind nearer the window is kept permanently down, even when visitors are in the room, and a second dark green or blue blind, fitted on the room side of the cream blind, can be lowered to reduce the light levels still further. It can also be used as a black-out when the room is empty during open hours.

The tops of windows with fanlights or gothic arches can be obscured by fitting into them a shaped piece of blind material. This can either be stretched over a frame which fits the window, or it can be fixed around the window frame with Velcro.

If an alarm system is to be fitted before sun-blinds or sun-curtains are in position, the security company should be warned. On a windy night, draughts coming through the closed window may move the blind or curtain. The type of alarm fitted should not be so sensitive as to be set off by this movement.

See also Selecting and fitting sun-blinds, p. 303, and Appendix 4.

Sun-curtains

In some cases, as for instance with the huge mullion windows at Hardwick, blinds are inappropriate and it may be possible to fit sun-curtains instead. The disadvantage of these is that they obscure the view from the window and tend to be claustrophobic. The advantage of sun-blinds is that they can be pulled down so that they block out the sky, while allowing the view below the skyline to be enjoyed.

There is a wide choice of sun-curtain material. The thicker and denser the material the more light it obscures. When making and hanging sun-curtains it is essential that the curtains overlap in the centre and come right to the window-frame edge, otherwise great shafts of light come into the room. The fullness of the curtain also lowers the light level.

Treatment of windows with ultraviolet (UV) filters

The windows of all rooms with light-sensitive contents should be treated with UV-absorbent varnish or film. Suppliers will apply the filters to the glass and will provide special cleaning instructions. Details of windows treated and dates should be kept at the house, so that the deterioration of the UV filter can be monitored. The efficacy of the filters should be checked twice a year using a UV monitor.

UV-absorbent varnish

This has to be applied by a specialist, who cleans the window and then treats it by running the varnish over the glass so that it forms a continuous coating. The treatment is not recommended for windows which have a history of condensation, because the water gets under the varnish at the edge of the pane and lifts it off, especially during freezing weather. Nor is it recommended for windows that suffer extreme temperatures, as the varnish crazes and lifts off the windows, leaving a disfiguring pattern of varnish remnants behind. The varnish can easily be damaged by abrasion and chemicals when cleaning windows (see Windows, p. 287).

UV-absorbent film

These self-adhesive polyester films are the preferred type of UV filter, except for windows with tiny panes of glass, to which it is easier to apply the varnish, or large panes of glass where a join in the film would be necessary. The film is usually applied by a specialist, although it can be purchased and applied by D I Y enthusiasts. It is supplied in sheets which can be cut to the size of the window panes. As there have been problems in National Trust houses with quality control in the past, it is recommended that the transmission properties (in other words, the effectiveness) of filters are checked before the film is applied to windows.

UV-absorbent jackets for fluorescent tubes

Although there is a considerably higher proportion of ultraviolet in daylight than the light from fluorescent tubes, it is recommended that all fluorescent tubes should be fitted with UV-absorbent sleeves. These sleeves are supplied as lengths of tubular polyester film containing a UV-absorbent filter; they should be changed every two or three times that the fluorescent tube is replaced.

Selecting and fitting sun-blinds

It is unwise to accept the lowest estimate for fitting sun-blinds without first checking exactly what you are being offered. Blinds are expensive and if they jam or do not run smoothly they will not be used. The expense of a blind is divided fairly evenly in three: the cost of the roller, the cost of the material, and the labour for making up and fixing. They must be accurately measured, otherwise gaps of light occur down the side of the window. Good-quality blinds should last many years without renewal, though it is advisable to have them serviced by the original supplier from time to time.

Rollers

Selecting a roller suitable for the job is essential to the long life and smooth functioning of the blind.

Spring roller

To raise the blind, it must be pulled down slightly by the centre cord in order to release the check action on the end of the roller.

Rollers of strong aluminium tubing should be selected. Diameter varies, according to drop, from 40 to 65 mm. The larger the diameter of the roller the stronger the spring which can be fitted. *Never* fit cheap mass-produced aluminium rollers, which are not adequate for a long drop of the heavier holland-substitute material or for constant use. Some manufacturers produce a spring roller with automatic stop action which prevents blinds from shooting up when released, and allows fine adjustment when pulled down.

Cap-and-rack roller

A cap-and-rack roller has a brass ratchet at one end and requires both hands to operate the blind. One hand controls the blind by the centre cord, while the other pulls the cord at one end of the roller about half an inch to release the blind. *Never* release the ratchet at the side without controlling the movement of the blind by the centre cord or the blind will zip up at terrific speed and wind the centre cord round and round the roller.

Old cap-and-rack rollers are often found stacked away somewhere in a house, usually with broken blinds attached. These rollers, with their brass ratchets, are well worth recovering for re-use. A lot of money can be saved in this way.

Flange-end roller

This type of blind can be virtually any size. The rollers can be supplied with or without a spring incorporated inside the barrel. Without a spring the blind is constantly dropping, unless secured by its cord on a K-cleat. It can be useful when access to the blind is difficult as the cleat can be some distance from the blind. If a spring is fitted, when the side cord is released and the blind begins to draw, the spring becomes tensioned, slowing the rate of fall. Careful fitting and spring tensioning will ensure that the blind stops travelling at the extent of the required drop.

Self-acting spring roller

For a glass roof, either sloping or flat, self-acting seamed metal spring rollers should be used. These have no check action but are always under tension. The blind is prevented from closing by a cord anchored on a K-cleat.

Any blind which does not hang vertically must be on a self-acting spring roller. Guide lines are fitted so that the blind travels in the direction of the glass instead of dropping vertically.

Side-winder

This is a mass-produced side-action roller made of white or beige plastic and controlled by a white or beige plastic bead string. The plastic is unattractive and difficult to fit into a historic house setting, but, in unobtrusive areas and in storage areas, could be considered. They are efficient and, if used carefully, can last many years, as there is no spring mechanism or stop-action to wear out.

Material (or drop)

All blinds used to be made of window holland, a glazed linen which is now unobtainable. The best substitute is a synthetically treated cotton which is virtually indistinguishable from holland.

The drop should have tabling or side hems and it is important that the stitching is zig-zag or cross-stitch; a straight running stitch can buckle the edge. It is sometimes said that side-hems are not necessary on blinds made of the synthetically treated cotton because the material is less likely to fray. However, blinds traditionally had side hems and on important windows they look rather mean without them.

The drop normally falls from the roller on the side nearer the window. Where fittings and handles would bruise and distort the blind, the drop can fall on the room side of the roller, which gives an extra two inches or so clearance.

71. Examples of the wooden acorn that is traditionally attached to blind cords

The bottom edge of the blind should be fitted with a strong, pear-shaped stick, which should be stitched into its own pocket in the hem. It is to this stick that the knot holder is attached; many of the sticks now fitted are too thin and snap easily.

The knot holder, fixed through the bottom edge of the blind on to the stick, should be fitted on the side nearer the window, out of sight.

The cord from the knot holder should be in cotton or flax, *not* nylon. It is fitted with a wooden acorn (with a rubber band to prevent tapping), or a tassel, or a Turk's head. A tassel has a knot of 'silk' and fringe. A Turk's head has a bulbous 'silk' knot and no fringe. The cord should not have plastic fittings.

It is never worth renewing the drop on existing cheap aluminium rollers, but it is well worthwhile renewing the material on the recommended types of seamed metal rollers.

Any existing blinds that are in constant need of attention should be renewed. However, a programme of work should be drawn up, as a fitter can measure or fit about ten or twelve blinds in a day and the manufacturer will charge a day's time whether one or a dozen blinds are measured or fitted. The fine adjustment of a blind is of great importance and so it should be fitted by a craftsman.

The fitting of double blinds

The metal bracket into which the rollers fit should be extended so that the two rollers can lie one on top of the other. The drop of the upper blind should fall outwards towards the window, and the drop of the lower blind inwards towards the room (see fig. 23).

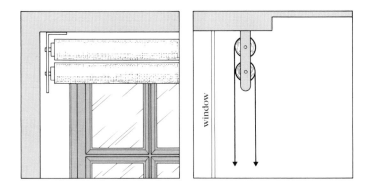

Fig. 23. Fitting double blinds: top roller (cream sun-blind) unrolls towards the window; lower roller (blue/green blackout blind) unrolls towards the room

SPECIAL EQUIPMENT AND PROTECTION

LIGHT METERS

The light levels recommended by museums are:

50 lux
Textiles (costumes, rugs, tapestries, curtains, etc.)
Water-colours, prints, drawings, letters and documents
Photographs
Marquetry furniture
Miniatures
Natural-history specimens

200 lux
Oil paintings
Wall-paintings

Using light meters

The sensor of the light meter should always face the light and must not be obscured by a hand or shadows of bodies, etc. Remember that it is the amount of light falling on the object which should be read, not the light reflected from it. The meter should be held facing the light source and parallel to the object without touching it. The light level is measured in lux units.

Photometer S511

This instrument consists of a scale and a round light sensor over which can be fitted two black caps marked 2500 and 5000.
Without a cap, read the lower set of figures, 1–500
With 2500 cap, read the upper set of figures, 1–2500
With 5000 cap, read the lower set of figures, 1–5000

Digital pocket light meter DL3

Digital light meters are now as cheap as or cheaper than the analogue type and have the advantage of being more robust as they have no moving parts. The DL3 instrument measures lux levels in three ranges:

o–100 lux, step size 0.1 lux
o–1000 lux, step size 1 lux
o–10000 lux, step size 10 lux

Further information

For further information consult: Garry Thomson, *The Museum Environment*, second edition, Butterworths 1986.

HYGROMETERS

Hygrometers are used to measure relative humidity.

Pocket whirling hygrometer

Before use

1. Buy distilled water (from any chemist), an eye-dropper bottle (or equivalent) and a magnifying glass.
2. Cut the sleeve just below the wet bulb (making sure that the bulb is covered by the sleeve).
3. Store spare length of tubular wick (sleeve) in the reservoir tank (dry).

Using distilled water keeps the sleeve free of salts and other deposits. As the instrument is going to be used only once a week, it is not recommended that the reservoir tank is used as it would have to be emptied after use. It is also easier to keep the sleeve on a wet bulb clean if the wick is used in short lengths. Using the magnifying glass speeds up readings and helps prevent breathing on the bulbs.

Use

1. Push the adjustable ring on the handle into position so that the joint is firmly held.
2. While both bulbs are dry, it is important that the two thermometers should agree in their reading to within 0.2°C.
3. Drop distilled water on the sleeve covering the wet bulb and allow time for it to soak in. (See that drops of water do not fall on the dry bulb, which must be dry – or dried – before the reading is taken.)
4. Whirl the hygrometer at arm's length for about half a minute.
5. Read the temperature of the wet bulb to a quarter of a degree.
6. Repeat whirling and reading the wet bulb until three successive readings agree.
7. Record readings of wet bulb and dry bulb, taking care to keep hands away

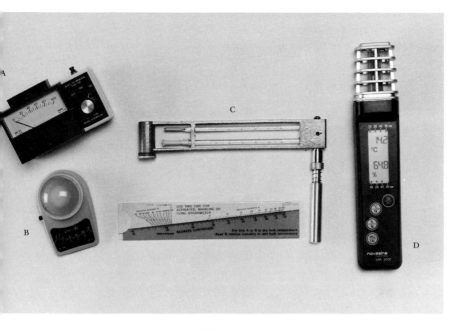

72. (A) An ultraviolet monitor; (B) a light meter; (C) a whirling hygrometer; (D) an electronic thermohygrometer

from the thermometers and not to breathe on the bulbs. Note the wet bulb first as it is less stable than the dry bulb.

8. Add drops of distilled water on the sleeve of the wet bulb before moving on to the next room to allow time for it to soak in. (It is essential that the wet bulb sleeve remains fully moistened throughout the operation.)

Directions for working out the relative humidity are given with every instrument.

Dial hygrometers

Dial hygrometers rely on the expansion and contraction of a moisture-sensitive element with changes in relative humidity. Hair and paper react quickly enough and with a large enough change in dimension to be used for this purpose. In a paper-dial hygrometer, two strips of paper which respond differently to changes in relative humidity are glued together and coiled so that when the relative humidity changes, the coil twists and moves a pointer attached to the end of it. In hair-dial hygrometers, a hair element is connected to a pointer, which moves as the element expands and contracts with changing relative humidity.

Both types of dial hygrometer require frequent calibration, at least monthly, with an accurate hygrometer such as a whirling hygrometer. Better dial hygrometers have a screw that adjusts the position of the pointer, until it reads the correct relative humidity, and only this type should be used. Cheap instruments that cannot be calibrated are worthless.

Electronic thermohygrometers

Novasina MIK 3000-C

The Novasina MIK 3000-C displays temperature in °C or °F, relative humidity in % and the dewpoint temperature in °C or °F. The humidity sensor is available in two types. The MIK 3000-C, which has a capacitive type sensor, is recommended. It is intended for arduous everyday duty and will tolerate condensation and chemical pollution (the latter should not be a common problem). It is accurate to ±2%. (The MIK 3000-E has an electrolytic measuring cell, is very accurate, but is damaged by condensation and is therefore not suitable for use in National Trust houses.)

Part of the display shows when the temperature and relative humidity have been stable for time intervals of 10, 20, 40 and 80 seconds. The stable temperature display will tell the user for how many seconds the temperature has not changed more than 0.3°C while measuring. The stable relative humidity display tells the user for how many seconds the relative humidity has not changed by more than 0.4% while measuring. Readings should not be taken until both displays show stable readings for 80 seconds. This may mean leaving the instrument in a room for up to half an hour before taking a reading. Changes in temperature between rooms are likely to cause the instrument to take the longest time to stabilize.

To calibrate the Novasina MIK 3000-C

The calibration of the hygrometer should be checked monthly. The instrument is supplied with a humidity standard at 75%, this is called the Sensor-check SC-75, and the salt it contains is coloured pink.

Temperature calibration of the instrument is not necessary. The cap should be kept on the Sensor-check when not in use. There should be a small excess of liquid visible above the salts in the transparent tube. The salt solution should fill at least two thirds of the outer chamber. The Sensor-check should be shaken before use to mix the solution thoroughly. If the solution dries out, with no water visible, it can be regenerated by removing the screw at the bottom and adding distilled water until a usable solution is formed. These instructions are intended to clarify the manufacturer's, not to replace them. It is a good idea also to read the latter, as there is additional information given.

1. Take the Novasina, capacitive sensor, Sensor-check and expanded poly-styrene casing out of the box and leave sitting for an hour in an even-temperatured room.
2. Remove the protective cage from the Novasina and insert the sensor into the socket (if it is not already on the instrument).
3. Look inside the Sensor-check and make sure that there is no sign of any liquid leakage. If there is then it must be thrown away and a replacement bought.
4. Place the Sensor-check over the sensor and the expanded polystyrene casing over the Sensor-check.
5. Leave until the temperature and relative humidity have stabilized, then take the readings.
6. Look on the label of the Sensor-check to see what the relative humidity should be at that temperature (approximately 75%).
7. If the relative humidity is within 2% of what it should be, the instrument is within the advertised accuracy of ±2%. If it is more than 2% from the right reading, it requires calibration.
8. Press the button labelled MES/CAL. The display will read HI CAL. When the calibration is complete the display will go blank. The Sensor-check can then be removed and the protective cage replaced.

The Novasina MIK 3000 range was discontinued in 1991 and replaced with the Novasina MS-1. This is only available with an electrolytic measuring cell.

Vaisala HM34

This pocket-size electronic thermohygrometer is fitted with a capacitance sensor. It is straightforward to use but there is no automatic method of telling when the temperature and relative humidity readings have stabilized. It is important to check that the display has remained constant for at least one minute before recording the reading. Calibration is best left to the manu-facturer.

Recording thermohygrograph

The three types of instrument described above are suitable for taking spot readings, that is measuring the temperature and humidity at a single moment in time. These readings will almost certainly be taken during the day. It is quite probable that relative humidity will change significantly during a twenty-four hour period, and it is impractical to expect to record changes with the use of spot readings. However, it is very important to have a record of daily fluctuations in relative humidity and for this recording instruments are needed. Two types are used in National Trust houses.

The recording thermohygrograph continuously traces temperature and relative humidity readings in different coloured inks on a rectangular paper chart wrapped round a slowly rotating drum. The drum is turned by a clockwork motor or, in the more recent models, a battery-powered quartz movement. A complete rotation of the drum takes one week or one month to complete, depending on the gearing of the motor.

A bundle of hairs is attached by a series of levers to a pen. As the relative humidity changes the hairs expand or contract which makes the pen rise or fall on the chart. The temperature is recorded using a pen that is moved by the twisting of a coiled bimetallic strip. The hygrometer part of the instrument requires frequent calibration, and this should be done at least once a month. The position of the pen on the chart can be adjusted by turning a screw, until the pen registers the correct relative humidity as determined by an accurate hygrometer, such as a whirling hygrometer or a recently calibrated Novasina MIK 3000-C. The recording thermohygrograph is quite labour-intensive, since the paper chart must be replaced once a week or once a month.

Electronic recording thermohygrometers

Squirrel meter/logger

These solid-state memory temperature and relative humidity recorders have been used in National Trust houses since 1985. They have the major advantage of needing no attention during recording periods. Models are available that can collect 16,000, 32,000 or 64,000 readings on four channels, two of temperature and two of relative humidity. The temperature and humidity sensors are in one probe, which can be positioned on the end of an extension cable up to 25 metres from the logger. This means that simultaneous readings can be collected in two rooms, or one room and outside.

Recording intervals can be set between one second and ninety-nine minutes. Hourly readings are usually recorded in National Trust houses, and these will fill a memory of 16,000 readings in just under six months. The 9V battery used to power the Squirrel also lasts for about six months. During this time the logger requires no attention, but it can be used as a meter while it is recording, and can display the readings in memory on its liquid crystal display, without affecting the recording. Instructions on how to do this are given to house staff when a Squirrel is installed.

The temperature sensors used are thermistors (electronic thermometers) with a range of −10°C to 40°C. The humidity sensors are of the capacitive type. They need occasional recalibration, which is done when the data is collected from the loggers.

The data is loaded into a computer, and software is available to calculate statistical information and print-out graphs of temperature and relative humidity for the recording period.

CARPET PROTECTION

Druggets

The International Wool Secretariat carried out tests over two years at the Treasurer's House, York, and at Erddig in North Wales to determine the best type of drugget. This research has led to the following conclusions:

1. Druggets protect a carpet from dirt and wear by absorbing and dissipating impact. The thicker the drugget, the better the protection.
2. They should be used especially in areas through which visitors are channelled or at any point where there is a turn in the route.
3. The druggets recommended are:
   (a) *Wilton* This lets through least dirt and its thickness gives the best protection from impact. It should be used on the longer-pile carpets.
   (b) *Feltlux* This came second to the Wilton and is recommended for short-pile carpets.
4. *Never* use plastic druggets because they can cause permanent structural damage to the carpet and may encourage mildew attack through condensation.

Practical points

1. Underfelt beneath a carpet is essential. Wear marks showed on a trial carpet without underfelt within six weeks. Good contract-quality hairfelt mixed underlay took up all the unevenness of the floor, leaving a smooth surface for the carpet. Rubber underlays merely followed the contours of the floor.
2. The druggets should:
   (a) be wide enough to enable the stanchions of the ropes to stand on the drugget;
   (b) cover all edges and ends of the carpet, which are very vulnerable areas – this is particularly important in window embrasures;
   (c) be laid with as few joins as possible, because any uneven line or roughness will cause wear. The seams should be stitched. Avoid modern joining methods which use adhesive tape; this gives a smooth finish but the adhesive can leach out, marking the carpet.
3. Druggets should have underfelt too, as, like carpets, any unevenness will cause them to wear. Where a drugget lies half on the carpet and half on the floor, it is important to continue the underfelt from under the carpet to the far edge of the drugget, building up the thickness with another layer of underfelt so that the drugget lies flat (see fig. 24).

4. All druggets should be taken up each winter, so that the carpets can be well vacuumed and the pile, if flattened, restored.

Fig. 24

Fixing of druggets

1. If possible druggets should not be nailed through a carpet.
2. Short straight lengths are less likely to move. Rugstop, a special polyester wadding, has proved effective in stopping movement.
3. As druggets should be lifted each winter, the fixing must be simple and not damage the floor. Recommended methods are:
   (a) a heavy metal bar sewn into a pocket at each end (suitable for felt druggets);
   (b) large-headed brass carpet pins and sockets fixed at approximately 150 mm intervals;
   (c) a bar of wood (see fig. 25) – this is better than the more easily available narrow metal bars.

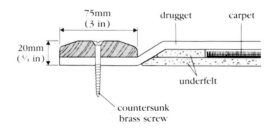

Fig. 25. Wooden bar used to fix drugget. It is held at 150 mm intervals by brass screws in brass sockets. The carpet should not go under the bar; underfelt should be used to fill any space between the carpet and the bar

Castor cups to protect carpets and floors

Protect carpets and delicate floors by placing small discs under the legs of furniture with metal feet or fitted with metal castors. Cut two circles of the same size out of plywood with a tank cutter. Create a ring out of one of the circles by cutting out the centre. Then glue the two circles together and smooth all rough edges with sandpaper before applying a primer. The 'cup' in the centre is essential as castors run off a flat disc. Apply emulsion paint to blend in with the tone of the carpet on which the furniture stands. Crown or Sanderson colour charts, for example, have wide ranges of shades.

The following two sizes have been found suitable for most castors and metal feet found on chairs, tables, beds, etc.

Large disc Use 6 mm plywood
    Cut two circles of 60 mm diameter
    Internal diameter of top ring 40 mm
Small disc Use 6 mm and 4 mm plywood
    Cut one circle of 50 mm in 6 mm plywood (base)
    Cut one circle of 50 mm in 4 mm plywood (top ring)
    Internal diameter of top ring 30 mm
 See Textiles, p. 259, and plate 59, p. 259.

Protective Footwear

In historic buildings on the continent, felt or canvas overshoes have traditionally been worn to protect marble, tiled or polished-wood floors.

No visitor should walk around a house in unsuitable footwear, such as walking boots, gumboots or sharp-heeled shoes. Shoes with 'track' soles harbour stones and grit, which can be scattered throughout the house, scratching polished floors.

There are three types of slipper which can be offered to visitors who have no suitable footwear:

(a) Blue plastic slippers – these stretch to fit most feet, and can also be worn over dirty shoes. Plastic slippers may be slippery on some floors. They are available at such low cost that they can be given away.

(b) Brown slipper socks (airline-type) – are available in one size to fit most feet.

(c) 'Pillow Paws' (polyurethane foam slippers) – are non-slip, and often used in hospitals. Available in seven colour-coded sizes from small child to large adult.

The slipper socks and 'Pillow Paws' can either be sold to visitors who may wish to keep them or be machine-washed and reused.

73. The Linen Room and (below) the Housemaids' Room in Queen Mary's Dolls' House

THE HOUSEMAIDS' CUPBOARD

A housemaids' cupboard is essential for equipment and materials in constant use. It should be well lit, with adequate shelving space for materials, dusters, polish, etc., and an area for hanging mops and brushes. In a really large house there should be one of these cupboards on each floor.

ELECTRICAL EQUIPMENT

The larger pieces of equipment are heavy and so difficult to move from floor to floor. They should therefore be stored near the largest area that has to be cleaned.

If the rooms open to the public cover several floors it is better to duplicate the smaller pieces of equipment such as the Dustette and domestic cylinder vacuum, so that each floor has its own. Much time can be lost searching for the equipment and carrying it to the area where it is needed.

Each house should decide on the type and quantity of equipment needed for the number of cleaning staff. The following electrical equipment has proved to be the most useful.

Vacuum cleaners

SMALL: Hoover Dustette: ideal for most textiles, including tapestries, upholstery and fragile carpets, and useful too for collecting the dust brushed out of nooks and crannies of furniture, sculpture and ornate plasterwork. It is supplied with the general-purpose head. The attachments, which are sold separately, are essential for getting the most use out of this vacuum. They consist of the flexible extension hose, crevice head and round brush head. The Hoover Dustette is light enough to be hand-held and when fitted with the flexible extension hose can be tied to the waist or hung from the shoulder, enabling both hands to be free.

Hoover Dustette S1122
Attachments (sold separately) S1914

MEDIUM: a domestic cylinder vacuum cleaner with variable suction and flexible hose for robust carpets, druggets, and small areas of wooden, stone and marble floors. The flexible hose makes it ideal for vacuuming stairs and stair-carpets.

Electrolux 1820
Electrolux 2230

INDUSTRIAL: industrial vacuum cleaner for modern carpets, druggets, large areas of floor surfaces, doormats and dustmats.

Electrolux UZ930 complete with attachments
Nilfisk IGS80 Attachments sold separately
  The most useful are:
      3-in-1 nozzle
      400 mm nozzle
      crevice nozzle
      crevice brush
      (power brush *only* for large areas of modern carpet and drugget)
Numatic NV250 complete with attachments

Polishers

DOMESTIC: *Electrolux* B 37
INDUSTRIAL: *Columbus Dixon* UB 853

Scrubbing machines

Columbus Dixon UB 853

Wet suction machines

Columbus Dixon UZ 876

BRUSHES

Brushes must be kept for the job specified. *Never* use one brush for different purposes. For example, *never* use a Silver Dip brush for dusting bronze; *never* use a furniture-polish brush on gilding. As it is important to distinguish the purpose of a particular brush, mark the handle of the brush so that it is readily recognizable.

To prevent metal ferrules scratching surfaces, isolate them by wrapping insulating tape round the top of the metal ferrule.

Brushes must be washed periodically. If waxy, first rinse in white spirit, then wash thoroughly with soap and water, rinse well under running water and allow to dry naturally (without heat) before storing.

The following brushes have proved to be the most useful. (The letters correspond with the brushes in plate 74.)

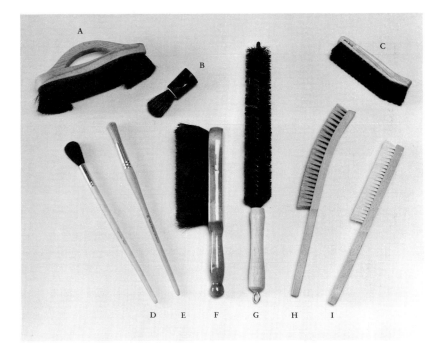

74. Brushes: (A) blackhead; (B) shaving; (C) furniture; (D) pony; (E) hogshair; (F) banister; (G) radiator; (H) curved plate; (I) straight plate

A Blacklead brush, for applying and removing Zebrite polish from iron grates.
B Shaving brush for dusting books.
C Furniture brush, bristle shoe brush with upturned end, for applying and removing wax on carved surfaces.
D Ponyhair brush, round-headed artist's fitch for dusting gilt furniture and frames, and gold and silver plated metalwork. (One brush for each type of material or metal.)
E Hogshair brush, round-headed artist's fitch for dusting in nooks and crannies – useful on plasterwork, sculpture, ceramics, plain furniture and robust metalwork such as iron, steel, copper and brass. (One brush for each type of material or metal.)
F Banister brush, soft hand-brush for dusting veneered, lacquer and marquetry furniture, where a duster would catch on uneven surface.
G Radiator brush, for radiators and banisters on staircases.
H, I Curved and straight plate brushes, for burnishing decorated surfaces on silver, copper, brass and steel (one brush for each type of metal).
   See also Appendix 4, p. 323.

STEP-LADDERS AND TOWER SCAFFOLDING

Cleaning in a historic house entails much work at high levels, so it is essential to have the right step-ladders and tower scaffold.

Aluminium step-ladders

Each house must choose the type and size that suits its needs. Both a seven-step and a four-step ladder are usually required, except in smaller houses. They should be made of aluminium and must be tested before they are bought, as some have very unstable back legs which slip and bend.

Tower scaffolding (lightweight)

Tower scaffold is essential for cleaning at high levels in large rooms and for use when moving and hanging tapestries and pictures. It is far easier and much safer to work from a scaffold than from ladders. The lightweight scaffolding is easy to erect. Choose the type with rectangular rather than square platforms so that the tower can be pushed from room to room without being completely dismantled.

MISCELLANEOUS

Dust-sheets and winter covers

Dust-sheets must be lightweight, closely woven cotton and should be washed every year. This is particularly important if there have been builders in the house.

When the house is 'put to bed', furniture can be covered with loose cotton case covers. These can be made of calico, sheeting, gingham or cotton lawn. For more fragile pieces, use lighter-weight material. Edges can be bound with bias binding, choosing a different colour for each room. Any joins in the fabric should be made with flat seams or French seams. There must be no loose threads or raw edges, as they can stick to upholstery, or catch and pull off pieces of veneer and metal decoration. The covers should be marked according to their position in the room or the inventory number of the furniture and stored in the room when not in use.

Care of chamois leather

Never use any detergents (powder or liquid) on chamois leather. They will react with and destroy the natural oils in the skin. Fairy soap is acceptable but

75. A modern housekeeper's room at Dunham Massey

Fairy liquid is a detergent. Wash chamois leather in warm soapy water; rinse out well in clean water; never wring out excess water but squeeze gently and shake out flat; allow to dry slowly away from direct heat and never in sunlight, as heat and sunshine will also destroy the natural oils in the skin. Rub together to bring back the softness of the leather.

Synperonic N

This is a neutral (non-ionic) detergent which acts as a wetting agent, breaking the surface tension of the water and enabling it to penetrate more easily. It comes in a highly concentrated form and must be used very sparingly: 5 ml to 20 ml to 4.5 l, depending on the type and amount of dirt. It froths very easily. If too much is used it is extremely difficult to rinse off. Pure Synperonic N is colourless and practically odourless.

SUPPLIERS OF EQUIPMENT AND MATERIALS

While believing the information given in the Manual to be correct at the time of going to press, the National Trust can take no responsibility for any shortcomings in service by the suppliers listed below or any deficiencies in their products.

Addresses of suppliers given in *italic* type will be found in Appendix 5, pp. 331ff.

Acid-free blotting paper
Atlantis Paper Company (Heritage)

Acid-free envelopes, folders
Made to order, any size
C. A. Coutts Ltd

Acid-free mounting card and board
Atlantis Paper Company
Conservation Resources (UK) Ltd
Lawrence & Aitken
Falkiner Fine Papers Ltd (single sheets and quantities)

Acid-free paper – cartridge paper
Falkiner Fine Papers Ltd (single sheets and quantities)

Acid-free tissue paper
Chinese unglazed tissue 18gsm
Fist Fast Packaging plc
Kendon Packaging Group plc
Small quantities from stationers – but make sure that it is acid-free

Aluminium step-ladders (lightweight)
Local ironmonger
T. B. Davies (Cardiff) Ltd

Anti-static liquid spray for Perspex
Amari Plastics

Artist's portfolio
A specialist art shop

Aubo Bronze picture wire
Frank B. Scragg & Co.
J. Shiner & Sons Ltd

Balsa wood
Model aeroplane shop

Bamboo satay sticks
Chinese supermarket
Department store
Hardware shop

Bias binding
Standard widths
Local haberdasher
Made to order, any size
W. Attwood Ltd

Black lead see **Zebrite**

Boxes
Acid-free, and specialist boxes
Atlantis Paper Company
C. A. Coutts Ltd
Conservation Resources (UK) Ltd
Solander boxes, invented by a Dr David Solander for storing prints and drawings at the British Museum; made to order, any size
G. Ryder & Co. Ltd
Wire-stitched record boxes
C. A. Coutts Ltd

Brass framing plates
To be used instead of nails; available in four sizes: use with round-head brass screws $\frac{3}{8}$ in. × No. 4.
J. Shiner & Sons Ltd

Brushes
Banister brush
Black lead brush
Furniture (bristle shoe brush, curved end)
Hogshair brush (firm but soft)

Plate brush (curved, 4-row)
Plate brush (straight, 6-row)
Ponyhair brush (very soft)
Radiator brush
   All above available by post from *The
   National Trust (Enterprises) Ltd*
Shaving brush
   Local chemist
Paint brush (25 mm–50 mm)
Wallpaper-hanger's brush
   Local ironmonger or D I Y shop

Bubblewrap
   Costerwise Ltd (bulk order)
   Fist Fast Packaging plc

Calico
   Local store
   MacCulloch & Wallis Ltd
   Quarry Bank Mill Museum Trust Ltd
   H. Wolfin & Son Ltd

Cardboard rollers see also **P V C pipes**
   Local carpet or dress-fabric shops

Carpet paper
   Local carpet shop

Carpet pins and sockets (brass)
Size 30 mm and 50 mm
   James Smith & Son (Redditch) Ltd

Castor cups
3-ply wood
   Local ironmonger or D I Y shop
   Charles Road Day Centre

Chamois leathers
   Advance Wipers Ltd

**Coconut matting (treble plain quality) and
coir fibre mats**
   Local manufacturers
   Norfolk Industries for the Blind Ltd

Cotton bump
   Department store

Cotton cambric
   H. Wolfin & Son Ltd

Cotton glacie picture cord
   Frank B. Scragg & Co.
   J. Shiner & Sons Ltd

Cotton sheeting
   H. Wolfin & Son Ltd

Cotton wool B P Quality
   Local chemist

Cuprinol Low Odour Woodworm Killer
   Local ironmonger
   Cuprinol Ltd

Curtain rings and hooks
   Hallis Hudson Group Ltd

Cuticle-sticks – round, wooden
   Local chemist

Dehumidifiers
Desiccant
   Munters Ltd
Refrigerative
   Trion Ltd

Detergent – neutral, non-ionic
Synperonic N
   Arcesso Conservation Materials

Dichlorvos strips see **Vapona, Mafu**

Distemper
National Trust paint range
Oilbound Distemper & Soft Distemper
   Farrow & Ball Ltd
   Potmolen Paints

Distilled water
   Local chemists; *not* from a garage

Doormat see **Coconut matting**

Downproof cambric
   H. Wolfin & Son Ltd

Druggets
Feltlux
   Bury Cooper Whitehead Ltd

Herdwick – heavy duty loop pile
Gaskell Carpets Ltd
Wilton
Local carpet shop

Dusters (all varieties)
Local supplier
Advance Wipers Ltd

Dustmats
Threshold Floorings
Herdwick – heavy duty loop pile
Gaskell Carpets Ltd

Dust-sheets
Advance Wipers Ltd

Eraser pencil
Venus Type-e-Rase
Art shop

Evostick Resin W
Local ironmonger

Felt
Local haberdasher or craft shop

Feltux
Local carpet shop
Bury, Cooper, Whitehead Ltd

Fibre optic lighting
Absolute Action

Filtration fabric
Picreator Enterprises Ltd

Foam plastic see **Polyurethane foam,
Polyethylene foam**

Foam plastic sheeting (5 mm–10 mm)
Local supplier

Foam plastic slippers see **Polyurethane
Foam slippers**

Gingham
MacCulloch & Wallis Ltd

Glass mats
Must have a bevelled edge
Department store or glazier (made to
measure)

Gloves
Cotton (without cuffs)
Advance Wipers Ltd
Selwyn Safety Services
Rubber
Local ironmonger
Vinyl (disposable)
Arcesso
Selwyn Safety Services
Totector

Goggles or safety spectacles
Local ironmonger or D I Y shop

Hair dryer (heavy duty)
Ogee Ltd

Hardboard
Local D I Y shop

Hide food (Connolly's)
Local saddler
Connolly Leather Ltd

Hoover Dustette S1122
Attachments S1914
Local electrical shop
Hoover plc

Humidifiers
Evaporative
Air Treatment Technology Ltd

Humidistat
R S stock number 331–118
R S Components Ltd

Hygrometers
Recording electronic thermohygrometer
(Squirrel)
Grant Instruments (Cambridge) Ltd

Recording thermohygrograph
  Casella London Ltd
Electronic thermohygrometer
Novasina MIK 3000C
  Air Treatment Technology Ltd
Vaisala HM34
  Vaisala
Dial
  Casella London Ltd
Whirling
  Russell Scientific Instruments Ltd
  Casella London Ltd

Impregnated cloth bags
Tarnish-inhibiting
  The Tarnprufe Co. Ltd

Impregnated polish cloths
Silver
  J. Goddard & Co. Ltd (see S. C. Johnson)
  Lees-Newsome Ltd
Brass & Copper
  Lees-Newsome Ltd

Industrial methylated spirits
  Chemist
I M S is a grade of alcohol for which a
Customs Licence is required. Apply to
Custom & Excise Dept, 071 620 1313,
'General Enquiries', for local Customs
Office

Insulating tape
  Electrical and D I Y shops

Ladders see **Aluminium ladders**

Lead sheeting
  Builder's merchant

Light meters
Digital D L 3
Photometer S511
  Megatron Ltd

Long Term Silver Cloth
  Local ironmonger
  J. Goddard & Co. Ltd (see S. C. Johnson)

Mafu
  Local ironmonger/hardware store

Mask (respirator)
RQ 2000 twin cartridge
twin exhaust valve to be used with R C 86
filters
  CLE Design Ltd

Masking tape (paper)
  D I Y shop, stationers
  Never use parcel tape or Sellotape

Melinex
Type '5' polyester film
  P. S. G. Group Ltd

Metal scraping grid
  Weetman & Co.

Methylated spirits
  Local chemist or ironmonger

Midas Touch
Mild cream polish for copper, brass & steel
  Rolite UK Ltd

Mops
  Local ironmonger

Muslin, butter
  MacCulloch & Wallis
  H. Wolfin & Son Ltd

Mutton cloth
  Advance Wipers Ltd

Nylon line
  Local fishing-tackle shop

Nylon net
20 denier bobbinet
  Dukeries Textiles and Fancy Goods Ltd

Opal glass candle tubes
  Wilkinson plc

Paint (see also Distemper)
National Trust paint range
Dead Flat Oil
Oil Eggshell
Oil Full Gloss
Estate Emulsion
Oil Bound Distemper
Soft Distemper
Oil based primers and undercoats
Traditional Lead (restricted use)
  Farrow & Ball Ltd
International Matt Black
Manders Black Ebony, Finish M.757
  Local paint shop
  Manders Paint Ltd
Joy Craftsman's Choice
  Huntings Specialised Products Ltd

Paper towels
Always choose extra-soft white kitchen
paper towels; some makes can be very
harsh and abrasive
  Local supermarket

Peek
Mild cream polish for copper, brass and steel
  Tri-Peek International

Perspex mounts
  Marchmade Ltd

Picture chain, cord and wire
  Frank B. Scragg & Co.
  J. Shiner & Sons Ltd

Picture hooks
  Frank B. Scragg & Co.
  J. Shiner & Sons Ltd

Picture rail
20 mm gas pipe
  Local builders' merchant

Picture rail hooks and fittings
  Frank B. Scragg & Co.
  J. Shiner & Sons Ltd

Pins
Lace and brass
  Local haberdasher
  MacCulloch & Wallis Ltd

Stainless steel
  MacCulloch & Wallis Ltd
  Watkins & Doncaster

Plastazote (black)
  BP Chemicals

Plastic slippers
  DRG Hospital Supplies
  H P C Group

Plastic tubing
  Local chemist

Plate hanger
  Department store
  Framemaker Products Ltd

Plate stand
  Acrylic Design Ltd (perspex)
  Department store (lacquered wood)

Plywood
  Local D I Y shop

Polish
1. Brass, copper: see **Midas Touch, Peek**
2. Floor polish
   Spirit based wax for wood and linoleum
   Johnson's Traffic Wax (liquid or paste)
     Small quantity – local ironmonger
     S. C. Johnson
   Water-based emulsion wax for vinyl
   floors
   Klear – litre tins
   Carefree – 5-litre tins
     Local ironmonger
     S. C. Johnson Wax Ltd
3. Furniture wax
   National Trust Furniture Wax sold in
   National Trust shops
4. Grates, black lead: see **Zebrite**
5. Silver: see **Silver Dip**
6. Steel: see **Midas Touch, Peek**

Polisher, electric
Small – B37
  Electrolux
Industrial – UB 853
  Electrolux Euroclean

**Polyester transparent envelopes
(photographs)**
  Secol Ltd

Polyester wadding
  Haberdasher
  Department store

Polyethylene Fast Foam
  Fist Fast Packaging plc

Polyethylene foam (10–20 mm)
  BP Chemicals

Polystyrene blocks
  Arrowtip Ltd

Polystyrene pellets or chips
  Costerwise Ltd (bulk orders)
  Arrowtip Ltd (by the bag)

Polythene bags self-sealing
  Supreme Plastics Ltd

Polyurethane foam
  For packing
  Local supplier
  BP Chemicals

Polyurethane foam slippers
(Pillow Paws)
  Henleys Medical Supplies Ltd

Portable plastic fumigation chamber
  Rentokil Ltd

P V C pipes (see also **Cardboard rollers**)
  Drainpipes
  Local builders' merchants

Renaissance Wax
  Picreator Enterprises Ltd

Rollers see **Cardboard rollers** and **P V C
pipes**

Rope (worsted), hooks and eyes
  *J. D. Beardmore & Co. Ltd (25 mm,
    30 mm, 40 mm)*
  J. Wippell & Co. Ltd

Rugstop
  Parkers Wholesale Carpet & Fitters

Rush matting
  Waveney Apple Growers Ltd

Sable brush
  An art shop

**Scaffold tower (lightweight) with
rectangular platforms**
  Yellow Pages
  T. B. Davies (Cardiff) Ltd
  Instant Zip-Up Ltd
  Access International Ltd – Hi-Way

Screening
  Picreator Enterprises Ltd

Scrubbing machine
  UB 853
  Electrolux Euroclean

Silica gel
  Crosfield Chemicals

Silver cloth see **Impregnated polish cloths**

Silver Dip – Goddard's
  Solution for removing tarnish from silver
  Local ironmonger
  J. Goddard & Co. Ltd (see S. C. Johnson)

Silver Drying Cabinet
  O V L-240-520Y
  Fisons Scientific Equipment

Slipper socks
  Delmore Manufacturing Ltd

Stainless steel brackets
  Local builders' merchant

Stanchions
  J. D. Beardmore & Co. Ltd
  Roblin & Sons
  J. Wippell & Co. Ltd

Steel wool – fine grades
  W. S. Jenkins & Co. Ltd

Stiletto heel guards
   Aztec Tooling & Moulding Co.

Stoddarts Solvent see **White spirit**

Sun-blinds
   Local specialist blind manufacturer
   Sun X (UK) Ltd
   Tidmarsh & Sons

Sun-curtains
Made from material of natural and/or
man-made fibre
   A department store or specialist fabric
   shop

Synperonic N see **Detergent**

Syringe for treating woodworm
   Rockets of London

Tank cutter
An attachment which can be fitted to an
electric drill
   Local ironmonger or DIY shop

Tape – broad white
   Local haberdasher

Tarnprufe bag see **Impregnated cloth bags**

Treasurers' filing tags
   Local stationer

Underfelt
Good heavy contract quality BS 5808:1991
Hair/jute blend: Gaskell Britannia 42 or 50
100% hair (for long-term resilience): Gaskell
Defender Plus FR or Defender Supreme FR
(FR = fire retardant)

UV-absorbent sleeves for fluorescent tubes
122 cm (4 ft) lengths
   The Morden Company (minimum order
   12)
   Sun X (UK) Ltd

**UV-absorbent treatment for window glass,
film and varnish**
   John Chamberlain
   Sun X (UK) Ltd

UV meter
Elsec Crawford UV Monitor Type 760
Elsec Crawford UV Monitor Type 762
   Littlemore Scientific Engineering Co.

Vacuum cleaners (see **Appendix 3, p. 317**)
Small, lightweight
   Hoover Ltd
Medium cylinder
   Electrolux Ltd
Industrial
   Electrolux Euroclean
   Nilfisk Ltd
   Numatic International

Vapona
   Local hardware store or ironmonger

Velcro
Nylon strip 'touch and close' fastener
   Local haberdasher
   Selectus Ltd

Watering can
   Local ironmonger or garden shop

Webbing (heavy duty)
When handling furniture, to hold doors and
drawers closed
   Local haberdashers
   Upholsterers

Weedkiller bar (for watering rush matting)
   Local ironmonger or garden shop

Wet suction machine – UZ 876
   Electrolux Euroclean

White blotting paper
   Local stationer
   Wiggins Teape Group Ltd (Fords Gold
   Medal)

White spirit
Supplied in various degrees of quality
   Local ironmonger

Wilton carpet
   Local carpet supplier

Wire trays (plastic-coated)
Sold for correspondence, vegetables and
freezers
   Local stationers or ironmongers

Zebrite (black lead, in tubes)
   Local ironmonger

SUPPLIERS' ADDRESSES

Absolute Action
Mantle House
Broomhill Road
London SW18 4JQ
Tel: 081 871 5005
Fax: 081 877 9498

Access International Ltd
South Way
Walworth Industrial Estate
Andover
Hampshire SP10 5AD
Tel: 0264 24014
Fax: 0264 358730

Acrylic Design Ltd
697 Harrow Road
London NW10 5NY
Tel: 081 969 0478
Fax: 081 960 8149

Advance Wipers Ltd
2 Centenary Road
Jeffrey's Road
Enfield
Middlesex EN3 7UF
Tel: 081 805 1000
Fax: 081 805 5805

Air Treatment Technology Ltd
34 Anyards Road
Cobham
Surrey
KT11 2LA
Tel: 0932 860600
Fax: 0932 860425

Amari Plastics
Holmes House
24–30 Baker Street
Weybridge
Surrey KT13 8AU
Tel: 0932 854 803
Fax: 0932 854 318

Arcesso Conservation Materials
194 Blue House Lane
Oxted
Surrey RH8 0DE
Tel: 0883 730304
Fax: 0883 716215

Arrowtip Ltd
Arrowtip House
31–35 Stannary Street
London SE11 4AA
Tel: 071 735 8848
Fax: 071 582 7248

Atlantis Paper Company
2 St Andrews Way
Bow
London E3 3PA
Tel: 071 537 2727
Fax: 071 537 4277

W. Attwood Ltd
13 Hague Street
London E2 6HN
Tel: 071 739 0091
Fax: 0787 312353 (factory)

Aztec Tooling & Moulding Co. Ltd
Buckholt Drive
Warndon Industrial Estate
Worcester WR4 9DN
Tel: 0905 754466
Fax: 0905 754475

J. D. Beardmore & Co. Ltd
3/4 Percy Street
London W1P 0EJ
Tel: 071 637 7041
Fax: 071 436 9222

BP Chemicals
Foams Business Croydon Division
675 Mitcham Road
Croydon
Surrey CR9 3AL
Tel: 081 684 3622
Fax: 081 684 7571

Bury, Cooper, Whitehead Ltd
Hudcar Mills
Hudcar Lane
Bury
Lancashire BL9 6HD
Tel: 061 764 2262
Fax: 061 797 1459

Casella London Ltd
Regent House
Wolseley Road
Kempston
Bedford MK42 7JY
Tel: 0234 841 441
Fax: 0234 841 490

John Chamberlain
88 Wensley Road
Woodthorpe
Nottingham NG5 4JU
Tel: 0602 269 424

Charles Road Day Centre
Charles Road
Holt
Norfolk
NR25 6DA
Tel: 0263 712451

CLE Design Limited
69–71 Haydons Road
London SW19 1HQ
Tel: 081 540 5772
Fax: 081 543 4055

Connolly Leather Ltd
Wandle Bank
Wimbledon
London SW19 1DW
Tel: 081 542 5251
Fax: 081 543 7455

Conservation Resources (UK) Ltd
Units 1, 2 & 4 Pony Road
Horspath Industrial Estate
Cowley
Oxford OX4 2RD
Tel: 0865 747 755
Fax: 0865 747 035

Costerwise Ltd
16 Rabbit Row
London W8 4DX
Tel: 071 221 0666
Fax: 071 229 7000

C. A. Coutts Ltd
Violet Road
Bow
London E3 3QL
Tel: 071 515 6171
Fax: 071 987 6839

Crosfield Chemicals
PO Box 26
Warrington
Cheshire WA5 1AB
Tel: 0925 416100
Fax: 0925 59828

Cuprinol Ltd
Adderwell
Frome
Somerset BA11 1NL
Tel: 0373 65151
Fax: 0373 74124

T. B. Davies (Cardiff) Ltd
Penarth Road
Cardiff
CF1 7RR
Tel: 0222 700723
Fax: 0222 702386

Delmore Ltd
Chiswick Avenue Industrial Estate
Mildenhall
Suffolk IP28 7AY
Tel: 0638 713 828
Fax: 0638 713 043

DRG Hospital Supplies
1–3 Dixon Road
Brislington
Bristol BS4 5QY
Tel: 0272 716111
Fax: 0272 723084

Dukeries Textiles and Fancy Goods Ltd
4 Fearfield Buildings
Broadway (off Stoney Street)
Lace Market
Nottingham NG1 1PU
Tel: 0602 507327/507488
Fax: 0602 506141

Electrolux Euroclean
PO Box 61
91 Oakley Road
Luton
Bedfordshire LU4 9QF
Tel: 0582 580120
Fax: 0582 579751

Electrolux Ltd
Oakley Road
Luton
Bedfordshire LU4 9QQ
Tel: 0582 491 234
Fax: 0582 574 255

Falkiner Fine Papers Ltd
76 Southampton Row
London WC1B 4AR
Tel: 071 831 1151
Fax: 071 430 1248

Farrow & Ball Ltd
Uddens Trading Estate
Wimborne
Dorset BH21 7NL
Tel: 0202 876141
Fax: 0202 892499

Fisons Scientific Equipment
Bishops Meadows Road
Loughborough
Leicestershire LE11 0RG
Tel: 0509 237371
Fax: 0509 231893

Fist Fast Packaging plc
Unit 3
Eastville Close
Eastern Avenue Trading Estate
Gloucester GL4 7SJ
Tel: 0452 500 471
Fax: 0452 309 962

Framemaker Products Ltd
Stanley Street
Burton on Trent DE14 1DY
Tel: 0283 47771
Fax: 0283 39163

Gaskell Carpets Ltd
Wheatfield Mill
Rishton
Blackburn, BB1 4NU
Tel: 0254 885566
Fax: 0254 888939

Gaskell Textiles Ltd
PO Box 10
Lee Mill
Bacup
Lancashire OL13 0DJ
Tel: 0706 878 787
Fax: 0706 877 351

Grant Instruments (Cambridge) Ltd
Barrington
Cambridge CB2 5QZ
Tel: 0763 260811
Fax: 0763 262410

Hallis Hudson Group Ltd
Bushell Street
Preston PR1 2SP
Tel: 0772 202 202
Fax: 0772 53305

Henleys Medical Supplies Ltd
39 Brownfields
Welwyn Garden City
Herts AL7 1AN
Tel: 0707 333 164
Fax: 0707 334 795

Hoover plc
Dragonparc
Abercanaid
Merthyr Tydfil
Mid Glamorgan
Wales CF48 1PQ
Tel: 0685 721 000 + Fax
Fax: 0685 721 000

HPC Group
30 Commerce Road
Brentford
Middlesex TW8 8LE
Tel: 081 568 7973
Fax: 081 847 3864

Hunting Specialised Products Ltd
European Headquarters
Prudhoe
Northumberland NE4Z 6LP
Tel: 0661 830000
Fax: 0661 838100

Instant Zip-Up Ltd
Audley Avenue
Newport
Shropshire TF10 7DP
Tel: 0952 811 779
Fax: 0952 825 635

W. S. Jenkins & Co. Ltd
Jeco Works
Tariff Road
Tottenham
London N17 0EN
Tel: 081 808 2336
Fax: 081 365 1534

Johnson S. C. (Goddard same address)
Frimley Green
Camberley
Surrey GU16 5AJ
Tel: 0276 63 456
Fax: 0276 683 654
Freefone: 0800 5255 525

Kendon Packaging Group Plc
Bow Paper Works
Bridgwater Road
Stratford
London E15 2JZ
Tel: 081 555 3188
Fax: 081 513 4333

Lawrence & Aitken
Albion Works
Kimberley Road
London NW6 7SL
Tel: 071 624 8135
Fax: 071 328 0760

Lees-Newsome Ltd
Ashley Street
Westwood
Oldham OL9 6LT
Tel: 061 652 1321
Fax: 061 627 3362

Littlemore Scientific Engineering Co.
Railway Lane
Littlemore
Oxford OX4 4PZ
Tel: 0865 747 437
Fax: 0865 747 780

MacCulloch & Wallis Ltd
25 Dering Street
London W1R 0BH
Tel: 071 629 0311/2/3/4
Fax: 071 491 2481

Manders Paint Ltd
PO Box 9
Old Heath Road
Heath Town
Wolverhampton WV1 2XG
Tel: 0902 871 028
Fax: 0902 452435

Marchmade Ltd
79 Dean Street
London W1V 6HY
Tel: 071 437 6241/3672
Fax: 071 734 6460

Megatron Ltd
165 Marlborough Road
London N 19 4NE
Tel: 071 272 3739
Fax: 071 272 5975

The Morden Company
Belt Cottage
Somerley
Ringwood
Hants BH 24 3QE
Tel: 0202 813 408
Fax: 0202 814288

Munters Ltd
Blackstone Road
Huntingdon
Cambs PE 18 6EF
Tel: 0480 432 243
Fax: 0480 413 147

National Trust (Enterprises) Ltd
Western Way
Melksham
Wiltshire SN 12 8DZ
Tel: 0225 704545
Fax: 0225 706209

Nilfisk Ltd
Newmarket Road
Bury St Edmunds
Suffolk IP 33 3SR
Tel: 0284 763 163
Fax: 0284 750 562

Norfolk Industries for the Blind Ltd
95 Oak Street
Norwich
Norfolk NR 3 3BP
Tel: 0603 667 957

Numatic International Ltd
Broadwindsor Road
Beaminster
Dorset DT 8 3PR
Tel: 0308 863413
Fax: 0308 862 766

Ogee Ltd
81 Shaftesbury Avenue
London W1V 7AD
Tel: 071 434 0064

W. R. Outhwaite & Son
Town Foot
Hawes
North Yorkshire DL8 3NT
Tel: 09697 487

Parkers Wholesale Carpet & Fitters
45a Derby Road
Southport
Lancs PR 9 0TZ
Tel: 0704 536404
Fax: 0704 500 333

Picreator Enterprises Ltd
44 Park View Gardens
Hendon
London NW 4 2PN
Tel: 081 202 8972

P. S. G. Group Ltd
49–53 Glengall Road
Peckham
London SE 15 6NF
Tel: 071 639 2075
Fax: 071 277 5654

Potmolen Paints
27 Woodcock Industrial Estate
Warminster
Wilts BA 12 9DX
Tel: 0985 213960
Fax: 0985 213931

Quarry Bank Mill Museum Trust Ltd
Styal
Cheshire SK 9 4LA
Tel: 0625 527 468
Fax: 0625 539 267

Rentokil Ltd
Consumer Product Division
Felcourt
East Grinstead
West Sussex RH 19 2JY
Tel: 0342 833 022
Fax: 0342 326 229

Roblin & Sons Ltd
112 High Street
Aylesbury
Buckinghamshire HP20 1RB
Tel: 0296 23099

Rockets of London
Imperial Way
Watford
Herts WD2 4XX
Tel: 0923 38791
Fax: 0923 30212

Rolite UK Ltd
72 Onslow Road
Mickleover
Derby DE3 5JG
Tel: 0332 512380
Fax: 0332 510704

R S Components Ltd
P O Box 99
Birchington Road
Weldon Industrial Estate
Corby
Northants NN17 9RS
Tel: 0536 201234
Fax: 0536 201501

Russell Scientific Instruments Ltd
Rashes Green Industrial Estate
Dereham
Norfolk NR19 1JG
Tel: 0362 693481
Fax: 0362 698548

G. Ryder & Co. Ltd
Denbigh Road
Bletchley
Milton Keynes
Buckinghamshire MK1 1DG
Tel: 0908 375524
Fax: 0908 373658

Frank B. Scragg & Co.
68 Vittoria Street
Birmingham B1 3PB
Tel: 021 236 7219
Fax: 021 236 3633

Secol Ltd
Howlett Way
Fison Way Industrial Estate
Thetford
Norfolk IP24 1HZ
Tel: 0842 752341
Fax: 0842 762159

Selectus Ltd
The Uplands
Biddulph
Stoke-on-Trent
Staffordshire ST8 7RH
Tel: 0782 522 316
Fax: 0782 522 574

Selwyn Safety Services
The Trading Estate
Old Road
Headington
Oxford OX3 8TA
Tel: 0865 751101
Fax: 0865 69985

J. Shiner & Sons Ltd
8 Windmill Street
London W1P 1HF
Tel: 071 636 0740
Fax: 071 580 0740

James Smith & Son (Redditch) Ltd
Ashley Works
24 Bromsgrove Road
Redditch
Worcestershire B97 4QY
Tel: 0527 62034/68826

Sun-X (UK) Ltd
2 Madeira Parade
Madeira Avenue
Bognor Regis
West Sussex PO22 8DX
Tel: 0243 826 441
Fax: 0243 829 691

Supreme Plastics Ltd
Supreme House
300 Regents Park Road
London N3 2TL
Tel: 081 349 3434
Fax: 081 346 1624

The Tarnprufe Co. Ltd
68 Nether Edge Road
Sheffield S 7 1 R X
Tel: 0742 553 652
Fax: 0742 509 887

Threshold Floorings
Vorda Works
Highworth
Nr Swindon
Wilts S N 6 7 A J
Tel: 0793 764301
Fax: 0793 765 319

Tidmarsh & Sons
1 Laycock Street
London N 1 1 S W
Tel: 071 226 2261
Fax: 071 226 4115

Totectors Ltd
Totector House
Rushden
Northants NN10 9SW
Tel: 0933 410888
Fax: 0933 410101

Trion Ltd
West Portway Industrial Estate
Andover
Hants S P 10 3 TY
Tel: 0264 364622
Fax: 0264 350983

Tri-Peek International
PO Box 18
Epping
Essex
CM16 7AJ
Tel: 0378 560454
Fax: 0378 560260

Vaisala (UK) Ltd
Cambridge Science Park
Milton Road
Cambridge CB4 4BH
Tel: 0223 420112
Fax: 0223 420988

Watkins & Doncaster
Four Throws
Conghurst Lane
Hawkhurst
Kent T N 18 5 E D
Tel: 058 075 3133
Fax: 058 075 4054

Waveney Apple Growers Ltd
Common Road
Aldeby
Beccles
Suffolk N R 34 0 B L
Tel: 050277 345
Fax: 050277 8134

Weetman & Co.
124 Ashley Road
Hale
Nr Altrincham
Cheshire W A1 4 2 U N
Tel: 061 928 0754

The Wiggins Teape Group Ltd
Gateway House
Basing View
Basingstoke
Hampshire R G 21 2 E E
Tel: 0256 842020
Fax: 0256 844272

R. Wilkinson & Son
5 Catford Hill
London S E 6 4 N U
Tel: 081 314 1080
Fax: 081 690 1524

J. Wippell & Co. Ltd
P O Box 1
88 Buller Road
St Thomas
Exeter E X 4 1 D Q
Tel: 0392 54234
Fax: 0392 50868

H. Wolfin & Son Ltd
64 Great Titchfield Street
London W 1 P 7 A E
Tel: 071 636 4949
Fax: 071 580 4724

PHOTOGRAPHIC ACKNOWLEDGEMENTS

1. John Bethell; 2. John Bethell/The National Trust; 3. The Art Institute of Chicago; 4. John Bethell; 5. David Kilpatrick; 6. Angelo Hornak; 7. Country Life/Alex Starkey; 8. Nicolette Hallett; 9. Jeremy Whitaker; 10. Judy Larney; 11. John Bethell; 12. Jonathan Betts; 13. A. C. Cooper; 14. Jonathan Betts; 15. Angelo Hornak; 16. Angelo Hornak; 17. Jeremy Whitaker; 18. The National Trust; 19. John Bethell; 20. John Bethell; 21. Angelo Hornak; 22. N T Waddesdon Manor; 23. N T Waddesdon Manor; 24. Angelo Hornak; 25. Angelo Hornak; 26. Angelo Hornak; 27. Jonathan Gibson; 28. A. C. Cooper; 29. Country Life; 30. Jeremy Whitaker; 31. John Bethell; 32. National Monuments Record for Wales; 33. Christopher Dalton; 34. John Bethell; 35. Molyneux Photography; 36. John Bethell; 37. John Bethell; 38. The National Trust; 39. Molyneux Photography; 40. John Bethell; 41. Will Curwen; 42. Sarah Staniforth; 43. Nicholas Pickwoad; 44. Fox Talbot Museum, Lacock; 45. Angelo Hornak; 46. Jonathan Gibson; 47. Jonathan Gibson; 48. Hawkley Studios/Angelo Hornak; 49. Jeremy Whitaker; 50. Angelo Hornak; 51. Angelo Hornak; 52. Angelo Hornak; 53. Paul Barkshire; 54. The National Trust; 55. John Bethell; 56. Angelo Hornak; 57. The National Trust/Anthea Palmer; 58. John Bethell; 59. Angelo Hornak; 60. Yale Center for British Art, Paul Mellon Collection/Angelo Hornak; 61. Angelo Hornak; 62. Angelo Hornak; 63. John Bethell; 64. Jeremy Whitaker; 65. Nicolette Hallett; 66. National Monuments Record; 67. Jeremy Whitaker; 68. Angelo Hornak; 69. John Bethell; 70. Angelo Hornak; 71. Molyneux Photography; 72. Angelo Hornak; 73. Country Life; 74. Angelo Hornak; 75. Angelo Hornak

INDEX

Acid-free *see* Boxes, Card etc.
Acidity in paper-supported works of art
 225, 229, 235
'Acorns' for sun-blind cords 305, 306
Acrylic paintwork surfaces 287
Adhesive tape for druggets (not
 recommended) 313
Adhesives
 animal-based 63, 64, 121, 172, 276
 epoxy-resin 64
 fish-based 276
 gelatine 48, 49
 rubber (not recommended) 200
 starch-based 48, 276
 water-soluble 64, 122
Advertisements (ephemera) 293
Aerosols not recommended near
 paintings 208
Alabaster 241, 242, 245
Algae on garden sculpture 249
Allotropy 171
Ambrotypes 200
Ammonia, damage caused by 77, 200
Animals, stuffed 179, 181–3, 194
Antlers 183
Aquatints 228
Arms, armour 27, 149
Artificial light 24–5
Ash furniture, woodworm in 114
Athletes' foot 191
Atmospheric pollution 21, 25, 30–31,
 32, 171, 200, 229, 231, 241
Atomizing humidifiers 30
Automata 295–6

Back-boards 199
Bacon beetle 180
Baize 142, 247
 in musical instruments 171, 172
Balustrades 241
Banners 266, 269
Bassoons 160
Bead embroideries 261, 266
Bed hangings 16, 256, 257, 264–5, 267
Beech, woodworm in 114, 172
Beetles 191, 193

Billiard tables 293
Birds
 eggs 179, 184
 mess on paintings 210
 stuffed 179, 180, 183, 194
Biscuit ware 68, 69
Black lead (Zebrite) 148, 329
Blinds *see* Dark, Double, Holland and
 Sun-blinds
Blueing 146, 149
Blunderbuss 149
Blu-tack (not recommended) 33
Board *see* Card
Bocage 65
Bookcases 51, 107
 glass-doored 50, 113
Booklice 49, 194
Bookmarks 41, 42
Books 35–59
 atmospheric conditions 47–50
 card wrappers for damaged 41, 52
 carrying 45–6
 clasps and bosses 52
 cleaning and routine care 39–43
 display 55–6
 dog-eared pages in 41
 dusting 39–40
 hand-painted initials and miniatures
 in 56
 handling 43–7
 insects and pests 40, 49, 194
 light affecting 47–8
 loose boards and spines in 41–2
 loose material in 41
 maps and documents in 41
 metal furniture on 52
 mould growth in 40, 48, 49
 paper-bound 46
 removal from shelves 43–4
 repair and special cleaning 56
 security for 54–5
 shelf list, shelf marks 37–8
 shelving for 50–53
 silk-bound 46
 stacking 46–7
 storage conditions 47–50

Books – *contd*
  ties, silk or linen 41
  temperature and relative humidity 48
  transporting 47
  ventilation 49–50
Bookshoes 52–3
Bosses on books 52
Boulle work
  cleaning 112
  lifting *112*, 113, 159, 169
Bows (violin, etc.) 174
Boxes
  acid-free 142, 184, 186, 200, 269,
    271, 323
  solander 57, 233, 293, 323
Braid on upholstery 266
Brass 138, 144–5
  fittings on furniture 111, 145
  inlay 113, 149
  miniatures on 221
  musical instruments 159, 169, 175
Brass-gilt 169
Bronze 142
  garden urns and statues 150, 152
Bronze disease 142
Brushes 318–19, *319*, 323–4
  banister 133, 285, 319
  blacklead 319
  furniture 319
  hogshair 110, 141, 142, 183, 185,
    242, 245, 285, 319
  paper hanger's 285
  plate 141, 144, 146, 319
  ponyhair 40, 113, 122, 123, 126, 133,
    139, 144, 183, 184, 216, 234, 319
  radiator 319
  sable 40, 328
  shaving 319
  to wash 318
Bubblewrap 47, 73, 121, 181, 214, 217,
    223, 235, 324
Busts 241, 245, 246, *248*
Butterflies 186, 191, 194
Byne's disease 184, *185*

Candelabra with ormolu mounts 144
Candle-grease catchers 144
Candlesticks, ormolu 144
Canvas, paintings on 25, 209, 219; *see
    also* Paintings

Canvas, printed, floor covering 98–9
Card albums 199
Card mounts, acid-free 41, 52, 57, 199,
    200, 233, 270, 323
Card tables 113, 267
Card wrapper 41, 42
Cardboard tubes, rollers 269, 324
Carpet beetle 179, 193, 194, 267
Carpet paper 93, 98, 258, 324
Carpeting, modern 262
Carpets 16, 193, 257, 258, 267
  cleaning 262, 263–4, 317
  fringes 263
  handling 268
  protecting 258, 259, 259–61, 312–15
  rolling 269–70
  turning and moving 259
Cartes-de-visite 199
Case covers 16, 17, 260, 261, 320
Case curtains 16, 17, 265
Cast-iron 138, 150, 151
  kitchen ranges 149
Castor cups 259, 259, 314–15, 324
Castors 259
  on musical instruments 162
Casts 252
Ceiling
  paintings 284
  plasterwork 283
Cement statuary 252
Ceramics 21, 61–73
  accidents to 63, 70
  carrying 67
  cleaning 67–71
  cracks in 64, 65
  display 71–2
  dusting 67
  environment and 63
  fillings 64
  glazes, damaged 69
  gold decorated 69
  greasy dirt on 71
  handling 65
  hanging, hangers 72
  hard-paste 'true' porcelain 68
  high-fired pottery or stonewares 68
  inspecting for old repairs 63–4
  low-fired pottery or earthenware 63, 68
  mats for 71
  metal and ormolu mounts on 69

overpaint 63, 64
rivets on 63
soft-paste 'imitation' porcelain 68, 69
spring-cleaning 67–8
stains on 71
storing 72–3
transporting 73
types of 68
washing 70–71
Chairs 16, 17, 106, 264, 266
Chalk drawings 226, 227, 231, 234
Chamois leather 108, 133, 324
care of 320–21
mats for ceramics 109
Chandeliers 16, 123–8, *136*, 208, 289
cleaning 126
dismantling 127–8
inspection 125–6
muslin bag for 126–7
re-assembling 128
washing 128
Charts 57
Chewing gum, to remove from floors 97
Chimneypieces 244, *245*
China *see* Ceramics
Chitarrones 173
Clasps on books 52
Cleaning equipment 317–21
electrical 317–18
Cling-wrap (not recommended) 142
Clocks and watches 77–87
care and maintenance 77–80
display 77
handling 80–86
hooded 81, 84
lantern 81, 83
long case 81, 84, *85, 86*
moving 81–3
ormolu mounts on 144
pendulum controlled 79–80, 81
platform escapement 80, 81
regulating 79–80
setting up after moving 84
spring-driven 81
stable 78–9
storing 87
temperature and relative humidity 77, 87
tower 78–9
'tripping' 81, 84

weight-driven 81–3, 84
winding and setting 78–9
Clothes moth 193–4
Coade stone 252
Coconut matting 92–3, 324
Coir matting 93, 98, 324
Condensation 27, 29
alabaster 241
armour and weapons 27, 149
furniture 116
mirrors 130
pictures 27, 211
wall-paintings 281
water-colour miniatures 224
Copper 138, 144–5, *145*
miniatures on 221
paintings on 219
statuary 152
Copperplate engraving 228
Coral 184, *185*
Cord
cotton glacie 234, 324
nylon (not recommended) 234, 306
Cork pieces for protection 27, 149, 211, 233
Cornices, carved 284–5, 289
Corrosion 137, 150, 152, 153, 224
Costume display and storage 270–71, 307
Craquelure 218
Crayon drawings 227
Curtains 257, 261, 289, 307
Case *see* Case curtains
cleaning 264–5
festoon or draw 261
linings 32, 267
protecting 261, 266
sun *see* Sun-curtains
Cushions, squab 110
Cuticle sticks 141, 142

Daguerreotypes *198*, 200
Damp 29, 191, 193
in books 49, 55
documents 56, 57
furniture 108, 116
mirrors 130
parchment and vellum 235
stored paintings 214
stored sculptures 249
wall-paintings 208, 281

Dark blinds 24, *300*, *302*, *306*
Daylight 23, 24, 31, 219, 257; *see also*
    Light
Death watch beetle 49, 190
Dehumidifiers 28–9, 154, 214, 324
Desiccant humidifiers 29, 324
Dichlorvos fumigant 180, 324
Display cases 21, 24, 31–3
    for books 55
    cleaning 32
    for documents 58
    labels for 33
    lighting 24, 25, 31
    for miniatures 222, 223
    new 32
    pollution in 32
    relative humidity in 24, 31–2
    removing objects from 33
    rigidity of objects in 32
    ventilation in 32
Distemper 286, 324
Documents 50, 55, 56–9, 224
    in books 41
    displaying 58
    handling 57
    light and atmospheric conditions 56,
        57, 307
    mould and mildew 58
    routine examination 58–9
Dog-eared pages 41
Door catches on furniture 107
Door furniture 138, *143*, 144
    cleaning dirty marks round 287
Doormats 30, 92–3
Double blinds *300*, 301, 306
Drawers, to make run smoothly 107
Drawings 209, 224, 226–7, 231, 233, 307;
    see also Paper-supported works of art
Dried flower arrangements 187
Drop-in chair seats 106, 110, 264
Druggets 16, 17, 93, 258–9, 262,
        312–14, 317
Dry mounting (not recommended) 200
Dry scrubbing 91
Dust mats 93
Dust-sheets 116, 154, 171, 208, 261,
        269, 320, 324
Dusters 324
    feather (not recommended) 108, 138,
        216

Earthenwares 68
Electrical cleaning equipment 317–18
Electronic dataloggers 48
Electroplate 139
Elephants, stuffed 183
Embroideries 261, 266, 270
Enamel, miniatures on 221, 224
Enamelled glass 287
Enamels 123
'English accent' 173
Engraving 230
    on armour 149
    on steel 146
Engravings, copperplate 228
Envelopes, transparent 199, 200, 327
    acid-free 57
Environmental conditions 25–31; *see*
    also Condensation, Humidity,
    Relative humidity, Temperature
Ephemera 293
Etchings 228
Ethnographic artefacts 294
Evaporative humidifiers 30

Feathers
    cleaning 183
    effect of light on 23
Felt 109, 325
    on card tables 113, 267
    mats for ceramics 71
    in musical instruments 159, 169, 171,
        172
    for wrapping 109
Feltback floorcloth 99
Fibre optic lighting 24, 31, 325
Figurines, ceramic 65, 70, 73
Filming and photography, care of
    pictures during 208–10
Finger-plates 138
Fire-arms 149
Fire irons 145
Fireplaces
    metal 145, 146, *147*, 148
    stone or marble 241, 244, 245, 246
Fish, mounted 179, 180, 184
Flags 266
Flaking
    in gouache 226
    in paintings 217, 218, 219
    in sculpture 245–6

Floodlighting 209
Floor cloths, impregnated 96
Floor coverings 93, 98–100; *see also*
　　Carpets, Druggets, Matting, Rugs
Floors 89–100; *see also* Marble, Stone,
　　Tiled and Wood floors
　cleaning 94–7, 317
　dust prevention 92–3
　historic ways of cleaning 91
　moving heavy objects across 92
　polishing 96–7
　protecting 91–2, 314–15
　scrubbing 94–6
　sealing (not recommended) 97
　vacuuming 94
Flower vases standing on furniture 71,
　　109
Fluorescent lamps 23, 24, 25, 31, 48,
　　57, 303
Flutes 165, 174
Fly dots 234
Foam plastic
　packing 247
　sheeting or squares 70, 325
Folders, acid-free 57, 323
Fossils 186
'Foxing' 229, 231
Frames
　mirror 16, 107, 129, *129*, *131*, *133*
　picture 208, 214, 215, 216–17, 232,
　　234, 289
Fretwork on musical instruments 169
Friezes, decorative 241
Fringes 262, 268
　on carpets 94, 263
　hangings 94
　upholstery 94, 106, 264, 268, *268*
Fungi 191
Fungicides 191
Furniture 16, 103–16
　avoiding damage from objects standing
　　on 71, 109
　Boulle 112, 113
　brass fittings on 116, 145
　carved 110
　case covers for 16, 17, 260, 261, 320
　cleaning 108–13, 317
　dust-sheets for 116, 154, 171, 208,
　　261, 269, 320, 324
　dusting 108, 109

gilded 16, 105, 106, 112–13, 115
glass-topped 107
glazed 113
handling 105–8
heat, effect of 105
japanned 112
lacquered 105, 112, 113
legs, rickety 113
light affecting 105, 116, 307
looking out for damaged 113
marble-topped 106, 107
ormolu mounts on 106, 144
painted 112
papier mâché 112
polishing 108, 109–11
seat *104*, 106
security for small objects on 116
storage 116
temperature and relative humidity 25,
　　105
tortoiseshell 112
washing 111
woodworm in 114–15
Furniture beetle 49, 114–15, 192–3; *see
　　also* Woodworm
Furniture cream (not recommended) 110
Furniture polish *see* Polishes

Garden furniture, metal 151
Garden sculpture and ornaments
　metal 152–4
　stone 249–52
Gaseous air pollutants 30–31
Geological specimens 186–7
Gesso 105, 111, 112
Gilding
　on furniture 16, 105, 111, 112–13,
　　115
　on glass 121
　on steel 146
　water 216
Gilt-bronze *143*, 146
Glass 21, 119–33
　accidents to 121
　chandeliers *see* Chandeliers
　cleaning 121–2
　display 123
　draining and drying 122
　handling 121
　metal and ormolu mounts on 122

Glass – *contd*
 mirrors *see* Mirrors
 negatives 201
 painted 121
 storing 123
 topped furniture 107
 washing 122
Glazed furniture (bookcases etc.) 113
Gloves, cotton 81, 106, 137, 325
Glues *see* Adhesives
Gold 139; *see also* Gilding
 decoration on ceramics 69
Gold leaf 150, 171
Gold-work embroidery 266
Gouache 226
Grained surfaces, to clean 286
Grand pianos 159, 162, 164, 167
Grates 145–8
Green corrosion 221, 224
Grids, metal or rubber, at entrance door 92
Guitars 159, 169, 173
Gum arabic 222, 226, 227
Gum tragacanth 227
Gumboots, avoiding damage to floors
 from 93

Handstops on musical instruments
 165–7
Hanging
 drawings, prints, water-colours 233–4
 miniatures 223
 paintings 208, 209, 211–14
Hangings 264–6; *see also* Bed hangings,
 Curtains etc.
Harp 167, 168
Harp-guitar 168
Harp-lute 168
Harp rack 166
Harpsichord 159, 160, 161, 163,
 163–4, 165, 165, 166, 167, 169,
 171, 173, 174
Headbands, detached, on books 41, 42,
 43
Heat caused by light 21, 24, 31; *see also*
 Temperature
Heating 27, 28
 central 222
Holland blinds 24, 301, 305
Horns and hooves 183
House moth 193–4, 267

Housemaid's cupboard 317–21
Humidifiers 29–30, 325
Humidistat 29, 30, 214, 325
Humidity 159, 169, 179, 187, 222; *see*
 also Relative humidity
Hydrogen sulphide 142, 200, 224
Hygrometers 27, 29, 32, 308–12, 325

India papers 276
Infra-red radiation 21, 24
Initials, illuminated 56
Ink
 affecting paper 58, 229
 drawings in 226–7, 231
 stains on stone or marble surfaces 242
 types of 226–7
Inlay
 brass 113, 149
 loose, on musical instruments 169
 tortoiseshell 112
Insect attack 25, 29, 172, 179–80, 186,
 191–4; *see also under individual*
 names
Insect collections 186
Insecticides
 for books 49
 furniture 115
 musical instruments 172
 natural history collections 180
 paintings and (not recommended) 208
Intaglio printing 228
Iron-staining on sculpture 241, 242,
 245, 249
Ivories (keyboard) 159
Ivory 294
 flute 159
 light and 23, 294
 model ships 294
 water-colour miniatures on 222, 224

Japanned surfaces 112
Jardinières 109

Keys
 for clocks 78
 for furniture 108
Kitchen range (cast-iron) 149

Labels for display cases 33
Lace 270

Lacquered furniture 105, 112, 113
Lacquering metalwork 138, 139, 142, 144
Ladders *see* Step-ladders
Lantern slides 201
Lead
  statuary and urns 137, 150, 152–4
  water cisterns 150, 153
Leaded windows 287, 288
Leather
  book bindings 37, 48, 49
  bureau-falls 111
  desk tops 111
  dyed 23
  in musical instruments 159, 166, 169,
    171
  upholstery 110–11
  wall-hangings 23, 275, 278, 279
Leather beetle 49
Lettering pieces, detached, in books 41, 42
Lids
  ceramic 65
  glass 121
  of musical instruments 160–61
Light 15, 17, 21–5, 301–6; *see also*
    Daylight, Sunlight
  and books 47–8
  ceramics 63
  documents 56, 57, 307
  ephemera 293
  ethnographic artefacts 294
  furniture 105, 116, 307
  ivory 23, 294
  methods of protection against 23–5,
    301–6
  and miniatures 23, 222, 307
  model ships 294, 295
  natural-history specimens 23, 179,
    184, 187, 307
  paintings 23, 214, 219, 307
  paper-supported works of art 23, 225,
    226, 231, 307
  parchment 235
  photographs 199, 202, 307
  textiles 20, 23, 257, 307
  wall-paintings 282, 307
  wallpaper 23, 277
Light-meters 24, 307–8, 309
Lighting; *see also* Light
  for display cases 24, 25, 31
  fluorescent 23, 24, 25, 31, 48, 57, 303

spotlights 24, 105
  tungsten 24, 63, 199
  tungsten halogen 23, 24, 199, 209
Limewashed surfaces 286
Linings for textiles 32, 267
Linoleum 99
  cork based 100
Lions, stuffed 183
Lithography 228
Lustres 125, 128
Lutes 159, 168, 173

Mammals, mounted 179, 181–3
Maps and plans 57, 224
  in books 41
Marble
  causes of damage and decay in 241–2
  cleaning 242, 245
  fireplaces 241, 245, 246
  floors 92, 93, 94, 96, 97, 258, 317
  reliefs 246
  sculpture 240, 241–9
  topped furniture 106, 107
  urns and vases 250, 252
Marbled surfaces 286
Marquetry 307
Masking tape 179, 247, 326
Matting
  coconut 92–3, 324
  coir 93, 98, 324
  rush 97–8, 328
Menu-cards (ephemera) 293
Metal 21, 30; *see also* Metalwork
    inlays 111; *see also* Boulle
  miniatures on 221
  mounts on ceramics 69
  mounts on glass 122
  paintings on 217, 219, 220
Metallized plastic film 132
Metalwork 135–54; *see also* Brass,
    Bronze, etc.
  corrosion in 32, 137
  day-to-day care 138–9
  dusting 138
  handling 137
  lacquering 137, 138, 139
  outdoor 150–54
  patina on 137
  polishing 138
  tarnish on 140, 144

Methylated spirits 288, 326
  cleaning antlers, horns and hooves of
    stuffed animals with 183
  not recommended for bronze 142
Mezzotints 228
Mice 191
  in books 40, 49
  in documents 58
Mildew 191
Minerals (displayed) 186
Miniatures, hand-painted, in books 56
Miniatures, portrait 23, 221–4
  cabinets and display cases for 222
  categories of 221–2
  cleaning 223
  condensation in vellum and ivory 224
  displaying 222–3
  on enamel 221, 224
  hanging 223
  inspection 223–4
  light, temperature and relative
    humidity 23, 222, 307
  oil 221, 224
  storage and transport of 223
  sulphiding in 224
  water-colour on ivory or vellum
    221–2, 223–4
Mirror paintings 130, 131
Mirrors 107, 129, 130–33
Model ships 292, 294–5
Moth 25, 193
  in books 49
  furniture 113, 116, 267
  musical instruments 160, 172
  natural-history specimens 179
  textiles 267–8
  upholstery 264
Mother-of-pearl 185
Moths (displayed) 186, 194
Mould growth 25, 26, 29, 191
  on books 40, 48, 49
  ceramics 63
  documents 58
  furniture 116
  glass 121
  marble 241
  miniatures 224
  musical instruments 170, 171
  paper-supported works of art 226,
    227, 229, 235

parchment and vellum 235
pastels 227
photographs 199, 200
textiles 268, 269
in water-colours 26, 226
Mouldings, carved 284–5
Mounting card see Card
Mounts, metal 69, 122
Mushrooms (fungal growth) 191
Musical boxes 295–6
Musical instruments 157–75
  atmosphere and 169–72
  avoiding accidents 160–9
  cleaning, polishing and dusting
    167–9
  component parts 159
  conservators 174–5
  domestic environment 160
  dust and airborne pollution 160
  enemies and snags 169–74
  handstops, pedals, etc. 165–7
  legs and stands 162
  lids 160–62
  moving 162–5
  pests 172
  playing 175
  relative humidity 159, 160, 169–71
  string tension and distortion 160,
    173–4
  temperature 160, 171
  tolerances 160
  tuners 174

Natural history collections 177–87; see
  also Birds, Butterflies, etc.
  cleaning and handling 180–85
  environment 179, 184
  insect attack 179–80, 181, 186, 187
  insect collections 186
  light and 23, 179, 184, 187, 307
  mounted mammals, birds, reptiles and
    fish 179–84
  rocks, minerals and fossils 186–7
Netting for textiles 266
Nitrate film 200
Nitrogen dioxide 30
Nylon fishing line (security) 54, 116,
  326
Nylon screening 262, 263, 263, 264,
  265, 266, 326

Oak 184
  effect on pewter 143
  woodworm in 114, 172
Oboe 160, 165, 174
Oil-based paintwork surfaces 287
Oil paintings *see* Miniatures, Paintings
Oilcloth 98
Opal glass 'candle' tubes 126, 128, 326
Organ *158*, 167, 171
  pallets 160, 171
  tuners 174
Ormolu 69, 76, 106, 122, 144, 169
Ornaments standing on furniture 109
Overmantel mirrors 130
Ozone (pollutant) 30, 31, 200

Paintings 27, 207–20; *see also* Ceiling,
    Wall paintings
  accidents to 210
  birds' mess on 210
  canvas tension 218–19
  carrying 211
  crating and loading for transport 217
  damage to, action in the event of 210
  dusting frames 216
  environment for 217–20
  flaking 217, 218, 219
  floods and splashes 210
  frames *see* Frames
  framing and unframing 217
  hanging and taking down 208, 209,
    211–14, 289
  inspection, routine, of 218–19
  light and 23, 214, 219, 307
  numbering 217
  panel 25, 208, 211, 217, 218, 219
  picture lights for 24, 220, *220*, 226
  preventing accidental damage
    207–10
  relative humidity and 25, 208, 209,
    214, 219
  safety of, during photography and
    filming 208–10
  safety of, when building and
    decorating 208
  stacking 215
  storing 214–15
  temperature 209, 214, 219
  transport 217–18
Paintwork, to clean 285–7

Panel paintings 25, 208, 211, 217, 218,
    219
Panelling 285
Paper; *see also* Ephemera,
    Paper-supported works of art
  acid-free 32, 33, 200, 277, 323
  brief history of 205–6
  humidity and 48
  light and 23, 57
  rodents and 49, 58
  tinted 231
  tissue *see* Tissue paper
Paper-bound books 46
Paper-supported works of art 220,
    225–35; *see also* Drawings, Prints,
    Water-colours
  accidents to 234
  causes of deterioration 229–31
  cleaning frames 234
  conservation of 234–5
  hanging 233–4
  insect pests 229, 231
  light, temperature and relative
    humidity 23, 225, 226, 230, 231,
    307
  mould growth 226, 227, 229, 235
  storage of framed and unframed
    works 231–3
Papier mâché surfaces 112
Parchment 58, 235–6
Parian ware 68, 69
Pastels 226, 227, 231, 232, 233, 234
Patina 137, 142, 143
Pelmets 264, 289
Pendant seals 57, 58
Pests, moulds and insects 49, 172,
    189–94, 267, 269
Pewter 143
Pewter disease 143
Photo-flood lights 209
Photograph albums 199, 200
Photographic paper, resin-coated (not
    recommended) 200
Photographs 197–202, 224
  for archives 200
  atmospheric pollutants and 200
  autochrome 201
  black-and-white 199–201
  colour 201–202

Photographs – *contd*
  dry mounting (not recommended) 200
  fading colours in 202
  gelatine and albumin 200
  light levels for 199, 202, 307
  problems 200–201
  relative humidity and temperature
    199, 202
  storage and display 199–200, 202
Piano-tuners 174
Pianos 160, 161, 169; *see also* Grand,
  Square pianos
Picture frames *see* Frames
Picture lights 24, 220, 220, 226
Picture wire and cord 211, 213, 234,
  323
Pictures *see* Drawings, Miniatures,
  Paintings, Paper-supported works of
  art, Prints, Water-colours
Pier glasses 129, 130
Pine, woodworm in 114, 172
Pins 327
  for costume display 271
  for display cases 33
Planographic printing 228
Plans and maps 57, 224
  in books 41
Plant materials, dried 187
Plants standing on furniture, to water
  109
Plasterwork 245, 246, 283, 284, 284–5,
  289, 317
Plastic slippers 93, 94, 327
Plastic tubing 149, 327
Plate stands 72, 327
Polishers, electric 318, 327
Polishes 327
  aerosol (not recommended) 110
  floor 96, 100
  furniture 77, 108–10
  metalwork 138, 140, 141, 144
  silicone (not recommended) 110
  wax 100, 108, 109–10, 169
Polishing
  floors 96–7
  furniture 109–10
  metalwork 138
Polishing cloth, impregnated 96
Pollution *see* Atmospheric pollution
Polystyrene for packing 47, 247, 327

Polythene tents 29, 154
Porcelain 68; *see also* Ceramics
Portfolios 231, 233, 323
Portrait miniatures *see* Miniatures
Postcards (ephemera) 293
Posters (ephemera) 293
Pottery 68; *see also* Ceramics
Pressed flower pictures 187
Presses 107
Printing processes
  intaglio 228
  planographic 228–9
  relief 228
Prints 209, 224, 228–9, 231, 234; *see*
  also Paper-supported works of art
Programmes (ephemera) 293
PVC pipes, tubes 269, 328
Pyrite disease 186–7

Rats 191
  damage to books by 49
Recorders 165
Recording thermohygrographs 48
Refrigerant dehumidifier 29
Relative humidity 21, 25–7, 28, 30,
    191, 308–12
  and books 48
  ceramics 63
  clocks 77
  display cases 24, 31–2
  documents 57
  ethnographic artefacts 294
  furniture 25, 105
  miniatures 222
  mirrors 130
  model ships 294, 295
  musical instruments 159, 160,
    169–71
  natural history collections 179, 184
  paintings 25, 208, 209, 214, 219
  paper-supported works of art 23, 230,
    231
  parchment 235
  photographs 199, 202
  sculpture 241, 249
  textiles 257, 269
Relief printing 228
Reliefs, sculptured 246
Repoussé work on musical instruments
    169

Reptiles, mounted 184
Rhinoceroses, stuffed 183
Rickety legs on furniture 113
Rising damp 116, 249, 281
Rivets on ceramics 63
Rocks (displayed) 186
Rollers for sun-blinds 303–5
Roman cement 252
Roping off visitors' routes 257–8
Rots (fungal growth) 191
Rubber
    marks on floors 96
    underlays 313
Rugs 258, 262, 263–4, 267, 307
Rugstop 314, 328
Rush matting 97–8, 328
Russetting 149
Rust
    in musical instruments 166, 170
    in ironwork 150–51
    stains in stone and marble 241, 245
    stains in woodwork 285
    on steel 146, 148

Salt air 200
Screening, nylon 262, 263, 263, 264,
    265, 266, 326
Scrubbing floors 94–6
Scrubbing machines 96, 318, 328
Sculpture and structural decoration in
    stone, marble and alabaster 241–51
    casts 252
    causes of damage and decay 241–2
    cleaning 242, 317
    decorators and builders 247
    flaking or sugaring of surfaces 245–6
    garden 249–52
    handling and fixing 246–7
    inspection 245
    iron staining 241, 242, 245, 249
    pedestals and socles 245, 247, 247
    routine maintenance 242, 245
    spalling 242, 243
    stability 245
    stains on 241, 242, 245, 249
    storage 249
    temperature and relative humidity
        241, 249
    transporting 247
    winter covers for garden 250, 251

Seals on documents 57, 58
Seat furniture 104, 106; see also
    Upholstery
Security 54–5, 116
Sellotape (not recommended) 33, 179,
    199
Sequin embroidery 161, 266
Serpents (musical instruments) 175
Shadow box for miniatures 223
Sheffield plate 138, 139, 144
Shells 184, 185
Shoes, sharp-heeled, damage to floors
    from 93, 94
Shutters 17, 47, 116, 214, 257, 301
Silica-gel crystals 32, 328
Silk
    bound books 46
    linings 32
    ties in books 41
Silver 138, 139–42
    miniatures on 221
    in musical instruments 169
Silverfish 40, 49, 194, 200, 229
Silver-gilt 138, 139, 144
    skirting boards 287
Slate, paintings on 217
Slippers, plastic 93, 94, 327
Slush casting 153
Solander boxes 57, 233, 293, 323
Sostenuto mechanism 162, 167
Soundboards 159, 169, 179
Souvenirs (ephemera) 293
Spalling 241, 243
Spinets 164, 169, 172
Spotlights 24, 105
Spruce-fir, woodworm in 172
Square pianos 160, 162, 164, 166, 173
Stained-glass windows 287
Stair-carpets 262, 317
Staircases, decorated 280, 280
Statues see Sculpture
Steam humidifiers 30
Steel 138, 145–8
    grates 145, 147, 148
Steel wool (wire wool) 146, 328
Step-ladders 288–9, 320, 323
Stone 21, 30, 241–52
    fireplaces 245
    floors 92, 93, 94, 96, 97, 108, 258,
        317

Stone – *cond.*
  garden sculpture and ornaments
    249–52
  sculpture 241–9
  urns and vases 250, 252
Stonewares 68
Stools 106, 264, 268, 268
Stringed musical instruments 160, 169,
  173–4
String tension 160, 173–4
Stringers, loose 169
Stump work embroidery 266
Sugaring in sculpture 245–6
Sulphiding in water-colour miniatures
  224
Sulphur (atmospheric pollutant) 140
Sulphur dioxide 30, 171, 226, 229, 241,
  242
Sun-blinds 17, 24, 28, 47, 257, 277,
  282, 300, 301–306, 328
Sun-curtains 22, 24, 261, 282, 302, 328
Sunlight 24, 31
  and clocks 77
  documents 57
  ivory 294
  leather hangings 278
  musical instruments 160
  paintings 219, 223
  paper-supported works of art 233
  wall-paintings 282
Synperonic N 321, 324

Table carpets 261
Tapestries 15, 16, 262, 265–6, 267,
  269, 289, 307
Tapestry on chairs 266
Tarnprufe bag 142, 325
Temperature 25, 27, 28, 310, 311, 312
  and books 48
  clocks 77, 87
  documents 57
  furniture 105
  miniatures 222
  model ships 294, 295
  musical instruments 160, 171
  paintings 209, 214, 219
  paper-supported works of art 231
  parchment 235
  photographs 199, 202
  sculpture 241, 249

textiles 269
wall-paintings 282
Terracotta 245, 246, 249, 285
Textiles 110, 209, 255–71, 275; *see also*
  Bed-hangings, Carpets, Costume, etc.
  cleaning 261–6
  display 270
  fixings for 267
  handling 268–9
  light and 20, 23, 257, 307
  linings for 32, 267
  pests and moulds in 267–8, 269
  protection for 257–61
  repairs to 266–7
  storing 269–70
  temperature and relative humidity
    257, 269
Theorbos 159
Thermohygrograph, recording 311–12
Thermomhygrometers, electronic 309,
  310–11, 312
Thermoplastic floor coverings 100
Thrips (hay bugs) 229
Tiled floors 94, 96
Tissue paper 73, 215
  acid-free 33, 58, 67, 73, 87, 121, 142,
    180, 184, 186, 223, 231, 233, 235,
    247, 265, 269, 270, 271, 293, 294,
    323
Tortoiseshell 194
  inlay 112
Tower scaffolding 124, 126, 207, 285,
  289, 320, 328
Treasurer's filing tags 213, 329
Tribal art 294
'Tripping', to stop 81, 84
Tubes
  cardboard 269, 324
  PVC 269, 328
Tungsten halogen lights 23, 24, 199,
  209
Tungsten lights 24, 63, 199

Ultrasonic humidifiers 30
Ultra-violet absorbent filters 23, 57,
  226, 302–3, 329
Ultra-violet absorbent sleeves 23, 25, 47,
  303, 329
Ultra-violet radiation 23, 24, 30, 219
  monitor 302, 309, 329

Ultra-violet varnish or film 23, 48, 179,
    226, 257, 282, 287, 288, 302–3, 329
Underfelt, underlay 93, 193, 258, 313, 329
Upholstery 106, 192, 193, 257, 262,
    264, 266
Urns 250, 252
UV *see* Ultra-violet

Vacuum cleaners 262, 317–18, 329
Valances 264
Vases
    flower 71, 109
    stone or marble garden 250, 252
Velcro 267, 329
Vellum 43, 48, 49, 235–6
    documents 57, 58
    in musical instruments 169
    paintings on 220
    pastels on 227
    water-colour miniatures on 221, 224
Veneers, lifting or splitting 26, 77, *112,*
    113, 116, 169
Venetian swell 161, 165
Ventilation 29, 191
    for books 49–50
    display cases 32
    musical instruments 171
    stored furniture 116
    stored paintings 214
    in winter-covered sculpture 250
Verdigris 241
Verre eglomisé 130, *132*
Vinyl floor coverings 99–100
Viol family 174
Violin family 167, 168, 174
Virginals 164, *168,* 169, 174

Wall-hangings *see* Leather, Tapestries,
    'Wax' cloth
Wall-paintings 280–2, 284
Wallpaper 23, 275–8
    Chinese 274, 275, 276–7
    chinoiserie 276–7
    flock 278
    general care of 277
    history of paper-hanging makers 275–6
    India 276
    light and 23, 277
Walls 284–7
    equipment for cleaning 288–9

Walnut, woodworm in 114, *114,* 172
Watches *see* Clocks and watches
Water-colour miniatures 221–2, 223, 224
Water-colours 23, 209, 224, 225, 226,
    231, 233; *see also* Paper-supported
    works of art
Water-gilding 216
Water-staining in drawings, etc. 231
'Wax' cloth hangings 278–9
Waxcloth floorcovering 99
Wax polish *see* Polishes
Weapons *see* Arms, armour
Wet suction machine 96, 318, 329
White spirit 144, 146, 148, 287, 318,
    329
Windows 27, 29, 287–8
    treatment with UV filters 302–3
Windowsills, condensation on 77
Winter covers
    for furniture 320
    for garden sculpture 250, *251*
Wire brush 149
Wire wool (steel wool) 146, 328
Wood
    colour affected by light 23, 105
    floors 93, 94, 95, 96, 258, 317
    furniture surfaces, to clean 108–11
    model ships made of 294
    paintings on *see* Panel paintings
    relative humidity and 25, 169
    woodworm in *see* Woodworm
Woodcuts 228
Woodwind instruments 167, 175
Woodwork, carved 285
Woodworm 192–3
    in books 40, 49
    furniture 114–15, 116
    musical instruments 160, 172
    paintings and frames 216
    paper-supported works of art 229
    woodwork 285
'Woolly bear' 194, 267
Wrappers for damaged books 41, 42
Wrought iron 150, 151, *151*

Yeasts (fungal growth) 191

Zinc (spelter)
    gilded 144
    sculpture 154